글로벌 무역영어

고명규

Global Business English

도서출판 청람

■ 머 리 말 ■

지금 세계는 급변하는 국제통상환경이 각국의 개방화와 첨단화를 가속시키고 있고 국경도 총성도 없는 경제전쟁이 치열하게 전개되고 있다.

21세기에도 국제공통어(Lingua Franca)이자 글로벌 비즈니스 언어(Global Business English)인 영어에 대한 태양은 결코 지지 않고 있다(The sun never sets on the English language). 더욱이 부존자원이 풍족하지 않고 협소한 내수시장 등의 한계요인으로 무역의존도(110%)가 상대적으로 높은 우리나라에서 무역영어는 더 이상 외국어가 아니라 제2모국어라는 콘셉트로 보급하고 연구해야 할 필수교육과정이다.

필자가 지난 30년간 한국금융연수원과 대학에서 실무자들과 학생들을 가르치면서 배운 지식을 토대로 출판을 구상했으나, '통역자는 일을 맡은 전날 밤 잠을 못 자지만, 번역자는 반역자(Translator is a traitor)란 격언처럼 일을 끝낸 순간부터 영원히 잠을 못 잔다' 는 현상을 체감하였다.

본서가 미비하고 부족하지만 미래의 시선으로 글로벌 무역전문가 양성에 작은 물방울 역할을 하도록 책의 완성도를 위해서 독자들의 기탄없는 조언과 사랑을 기대한다.

'글로벌 무역영어' 의 특징은 거래제의부터 클레임에 이르기까지 대외무역거래절차에 따라 효율적인 비즈니스 커뮤니케이션 능력의 함양을 위하여 Sample Letter와 Useful Sentence로 구성하였다. 또한 국제무역사 · 무역관리사와 대한상공회의소 시행 '무역영어 국가검정시험' 에 대비하여 최근의 기출문제와 Fundamental English의 가로와 세로의 심화를 위하여 'Enrich Your Word Power' 를 부록에 첨가하였다.

국제무역을 전공하는 학생들에게 좋은 길잡이가 될 수 있도록 아낌없는 조언과 최신자료를 제공해 준 미국 Rider University 영문학과장인 오세웅 박사, 배화여자대학교 국제무역과 Jeffrey Cotter & Anis Eshragh 교수, 교정 작업을 도와준 조연호 간사, 김시내 · 민정원 조교와 도서출판 청람의 이수영 대표님께 깊은 감사를 드린다.

끝으로 필자와 아들 재현이를 위하여 항상 하나님과 동행하도록 기도해 주시는 영등포 중앙교회 김진두 담임목사님께도 심심한 경의를 표한다.

2016년 정월
캠벨홀 연구실에서
저자 고명규

■ 차 례 ■

●●● Part Ⅰ 총 설

Part Ⅱ 무역통신문의 체계

제1장 무역통신문의 구성요소

제6장 신용장

제7장 선적통지 및 선적지연통지

제8장 클레임 및 조정

Part Ⅳ 기타 관계통신문

제1장 기타 관계통신문

Part I

총 설

제1장 무역영어의 의의

제2장 무역통신문의 작성원칙

Global
Business
English

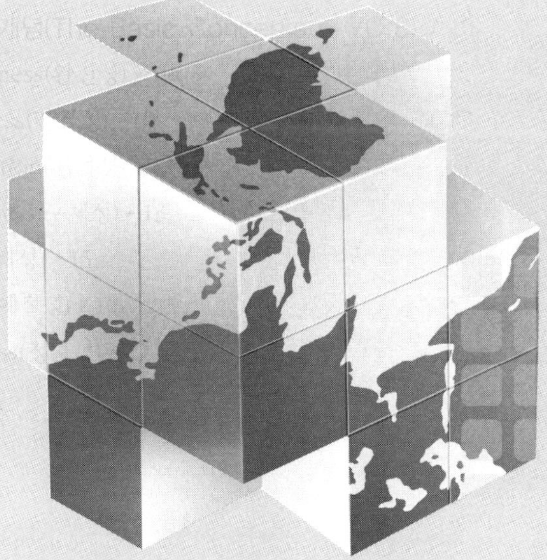

G l o b a l   B u s i n e s s   E n g l i s h

Chapter 01

무역영어의 의의

제1절 무역영어의 정의

무역영어는 대외무역거래의 효과적인 커뮤니케이션을 위해서 교역당사자 간에 사용되는 영어를 말한다. 구체적으로 말하면 무역영어의 범위는 상업통신문(Business Correspondence), 무역서식(Trade Documents), 전신문(Telecommunication), 광고문(Advertisement), 화환신용장 통일규칙 및 관례(Uniform Customs and Practice for Documentary Credits), 무역조건의 해석에 관한 국제규칙(Incoterms, 2010), 추심에 관한 통일규칙(Uniform Rules for Collection)과 계약보증에 관한 통일규칙(Uniform Rules for Contract Guarantee) 등이 포함된다.

영어를 공용어로 사용하지 않는 우리나라는 대외거래에만 주로 영어를 사용하므로 무역영어를 International Trade English나 Practical Business English for International Trade로 하는 것이 적절한 표현이지만 Commercial English(영국)나 Business English(미국)로 불러도 무방하다.

영어란 본시 5세기경 영국에 토착한 게르만민족의 언어를 가리키는데, 이 언어가 영국에 토착한 후에 여러 가지 변천과정을 겪어 오늘과 같이 문자 그대로 세계어(world language)로서 지위를 확보하고 있는 것이다.

따라서 대외무역거래에서 발생할 수 있는 커뮤니케이션 에러(communication error)를 줄이고, 효과적이고 성공적인 교역활동을 위해서 연구하는 것이 무역영어의 그 존재이유라 하겠다.

Key Concepts

Although the English Empire has long since slipped below the horizon, the sun never sets on the English language.

: 비록 대영제국이 쇠락한지는 오래되었지만 영어에 대한 태양은 절대로 지지 않고 있다.

제2절 무역영어의 특징

1. 학제적 연구(Interdisciplinary Approach)의 필요성

무역은 수출입, 외국환, 관세 영역의 연관효과(linkage effect)로서 이루어지는 역동적인 실천과학의 한 분야인 만큼 무역통신문을 정확하게 해독하고 작성하기 위해서는, 첫째 무역실무에 대한 기본지식, 둘째 일반영어의 구사능력(good command of the English language) 그리고 사고의 주파수를 항상 이질적 속성의 해외시장에 맞추고 무역인으로서 진취적이고(aggressive), 빈틈없고(astute), 유능한(competent) 소양과 국제적인 감각을 갖추는 것이 요구된다.

Key Concepts

We should know something of everything and everything of something.

–by Huxley, Harvard University–

2. 무역영어의 최근경향

모든 학문이 그러하듯 무역영어도 옛부터 전수되어 온 지식이 체계적으로 검증되고 거름과정(filtering)을 통해서 정리된 결과이다. 일반적으로 언어도 기존의 표현을 비평 · 반증하는 적자생존의 역학시스템에서 발전하게 된다.

언어는 항상 변화하기 때문에 3가지 수준(formal, informal, substandard)의 언어가 상존하고 있는데 무역영어에서도 formal language나 substandard language보다는 informal language를 사용하는 것이 최근의 경향이다.

Key Concepts

Formal language	공식적인 자료, 고위정부수준의 조약 및 법률문서 그리고 주로 학위논문 작성에 사용되는 언어 (long, unconversational, impersonal words)
Informal language	비즈니스 · 커뮤니케이션, 신문, 보고서, 서신에 사용되는 비즈니스언어(The language of business) (short, well-known and conversational words)
Substandard language	일반적으로 사람들이 사용을 기피하고 통용되지 않는 언어(ain't, young chicks)

(1) Latin어 사용의 감소 : instant → this month, ultimo → last month, proximo → next month, per day → a day

(2) 비차별적 표현의 선택(choose nondiscriminatory expressions) : salesman → salesperson, sales clerk, chairman → chairperson, head cameraman → camera operator

Man cannot live by bread alone.

→ People cannot live by bread alone.

(3) 진부한 표현(trite expressions)의 폐지 : favor(편지), kindly, beg to advise, with your esteemed company.

(4) 애매하고 불명확한(vague and indefinite) 단어의 회피 : early, soon, quick, many, high, slow

(5) 문체는 분사구문체(participle construction)보다는 진행형(progressive form)으로, 수동태(passive voice)보다는 능동태(active voice)로 작성하는 흐름이다.

(Passive) Tests were made by us.

(Active) We made tests.

3. 무역영어와 일반영어의 차이

일반영어에서 쓰이는 동일한 단어나 어휘가 무역영어에서는 다음의 예와 같이 다른 의미로 사용되는 경우가 많다.

	일반영어	무역영어
credit	신용, 학점	신용장, 대기(貸記)
draft	초고, 징집	환어음
information	정보	참고사항, 자료, 내용
instrument	기구, 악기	(법률상의)공식문서, 서류
fate	운명	행방
protect	보호하다	지불을 준비하다
honor	존경하다	지불하다
proceed	진행하다	(pl.) 수익, 매상고

4. 영어에 흡수된 주요 외래어(English loanwords of foreign origin)

1) 라틴어 계(Latin)

alumnus	[əlʌ́mnəs]	학생, 졸업생
alumna	[əlʌ́mnə]	여학생
de facto	[di:fǽktou]	사실상의
per annum	[pər ǽnəm]	1년에
per diem	[pər－dáiem]	하루에 수당

2) 프랑스어 계(French)

bon voyage	[bɔ́n vɔ́idʒ]	여행을 잘 다녀오세요
cafe	[kǽfei]	까페
debutante	[débju(:)tá:nt]	처음 사교계에 나오는 여성

attaché	[ətǽʃei]	대(공)사관원
fiancé	[fiá:nsei]	약혼자
bayou	[báiui]	지류, 하구(河口)
divorce	[divɔ́:rs]	이혼한 사람

3) 스페인어 계(Spanish)

pecan	[pikǽn]	피칸(열매)
chocolate	[tʃɔ́kəlit]	초콜릿
barbecue	[bá:bikjù:]	바베큐
matador	[mǽtədɔ́]	투우사
chihuahua	[tʃiwá:wə]	치와와(개)
rodeo	[roudéiou]	로데오(경기)
senorita	[sénjərí:tə]	아가씨

4) 독일어 계(German)

sauerkraut	[sáuəkráut]	배추 절임
frankfurter	[frǽŋkfɔ:rtər]	프랑크푸르트 소시지
delicatessen	[dèlikətésn]	조제 식품
meerschaum	[míəʃəm]	해포석

5) 이탈리아어 계(Italian)

pizza	[pí:tsə]	피자
ravioli	[rǽviə́uli]	라비올리(요리의 일종)
sotto voce	[sátou-vóutsi]	슬며시

6) 하와이어 계(Hawaiian)

aloha	[a:lə́uha:]	안녕(인사)
lei	[léii:]	레이(목에 거는 꽃다발)
luau	[lú:au]	로우오(요리의 일종)
poi	[pɔ́i]	포이(하와이 식품)
ukulele	[jù:kəléili]	우쿨렐레

7) 중국어 계(Chinese)

chop suey	[tʃɔ́p-sju(:)i]	챱수이(미국식 중국요리)
chow mein	[tʃáu-méin]	볶은국수(미국식 국수)

8) 화란어 계(Dutch)

cole slaw	[kə́ul-slɔ́:]	배추 샐러드
Santa Claus	[sǽntə-klɔ́:z]	산타클로스

9) 아메리카 인디언어 계(American Indian)

mocassin	[mɔ́kəsin]	(북미 인디언의) 신
opossum	[əpásəm]	주머니쥐

10) 일본어 계(Japanese)

harakiri	[hǽrəkíri]	할복
kamikaze	[kà:miká:zei]	무모함

11) 한국어 계(Korean)

ginseng	[dʒínseŋ]	인삼
kimchi	[kímtʃi]	김치
Bulgogi	[pulgogi]	불고기
Bibimbap	[bibimbap]	비빔밥

Chapter 02

무역통신문의 작성원칙

Business Communications Principles

효과적인 무역통신문을 작성하기 위해서는 구체적인 커뮤니케이션 원칙을 적용하는 것이 필요하다. 서신작성은 비대인적인 커뮤니케이션(Nonpersonal Communication)의 수단인 Letter를 통해서 ① 최초거래 시에는 상대방으로 하여금 호의적인 태도를 형성(Favorable Attitude Formation)케 하고, ② 기존거래고객에게는 호의적 관계를 더욱 강화(Favorable Attitude Reinforcement)하며, ③ 비호의적 상황인 경우는 호의적으로 태도를 변용(Attitude Change)토록 설득시키는 데 그 목적이 있는 것이다.

훌륭한 서신이 갖추어야 할 요소에 대해서는 다양한 학설이 있다. Abraham Ellenbogan은 "Letter Perfect"에서 The ABCD(Accuracy, Brevity, Clarity, Dignity)를 good letter writing의 구비요소라고 주장했으며, Urabe Shigeo는 "How to Write Business Letters"에서 5C'S(Clear, Concise, Correct, Concrete, Courteous)를 강조하고 있다.

본 장에서는 "Effective Business Letter"에서 다루는 7C'S(Completeness, Conciseness, Consideration, Concreteness, Clarity, Courtesy, Correctness)를 상론하고자 한다.

Key Concepts

Theory without application can be empty,
Application without theory can be folly :
- by Robert Hicks -

제1절 7C' S의 기본개념(The Basic Concepts of 7C' S)

1. Completeness(완전성)

무역통신문은 상대방에게 자기의 생각을 전달하기 위한 것이므로 필요한 내용을 충분히 효과적인 순서로 표현하여야 한다. 특히 상대방 서신에 대하여 답장을 하는 경우 상대방이 알고 싶어하는 사항을 빠짐없이 회답하여야 한다.

Guidelines

- Answer all questions asked.
- Give something extra, when desirable.
- Check for the five W's and any other essentials.

2. Conciseness(간결성)

Business person은 글자 그대로 항상 바쁘게 움직이는 사람이다. 그러므로 간결한 통신문은 서신작성자와 수신인 모두에게 시간과 경비를 절감시켜준다. 그러나 필요한 어구와 항목을 함부로 생략해서는 안 되고 장황한 것은 피하는 것이 좋다. 즉, 할말은 하되 간결하게 작성하여야 한다(Be complete, but be concise).

Suggestions

- Shorten or omit wordy expressions.
- Include only relevant statements.
- Avoid unnecessary repetition.

(1) 장황한 어구 대신 같은 의미의 단일어를 사용하는 것이 간결하다.

Wordy	Concise
along the line of(salary)	about(salary)
at this time	now
consensus of opinion	consensus
due to the fact that	because
during the time that	while
during the year of	during
few and far between	seldom, scarce
for a price of	for
for the purpose of	for, to
for the reason that	since, because
from the point of view	as
in accordance with your request	as you requested
have need for	need
in due course	soon
in many cases	often, frequently
in most cases	usually
in order to	to
in some cases	sometimes
in spite of the fact that	although
in(for) the amount of	for
in the city of	in
in the event that	if
in the neighborhood of $60	about $60
give consideration	consider
have a requirement	require
take a look	look
please don't hesitate to write	please write
under date of	dated
under the circumstances	because

(2) 가능하면 "Which나 That" 절을 사용하지 않는 것이 좋다.

Wordy : She ordered desks which are of the executive type.

Concise : She ordered executive-type desks.

Wordy : Bill said that he heard the news.

Concise : Bill said he heard the news.

(3) 문장서두에 "It is, There are, there is"의 과다사용을 피하자.

Wordy : There are four rules which should be observed.

Concise : Four rules should be observed.

Wordy : It is known that we must reduce the ⋯.

Concise : We must reduce the ⋯.

3. Consideration(배려성)

Consideration은 서신작성의 다른 6원칙(the six C's)을 모두 적용하는 것이다. 즉, 수신자의 입장에서 통신문을 준비하는 것이다. 또한 사려깊은 배려는 인간성의 이해, 감정이입 및 수신자본위(You-attitude)의 접근을 포함하는 것이다.

Specific Ways

- Focus on "You" instead of "I" and "We".
- Show reader benefit or interest in reader.
- Emphasize positive and pleasant facts.
- Apply integrity to your messages.

"You"에 초점을 둔 문장은 다음과 같다.

We Attitude : I want to send my congratulations.

You Attitude : Congratulations once again on your admission to MSU.

We Attitude : We will ship your May 4 order today.

You Attitude : You should receive the portable radio you ordered May 4 on or before May 9.

We Attitude : We have enclosed a reply envelope.

You Attitude : Just mail your check in the enclosed envelope.

그러나 상대방이 실수를 했거나 견해가 다른 경우는 "You"를 사용하지 않는 것이 상대방을 배려하는 것이다.

Poor : You failed to enclose your check in the envelope.

Better : The envelope we received did not have a check in it.

Poor : You are entirely wrong in your attitude.

Better : The proposed plan has three aspects which are extremely important and which we need to explain now.

또한 상대방의 기분을 상하지 않게 positive하고 pleasant한 함축어를 사용하는 것이 효과적이다. 그 예를 요약하면 :

Negative-unpleasant	Positive-pleasant
It is impossible to open an account for you today.	As soon as your signature card reaches us, we will gladly open an….
We don't refund if the returned item is soiled and unsalable.	We refund when the returned item is clean and resalable.
To avoid further delay and inconvenience, we are sending this report by special delivery.	So that you will get this report as soon as possible, we are sending it special delivery.
Second-hand car	Used car or Resale car

4. Concreteness(구체성)

구체성이란 애매하고 일반적인 표현보다 명확하고 구체적인 사실이나 숫자를 열거하는 것을 말한다.

Guidelines

- Use specific facts and figures.
- Put action in your verbs.
- Choose vivid and image-building words.

Vague, general, indefinite	Concrete and convincing
Our product has won several prizes.	Our product has won first prize.
This computer reproduces campaign letters fast.	This computer types 1,000 personalized 150-word campaign letters in one hour.

특히 a few, high, low, more, quick, soon, early, long, many, most, slow, tall 등과 같이 불확실하고 오해와 혼동을 초래하는 표현보다 for instance, for example, such as와 같이 예를 들어가면서 문장을 구체적으로 작성하여야 한다. 또한 business letter는 아래와 같이 수동형보다는 능동형으로 문장을 작성하는 것이 좋다.

Passive : A decision has been made.

Active/specific : The board of directors decided.

Passive : It will be noted ….

Active/specific : You will note ….

Passive : It is shown by figures ….

Active/specific : Figures show ….

Passive : A mile was run by the child.

Active/specific : The child ran a mile.

그러나 다음과 같이 행동의 주체나 목적을 강조할 때는 능동태보다 수동태로 작성하는 것이 바람직하다.

Don' t(active voice)	Do(passive voice)
We invite you~.	You are invited~.
He made three announcements~.	Three announcements were made before the meeting started.
You must attend~.	Attendance at the meeting is required.

Key Concepts

우리나라, 일본, 중동, 라틴아메리카는 High Context 문화권으로서 묵시적 표현이나 말 또는 그 사람의 사회적 신분을 중시하는 추상적인 배경을 가지고 있는 반면, 미국, 서구는 Low Context 문화권으로 명시적인 말, 계약, 법규를 중시한다. 따라서 마케터가 해외시장에서 실패하는 이유는 무의식적으로 주재국의 문화적 특성을 자국의 것과 같이 동일시하려는 소위 SRC(self-reference criterions)의 태도에 있다.

5. Clarity(명쾌성)

Clarity는 서신작성자가 전달하고자 하는 의미를 수신자가 쉽게 이해할 수 있도록 그 내용을 접근시키는 것을 의미한다. 대체로 사람들의 경험은 일치하지 않기 때문에 같은 단어라도 사람에 따라서 다른 의미로 해석될 수 있다. 따라서 명쾌한 통신문을 작성하기 위해서는 애매하고 오해를 불러 일으키기 쉬운 용어나 구문을 피하고 가능한 한 수신자에게 익숙한 단어를 사용하는 것이 필요하다.

Specific Ways

- Choose short, familiar and conversational words.
- Construct effective sentences and paragraphs.
- Include examples, illustrations, and other visual aids, when desirable.
- Achieve appropriate readability.

Say	Not
after	subsequent
big, large	substantial
error	inadvertency
issue	promulgate
home, house	domicile
pay	remuneration

show, uncover	disclose
use	utilize
about	circa
this is	i. e.(id est)
following	sequent
for example	e.g. (exempli gratia)

6. Courtesy(예절성)

예절바른 서신은 신규거래선의 개척뿐만 아니라 현재의 좋은 관계를 더욱 증진시키는 요소이다. 예의를 갖춘다는 것은 성실한 수신자본위(You-attitude)의 접근을 말한다.

따라서 courtesy는 thank you나 please 같은 기계적인 삽입어(mechanical insertions)로 구성되는 형식상의 정중함인 politeness와 구별된다. 그러므로 예절바른 서신 작성은 "I"나 "We" 대신에 "You"에 초점을 두고 positive하고 pleasant한 사실을 강조하면서 수신자의 입장에서 적절한 어기(語氣 ; tone)를 사용하여 회신을 신속하게 처리하는 것이다.

Suggestions

- Be sincerely tactful, thoughtful and appreciative.
- Omit expressions that irritate, hurt or belittle.
- Grant and apologize good-naturedly.
- Answer your mail promptly.

아래 좌측에 있는 표현을 피하고 우측컬럼에 있는 문장으로 고쳐 쓰는(rephrasing) 것이 좋다.

Tactless ; blunt	Tactful
Your letter is not clear at all; I can't understand it.	If I understand your letter correctly….
Obviously, if you'd read your policy carefully, you'd be able to answer these questions yourself.	Sometimes policy wording is a little hard to understand. I'm glad to clear up these questions for you.
Apparently you have already forgotten what I wrote you two weeks ago.	As mentioned in May 15 letter(or memo) to you, ….

7. Correctness(정확성)

서신작성 시 철자, 구두점, 문법 등의 정확성은 기본적인 요건이다. 무역통신문은 권리, 의무와 이해관계에 관련되는 거래가 많으므로 서신작성자는 다음과 같은 작문의 기법(The mechanics of writing)을 준수하여야 한다.

The Writer Should

- Use the right level of language.
- Include only accurate facts, words and figures.
- Maintain acceptable writing mechanics.
- Choose nondiscriminatory expressions.
- Apply all other pertinent C qualities.

정확성(correctness)에 대한 또 다른 중요요소는 인종이나 신체장애자들에 대한 무편견(nonbias)과 성(sexes)에 대한 동등한 대우이다.

Politically Correct Expressions

NO	YES
authoress, poetess, Jewess	author, poet, Jew
the better half, ball and chain	wife, spouse
mankind	humanity; human being; human race
man-made	synthetic, artificial
manpower	human power; human energy
men and ladies	men and women
	gentlemen and ladies, girls and boys
career girl or career man	Attorney Ellen Smith
	Jane Hills, a journalist
Mrs Brown and Smith	Ms. Brown and Mr. Smith
man and wife	husband and wife
Yes, for men	Yes, for men and/or women
businessman	business executives; business person;
	manager
Congress man	member of Congress
mailman, postman	mail carrier, letter carrier
hostess/host	server
house wife	home maker
policeman	police officer
weather man	weather forecaster
forefather	ancestor
foreman	supervisor
manhole	utility tunnel
craftsman	artisan
bell boy	bell captain
stewardess	flight/cabin attendant
showmanship	talentship
delivery boy	delivery person
repairman	repair person

또한 정확성은 서신작성의 필수적인 요소이므로 사용 시에 종종 혼동하기 쉬운 단어와 틀리기 쉬운 스펠링에 유의하여야 한다.

영국인들이 흔히 틀리는 영어 표현(BBC 방송 선정)

의미	그른 표현	옳은 표현
공짜로	for free	for nothing
정오	12 pm	noon, midday
변화를 초래하다	affect a change	effect a change
~와 다르다	different to	different from
빌리다	lend	borrow
걸어서	by foot	on foot

Korean Shortenings of English Words

NO	YES
Man to man t-shirts	Sweat shirts
Ball pen	Ball-point pen/Pen/Plain pen
Sack	Back pack
Note	Notebook
White	White-out/Correction fluid
Sign	Signature
APT	Apartment
Can	Canned beverage
Skin	Skin lotion
One-piece	Dress
Night club	Dance club
Aircon	Air conditioner
Remocon	Remote control
Trans	Transmission
Cassette	Tape recorder/player
Cunning	Cheating
Eye-shopping	Window shopping
Burberry coat	Trench coat
Back mirror	Rearview mirror
Kleenex	Tissue
After-service	After-care service, After-sale service
스치로플	Styro·foam or Styropor(독일어)
Social Network Service(SNS)	Social media
Skinship	Physical intimacy
Mixer	Blender

Some do's and dont's

Correct	Wrong
1. Ten tons of beef	1. 10 tons of beef
2. 10%(ten percent, 10 percent)	2. ten%
3. 10 a.m. 3 p.m.	3. ten a.m three p.m
4. Three o'clock	4. 3 o'clock
5. You are	5. You're
6. Will not	6. Won't

틀리기 쉬운 스펠링

낱말	발음기호	품사	뜻
accommodate	əkɔ́mədèit	vt.	수용하다
analyze	ǽnəlàiz	vt.	분석하다
auxiliary	ɔ:gziljəri	n.	보조적인
bankruptcy	bǽŋkrʌp(t)si	n.	파산
coliseum	kàlisi:əm	n.	대경기장
consensus	kɔnsénsəs	n.	합의
controversy	kántrəvə̀:rsi	n.	논쟁
extension	eksténʃən	n.	구내전화
February	fébuəri	n.	2월
forty	fɔ́:ti	n.	40
grammar	grǽmər	n.	문법
hygiene	háidʒi:n	n.	위생학
incidentally	insidéntəli	adv.	부수적으로
inoculate	inɔ́kjulèit	vt.	접종하다
interfered	intəfíə(d)	vi.	방해를 받은
license	láisəns	n.	면허
maintenance	méintinəns	n.	유지, 수리
nickel	níkl	n.	5센트짜리 주화
ninth	náinθ	n.	아홉번째
occasionally	əkéʒənəli	adv.	때때로, 가끔
occurrence	əkʌ́rəns	n.	발생
persuade	pə(:)swéid	vt.	설득하다
preferable	préfərəbl	a.	바람직한
psychological	sàikəlɔ́dʒikəl	a.	심리적인
questionnaire	kwèstiənέər	n.	질문지(앙케이트)
rhythm	ríðəm	n.	리듬
safety	séifti	n.	안전
separate	sépərèit	v.	분리시키다
shepherd	ʃèpəd	n.	양치기
sincerity	sinsèriti	n.	성실성
souvenir	sú:vəniə(r)	n.	기념품
transferable	trænsfɔ́:rəbl	a.	양도할 수 있는
usage	jú:zidʒ	n.	용법
vegetable	védʒitəbl	n.	야채
wednesday	wénzdi	n.	수요일

Error Detection

Detect the misspelled words in the following and correct the errors. Then check all words in a dictionary to see how many you had right.

1. aquainted
2. attatched
3. attendance
4. attornies
5. batchelor's degree
6. benefited
7. brosure
8. compliment
   (meaning supplement)
9. childrens
10. colledge
11. consede
12. concensus
13. congradulate
14. convience
15. correspondant
16. defendent
17. descendant
18. develop
19. disadvantage
20. dissatisfaction
21. envelop
22. excellente
23. existance
24. Febuary
25. heighth
26. incessent
27. insistence
28. interrupt
29. knowledge
30. labled
31. manageing
32. misspelled
33. occured
34. oppurtunity
35. paralel
36. preceed
37. prefered
38. proceedure
39. proceed
40. questionaire
41. recieve
42. referance
43. referred
44. recind
45. reccomodation
46. resistence
47. sargeant
48. seperate
49. servicable
50. stationary (paper)

혼동하기 쉬운 단어(Words often confused)

a, an	Use a before a word that begins with the consonant sound or long "u" sound. Use *an* before a word that begins with a silent "h" or a vowel sound.
amount, number, quantity	Whenever you count the units, use *number. Amount and quantity* refer to bulk, weight, or sums
anxious, eager	*Anxious* implies worry, whereas *eager* conveys keen desire.
between, among	*Between* involves two people or two groups; *among*, three or more.
biannually, biennially	*Biannually* means two times a year; *biennially*, every two years.
continual, continuous	*Continual* means to recur regularly(like lapping ocean waves). *Continuous* means without stopping.
counsel, council	*Counsel*(verb) means to advise, and(noun) means lawyer, advice. *Council*(noun) is an advisory or governing group.
data	*Data, plural of datum*, is now used informally with a singular verb(This data is) when all the facts are considered as a unit ; but the plural (These data *are*) is the more appropriate informal usage.
effect, affect	In business usage only *effect* is a noun; it means result, condition, or influence. Both words are verbs—to *effect* is to bring about, to *affect* is to influence.
imply, infer	*Imply* means to insinuate, or suggest; *infer* means to conclude. A writer *implies*; the reader infers.
lay, laid, laid lie, lay, lain	A person or a rug *lies* on the floor, but a person *lays* the book on the table or *lays* oneself of the floor. If you can substitute *place*(s) and answer *what*?, use the proper tense of *lay*.
principal, principle	*Principal* means "chief," "main," or (noun) sum of money, head of a school ; *principle*, rule or basic truth.
which, that, who	That refers to persons or things ; who to people; which only to things.

Maxim

A man who does not read good books has no advantage over a man who can't read them.

좋은 책을 읽지 않는 사람은 책을 볼 줄 모르는 사람보다 유리할 것이 없다.

Humor Parade

Man : Do you love me?

Woman : Madly.

Man : Do you need me?

Woman : Badly

Man : Will you marry me?

Woman : Gladly.

Man : Then would you take care of this check?

Woman : Sadly.

Part Ⅱ

무역통신문의 체계

The Arrangement of a Business Letter

제1장 무역통신문의 구성요소

G l o b a l   B u s i n e s s   E n g l i s h

Chapter 01

무역통신문의 구성요소

무역통신은 교역 당사자 간에 정보나 사상을 교환하는 쌍방향형(two-way type) 과정이다. 일반적으로 무역영어 통신문을 "상호 간의 이익을 위하여 수신자로 하여금 일을 수행하게 하는 낱말의 사용술이다(Business English is the art of using words so as to make men do things for the mutual benefit)"라고 정의하는데, 무역서신의 수신자로부터 좋은 인상과 호의적인 반응을 얻어내기 위해서는 적절한 용지, 정확한 구성요소 및 배치(layout), 정교한 타자 등이 요구된다. 대부분의 서신은 표준요소(standard parts)와 선택요소(optional parts)로 구성된다.

표준요소(Standard parts)	선택요소(Optional parts)
1. Letterhead 서두 2. Date Line 날짜 3. Inside Address 수신인 주소, 성명 4. Salutation 서두인사 5. Body or Message of Letter 서신의 본문 6. Complimentary Close 결미인사 7. Signature 서명	1. Reference No. or file No. 참조번호 2. Subject Line or Matter 서신의 제목 3. Attention Line 특정수신자 표시 4. Identification Marks 서신 관계자 표시 5. Enclosure Direction 동봉물 표시 6. Postscript 추신 7. Carbon Copy Notation 사본배부처 8. Additional Sheet 추가면

| 표 2-1 | 구성요소별 배열

(A diagram of a business with most of the possible parts)

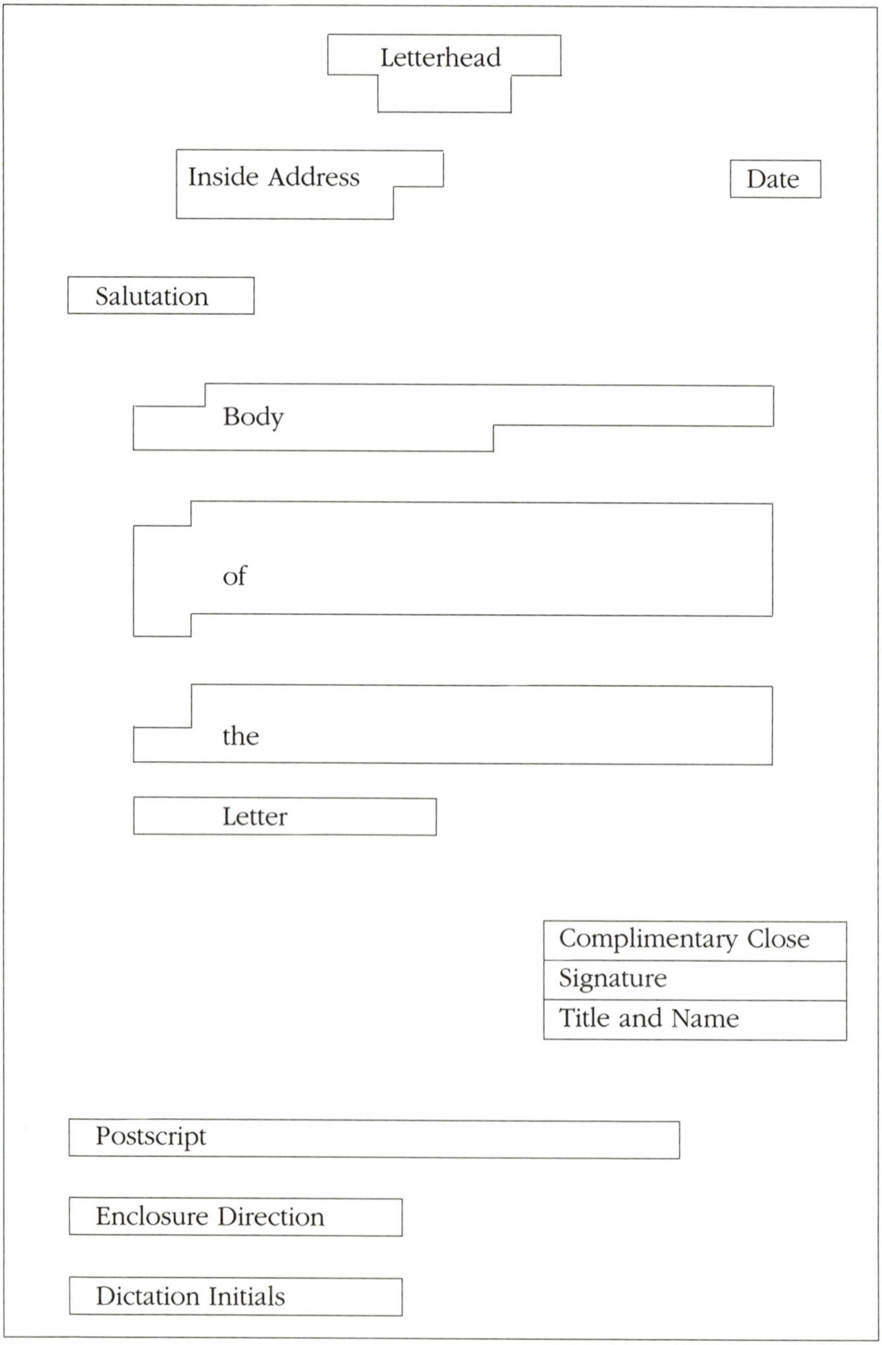

제1절 통신문의 표준요소(Standard Parts of the Letter)

1. Letterhead(서두)

무역통신의 서신용지(letter paper)는 일반적으로 흰색 또는 파스텔풍의 색조를 사용하고 8 2/1″×11″의 표준규격을 사용하는 것이 수신자에게 안정감과 좋은 이미지를 준다. 상단의 2″ 이내에 아래와 같은 사항을 간소하게 인쇄해서 사용한다. 이러한 인쇄부분을 printed letterhead라 한다.

(1) Name of the firm '회사명'

(2) Address '주소', P.O.Box No. '우편사서함번호'

(3) ZIP code '우편번호', Telephone No. '전화번호', Fax. No. '모사전송번호', 'e-mail'

(4) Line of business '업종' 등

강의노트

① P.O.Box No.(post office box number) C.P.O. Box No. (central post office box number : 중앙우체국 사서함번호) I.P.O. Box No. (international post office box number : 국제우체국 사서함번호).

② ZIP code(우편번호) : zone improvement program

③ Fax. No.(모사전송번호) : facsimile의 약칭으로서 불어 facere(make, do)와 similis(similar, like)의 합성어로 make similar의 뜻으로 쓰인다.

2. Date Line(날짜)

날짜는 보통 서신의 형식(styles of the letter)에 따라 서신의 우측, 중앙, 좌측 상단에 기재하며 여기에 사용되는 월명은 약자를 쓰지 않고 풀어쓰는(spellout) 것이 명확하며 연도 앞에는 반드시 comma를 찍는다.

그러나 date line 끝에는 period를 찍을 필요가 없다.

February 3, 20×× (American Style)
3rd February, 20×× (British Style)
3 February, 20×× (U.S.Military, Europe, Latin America)

| 표 2-2 |

PRICE WATERHOUSE FOUNDATION
60 BROAD STREET
New York NY 10004-2306

TWA — TRANS WORLD AIRLINES. INC
7001 WORLD WAY WEST
P.O.Box90909, AIRPORT STATION
LOS ANGELES, CALIFORNIA, U.S.A 90009

Weyerhaeuser Company
Tacoma, Washington 98477-0001
A.C206 · 383-3361

THE BOEING COMPANY
HEADOUARTERS OFFIES · PO BOX 3707 · SEATTLE. WASHINGTON 98124-3707.
IN REPLY REFER TO

ALLENITE PRODUCTS COMPANY,INC.
801 ADDISON STRET · BERKELEY CALIFORNIA 94710-2053 · (415)548-1252

ALUMINUM'
SCAFFOLDS
LADDERS
STAGING PLANKS
WORK PLANKS
ROLLING STEPS

STEEL
ROLLING STEPS

F W PETER McCHESNEY
president

Illustrations of letterheads.(All these are printed in black, except TWA initials, circles, and horizontal lines, in red; Weyerhaeuser outer triangle, in dark green : Allenite, all in medium green.

강의노트

① 날짜를 02/01/20×× 또는 2 · 3 · 20××와 같이 숫자(figures)로 쓰는 것은 메모용으로는 편리하지만 서신작성 시에는 혼동하기 쉬우므로 피하는 것이 좋다.
② Letterhead와 Date line을 합쳐서 Heading이라 한다.

3. Inside Address(수신인 주소 · 성명)

수신인의 상사명과 그 주소를 말하며, 봉투의 주소 및 성명과 동일하게 적는 것이 원칙이다. Date line으로부터 2줄 아래 좌측에 항상 기재한다. Inside address는 보통 3줄에서 4줄로 하지만 길면 6줄까지 타자한다.

(1) Mr. Charles W. Harper, President
Good Friends Trading Company
Empire State Building
345 Fifth Avenue
New York, NY 10016
U.S.A. (Block Form, Open Punctuation)

(2) Mr. Dallas Gordon,
Assistant Vice President,
Treasury Department,
ABC Banking Corporation,
P.O.Box 914167,
Augusta, GA 30915. (Indented Form, Closed Punctuation)

강의노트

① Inside Address는 여러 가지 요소가 피라미드 형태처럼 배열된다.

Person and Business(or Executive) Title
Commitee, section or other small group company
Building
P.O.Box number, Street, Address
City State ZIP Code
Country(자국 밖으로 가는 서신인 경우)

② 수신자의 성명, 상호, 구두점표기, 정관사 the의 유무 및 기타 요소에 대해서는 상대방의 서두 및 서명 등에서 사용하는 양식에 따라서 쓴다.

③ 주소에서는 St. Assn. Sq. c/o. Bldg 등의 약어를 많이 사용하는데, 미국의 주명을 약어로 표시할 때는 [표 2-3]과 같이 미국 우편성이 제안한 공식 약어를 사용해야 신속정확하게 배달될 수 있다.

| 표 2-3 | Official two-letter state abbreviations suggested by U.S. Postal Service

State	Abbr.	State	Abbr.
Alabama	AL	Louisiana	LA
Alaska	AK	Maine	ME
Arizona	AZ	Maryland	MD
Arkansas	AR	Massachusetts	MA
California	CA	Michigan	MI
Colorado	CO	Minnesota	MN
Connecticut	CT	Mississippi	MS
Delaware	DE	Missouri	MO
District of Columbia	DC	Montana	MT
Florida	FL	Nebraska	NE
Georgia	GA	Nevada	NV
Guam	GU	New Hampshire	NH
Hawaii	HI	New Jersey	NJ
Idaho	ID	New Mexico	NM
Illinois	IL	New York	NY
Indiana	IN	North Carolina	NC
Iowa	IA	North Dakota	ND
Kansas	KS	Ohio	OH
Kentucky	KY	Oklahoma	OK
Oregon	OR	Utah	UT
Pennsylvania	PA	Vermont	VT
Puerto Rico	PR	Virginia	VA
Rhode Island	RI	Virgin Islands	VI
South Carolina	SC	Washington	WA
South Dakota	SD	West Virginia	WV
Tennessee	TN	Wisconsin	WI
Texas	TX	Wyoming	WY

영국 및 기타 국가의 도시명 다음에 있는 숫자와 문자는 우편구역(Postal Districts)을 표시하는 것으로 E.C.2는 동부중앙 제2우편구역을 의미하며, 항상 대문자로 쓴다. 기타 런던시의 지역 구분은 다음과 같이 시행하고 있다.

The Points of the Compass :

N–North	S–South
E-East	W–West
NW–North West	NE–North East
SW–South West	SE–South East
EC–East Central	

4. Salutation(서두인사)

서두인사는 결미인사와 같이 고대 로마시대부터 전통적으로 사용해오고 있다. 우리나라의 배계 또는 근계에 해당하며 서신의 본문 2줄 위 좌측(left margin)에 타자한다.

(1) Gentlemen : 회사에 대하여 미국에서 일반적으로 사용되며, 구두점은 반드시 colon(:)을 찍는다. semicolon(;)을 사용하지 않도록 주의해야 한다.

(2) Dear Sirs : 회사에 대하여 사용되며, 영국에서 많이 쓰인다.

(3) Dear Sir : 한 사람의 남자에 대하여 쓰여지며, 미국에서 널리 사용한다.

(4) Dear Madam : 여자에게 기혼, 미혼을 불문하고 사용한다. Sir와는 달리 Madam에 s를 추가해서 Madams로는 절대 쓰지 않는다.

(5) Mesdames, Ladies : 여자만으로 구성된 사회, 단체에 사용한다.

(6) Sir, madam : Dear를 생략하고 Sir, Madam이라 하며 가장 formal한 것으로 공용문에서 많이 사용된다.

강의노트

① 서두인사에는 존칭어를 사용할 경우에 이름(given name or first name)을 쓰지 않고 성(surname or christian name)을 쓴다.

(ex)	Do	Don't
	My dear Smith	My dear Huntington J. Smith

서두인사	주소작성
Dear Mrs. Carter Dear Mr. Douglas Dear Mr. Smith	Mrs. Rosalynn Carter Mr. William O. Douglas Mr. Robert E. Smith, Jr.

② 존칭사용 요령

Mr. : 개인인 남자에게 붙이는 존칭이며 Mister의 약자이다. 우리나라와는 달리 미국에서는 대통령에게도 붙이는 최고의 존칭이다.

Miss : 미혼여성에게 붙이는 존칭이며 약자가 아니므로 period를 찍지 않는다. 복수형은 Misses.

Mrs.[misiz] : Mistress의 약자로 기혼여성에 붙이는 존칭이다.

Ms.[miz] : Miss와 Mrs.를 합친 여성의 경칭이다. 혼인 여부(marital status)에 관계없이 직책(title)이 없는 직장여성들에게 붙이는 것이 최근의 경향이다.

Messrs[mesəz] : Mr.의 복수형으로서 Messieurs의 약칭이다. 둘 이상의 남자나 인격적 요소가 있는 상사명 앞에 붙이나 대체로 생략하는 경향이 있다.

Esq. : Esquire의 약자로서 Mr.와 같이 한 남자에게 쓰이는 영국식 존칭이나 사용빈도수가 줄어들고 있으며 Mr.와는 달리 항상 성명 뒤에 붙인다.

일반개인으로부터 정부각료에 이르기까지 수신자가 다양하므로 정확한 서두인사 및 주소작성을 위해서는 [표 2-4]를 참고로 해서 사용하는 것이 좋다.

| 표 2-4 | Formal and Informal Salutations

Correspondent	Forms of Address	Salutations
Man	Mr. Huntington J. Smith Peter Campbell Brown, Esq.(A British title[Esquire] of courtesy and respect, becoming less common	My dear Sir(formal), My dear Mr. Smith(formal), Dear Sir(less formal), Dear Mr. Smith(less formal), Dear Hunt(informal)
Woman	Mrs. Fay T. Jones, or Mrs. John L. Jones(legal form of address) Miss or Ms. Fay T. Jones	My dear Madam(formal), My dear Mrs.(Ms. or Miss) Jones (formal), Dear Mrs. (Ms. or Miss) Jones(Less formal), Dear Madam(less formal), Dear Fay(informal)
Unknown gender	Jean Fredericks Hua Mei Lai L.C.Stewart	Dear Jean Fredericks Dear Hua Mei Lai Dear L.C.Stewart
Two men addressed jointly	Messrs. John Able and Jay Baker, or Messrs. Able and Baker	My dear Sirs,* Sirs*(formal) ; Dear Sirs,* Gentlemen*(less formal) : Dear John and Jay(informal, when first names are used in address)
Married couple	Mr. and Mrs. John LJones, or Mr. and Mrs. J.L.Jones	Dear Mr. and Mrs. Jones (formal), Dear Mary and John(informal)
Two married women or one married, one single	Mmes. Carr and Roth, or Mrs. Carr and Ms. M.Roth, or Miss Amelia Carr and May Roth, or Mrs A.Carr and Miss M.Roth	Ladies, Mesdames(formal) ; Dear Ladies, My dear Ladies Dear Mmes. Carr and Roth
Two single women	Misses Carr and Roth Miss A.Carr and Ms. M.Roth, or Miss Amelia Carr Ms.May Roth(two lines)	Same as above for formal ; Dear Misses Car and Roth, Dear Amelia and May
Two single women with same surname (give name of older first, if known)	Misses Hortense and Lila Skugs Miss Hortense and Ms. Lila Skugs Ms. Hortense and Lila Skugs, or	Same as above for formal ; My dear Miss Skugs, Dear Miss Skugs, Dear Hortense and Lila

	Miss Hortense Skugs Ms. Lila Skugs(two lines)	
Unknown	None	To Whom it May Concern : Dear Sir or madam,

Companies

A business firm (of men or of men and women) Hyer and Lowre, Inc.	Hyer and Lowre, Inc.	My dear Sirs*(formal)(use only when no women officers) ; Dear Sirs*(Less formal) ; Gentlemen*(less formal)
A specific person at a business firm	Mr. John L.Jones, title ; ABC Company	Same as for individual
A firm of two or more women	Carr and Roth, or Mmes, (or Ms.)Carr and Roth	Some salutations as for two or more married women ; when in doubt use "Gentlemen"

Professional people

Any person with a doctor's degrees (Ph.D., LL.D., D.V.M., etc.), or (PhD, LLD, DVM, DDS, etc.)	Dr. Leon Goldenberg, or Leon Goldenberg, M.D. or Md† Mr. John and Dr. Jane Hemple*	My dear Doctor, My dear Sir(formal) ; [My dear Madam (formal)] ; My dear Dr.Goldenberg, Dear Doctor(less formal); Dear Sir(less formal), Dear Leon(informal); Dear Mr. and Dr. Hemple
Two people with doctor's degrees not necessarily the same. Address senior person first, if known.	Drs. Leon Goldenberg and Jessie Holland, or Drs. Goldenberg and Holland	My dear Doctors(formal), My dear Drs. Goldenberg and Holland(less formal), Dear Drs. Goldenberg and Holland(less formal), Dear Doctors(less formal), Dear Leon and Jessie(informal)
An assistant, associate, or full professor in a college or university	Henry J.Morrow, M.A., M.Sc., or MA, MSc Professor Henry J.Morrow Professor Pauline J.Morrow	Dear Sir(or Madam)(formal); My dear Sir(or Madam)(formal) ; My dear professor Morrow (formal); Dear Professor Morrow(less formal); Dear

		Professor, Dear Henry (informal); Dear Pauline (informal)
Dean of a college or academy (without doctoral degree)	Dean Fullerton Briggs School of Optometry Columbia University	Dear Dean(formal) Dear Dean Briggs(informal)

* Do not use "Sirs" when a mixed group is addressed. "Gentlemen" is a softer word for this purpose.

† Strong trend to omit periods between letters recently.

Clergy

The Pope	His Holiness, Pope Paul VI	Your Holiness, Most Holy Father
A Roman Catholic cardinal	His Eminence, James Cardinal Montilla Archbishop of New Brunswick	Your Eminence
A Roman Catholic archbishop or bishop	The Most Reverend Gerald T. Bole Archbishop(or Bishop) of Chicago	Excellency, Your Excellency, Most Reverend Sir
A monsignor	The Right Reverned Monsignor James A. O' Leary	Right Reverend and dear Monsignor(formal), or either Half(less formal)
A Roman Catholic priest	Rev. Stanislave V.Bonawicz	Reverend and dear Father, Dear Reverned Father
A brother of an order of monks	Brother Jerome, C.F.X	Dear Brother, Dear Brother Jerome
A mother superior in an order of nuns	Mother Mary Kathleen, Superior St. Mary' s High School	Dear Mother Superior, Dear Reverend Mother
A nun	Sister Muriel Joseph, O.S.J	Dear Sister, Dear Sister Muriel
A Protestant Episcopal Bishop	The Right Reverend Francis Conne Bishop of Denver	Right Reverend and Dear Sir, Dear Bishop Conne, My dear Bishop Conne
A minister	The Rev. Harvey W. Noordsy	My dear Reverend Noordsy, Dear Reverend Noordsy, Dear Pastor Noordsy (Lutheran)

A minister, dean, or pastor with a D.D	Dr. John Henry Browne, or John Henry Browne, D.D(or DD)	Dear Dr Browne
A rabbi	Rabbi Aryeh Lev	Dear Rabbi, Dear Rabbi Lev, My dear Rabbi Lev

Government officials

President	The* President of the United States	Dear Mr. President, Sir, Dear Sir, Dear Mr.Bush
A member of the Supreme Court (the chief is referred to as Chief Justice)	The*Honorable William D.Douglas Justice of the United States Supreme Court, or Justice William O.Douglas United States Supreme Court	Dear Sir, Dear Mr. Justice, Dear Mr. Douglas, Dear Justice Douglas(Dear Mr. Chief Justice)
An ambassador of the U.S.	The* Honorable John Smith Ambassador to Denmark	Dear Sir, Dear Ambassador, Dear Mr. Ambassador, Dear Madam Ambassador, Dear Mr. Smith
An ambassador of a foreign country	The* Honorable(or title or rank if known) Hector Dubal Ambassador to United States, or His Excellency the French am-bassador(if name unknown)	Honorable Sir, Honorable Ambassador, My dear Ambassador, Dear Ambassador, Dear Mr. Ambassador, Dear Madam Ambassador, Dear Dr. Duval
A member of the President's cabinet	The* Honorable Robert E. Smith Secretary of State, or The Secretary of State (name omitted)	Dear Sir, Dear Mr. Smith, Dear Mr. Secretary
Wife of the President of the United States	Mrs. Rosalynn Carter White House Washington, DC 20500	Dear Madam(formal), Dear Mrs. Carter(informal)
The Vice President of the United States	The Vice President Senate Office Building Washington, DC20510	Dear Mr. Vice President, (formal), Dear Sir (formal), Dear Mr. Cheney (less formal)

Secretary General of the United Nations	His Excellency Kurt Waldheim Secretary General of the United Nations New York, NY 10017	Dear Secretary General (formal), Dear Sir(formal), Dear Dr. Waldheim (less formal)
President of a foreign country	(Name), President Republic of France Presidential Palace Paris, France	Your Excellency(formal), Dear Mr. President(formal)
United States Representative to the United Nations (Ambassador-rank position)	The* Honorable(name) United States Representative Mission to United Nations New York, NY 10017	Dear(name & title)(not position title)
A U.S or state senator	The* Honorable Richard Fields, or Senator Richard Fields Senate Office Building Washington, DC20510	Dear Sir, Dear Mr. Fields, Dear Senator Fields, My dear Senator
A member of Congress	The* Honorable Roberto B. Cendar, or Representative Roberto B. Cedar	Dear Rep. Cedar, Dear Ms. Cedar, My dear Rep. Cedar, My dear Ms. Cedar
A governor	The* Honorable John F.Jones Governor of Minnesota, or Governor John F. Jones	Dear Sir, Dear Governor, Dear Governor Jones
A mayor of a city or town or any local government official	The* Honorable Robert F. Green Mayor of Bingham-ton	Dear Sir, Dear Mr. Mayor(or other title), Dear Mr. Green

Military personnel

Except When "Mr." or "Chief" is used, the name may be omitted in all military salutations. In the address, rank is usually abbreviated. To insure good delivery, give all information possible in military addresses.

Navy and Coast Guard enlisted men and officers	rank and name	Dear Mr. Jones(enlisted man), Dear Lieutenant(or other rank) Brown. Except : the salutation for an ensign is "Dear Mr. Brown"; for a lieutenant junior grade, "Dear Lieutenant Brown"; for a lieutenant commander, "Dear Commander Brown"; for a rear, vice, or fleet admiral, " Dear Admiral Brown"; for a chief petty officer, "Dear Chief Brown."
Army, Marine Corps, and Air Force enlisted men	rank and name	Dear Private(or other rank) Smith. Except the salutation for all grades of sergeants is "Dear Sergeant Smith."
Army, Marine Corps, and Air Force officers	rank and name	Dear Captain(or other rank) Holmes. Except : the salutation for a lst or 2nd lieutenant is "Dear Lieutenant Holmes" ; for lieutenant colonel, " Dear Colonel Holmes"; for a lieutenant, major, or brigadier general, "Dear General Holmes"; for a warrant officer, "Dear Mr. Holmes."

* May be dropped entirely. When "The" is omitted, "Honorable" may be abbreviated as "Hon." before the person' s name, not the title.
* "Letter Perfect"에서 인용.

5. The Body of the Letter(서신의 본문)

무역통신문의 구성요소 중 가장 중요한 부분이다. 일반적으로 본문은 single space로 하고, paragraph와 paragraph 사이는 double spacing으로 타자하는 것이 원칙이다.

서두인사 다음 2줄 밑에서 시작하고, block form은 left margin에서부터 그리고 indented form은 왼쪽에 5~10 space의 margin을 둠으로써 paragraph가 바뀜을 표시한다.

강의노트

본문작성 시 지켜야 할 유의사항 :

① Organize according to an appropriate plan
② Keep your first and last paragraphs short-preferably less than 5 lines
③ Vary the intervening paragraph lengths; Maximum 8 to 10 lines
④ Make the average length of your sentence about 17 to 20 words
⑤ Achieve the C qualities
⑥ Avoid the use of quotation marks and underlining as much as possible
⑦ Syllabification(분철법)

Don't	Do
Mr. Bill Clinton	Mr. Bill Clinton
February 3, 20××	February 3, 20××
$1,123, 457.80	$1,123,457.80
35.3 milli- meters	35.3 millimeters (or 35.3mm.)
28 yards, 2 feet, 7 inches	28 Yards, 2 feet, 7 inches

6. Complimentary Close(결미인사)

Complimentary Close는 Salutation과 마찬가지로 관습적이고 경의적인 표현으로서 본문 2줄 아래 타자하고 첫 글자는 대문자로 써야 한다(Only the first letter of the first word is capitalized). 그리고 끝에 ","(comma)를 찍는 것을 잊어서는 안 된다.

Complimentary Close	Style
Yours truly, Yours very truly, Very truly yours,	Formal, Businesslike
Sincerely, Yours sincerely, Sincerely yours, Very sincerely yours,	Less Formal
Cordially, Yours cordially, Cordially Yours, Yours very cordially, Very cordially yours,	Less Formal, friendly
Yours respectfully, Respectfully yours, Yours very respectfully, Very respectfully yours,	Formal, to a superior

Traditional Style	Modern/Recommended Style
Yours very truly, Korea Trading Company J. H. Koh, Manager Purchasing Department	Yours truly, J. H. Koh, Manager Purchasing Department

강의노트

① Yours truly, Very truly yours,와 같이 순서가 바뀌는 것은 단조로움을 피하기 위해서이고 Truly는 미국에서, Faithfully는 영국에서 주로 많이 사용한다.
② 판매서한에서 가끔 Gratefully yours, Expectantly yours, At your service와 같은 Unusual complimentary close를 사용하는 것도 효과적이다.
③ 상용서신과는 달리 Personal letters에서는 상대방과의 친소관계에 따라 예의바르고 관례적인 것에서부터 지순한 감정을 나타내는 표현들을 사용한다. : Yours very sincerely, Yours affectionately, Ever yours, Yours as ever, Love, All my love, With my undying love.
④ capitalize[~을 대문자로 쓰다(인쇄하다)] ↔ lower-case[~을 소문자로 쓰다(인쇄하다)]

7. Signature(서명)

Signature Area(서명란)는 상사명, 육필서명(pen-written), 타자한 서명자명(typewritten name) 및 직명(business title)로 구성된다.

서명은 반드시 자필(manual)로 일정하게 해야 하다. 수신인이 서명자의 성(gender)을 구분할 수 있도록 가끔 여자 앞에 Mrs., Miss를 붙이나 Mr.는 절대 사용하지 않는다.

Very truly yours,	Sincerely.	Cordially yours,
Thomas L. Sutton	BRONSON COMPANY	*Roy*
Thomas L. Sutton	*Mary P. Tracy*	Roy Layton, President
Manager, Plant 2	Mary P. Tracy	
	Personnel Manager	

서명권이 없는 사람이(unauthorized signer) 대리로 서명하는 경우에는 회사명 앞에는 For, 사람 앞에는 By를 붙인다. 법률적으로 대리서명이 위임된 경우 P.P. 또는 per pro.를 사용하는데, 라틴어 per procurationem의 약어로서 by proxy, as agent for를 쓰는데 '대리로' 라는 의미이다.

강의노트

Signature는 Sign의 명사형으로서 '서명' 이란 뜻이다. Sign은 '표시, 부호, 기호' '서명하다, 기명날인하다'

Don't : We need your sign.

Do : We need your signature.

Don't : Authorized Sign Booklet.

Do : Authorized Signature Booklet.

Don't : Please signature on the back of the check.

Do : Please sign on the back of the check.

제 2 절 통신문의 선택요소(Optional Parts of the Letter)

1. Reference No. or File No.(참조번호)

업무처리를 용이하게 하기 위한 것으로 서신의 우측 Date line 위나 아래 또는 Inside address 위에 타자한다.

	Date line Our Ref No.
Inside Address	

보통 Letterhead에 인쇄를 해두고 서신의 참조번호나 부호를 타자토록 한다.

- Please quote our reference No. 1234, when corresponding with us.
- In response, please refer to our file No. SP-9001.
- Please mention our file reference No. 1234 when answering this letter.
- For our future communications, please cite our stenographic reference No. JH 1001.

2. Letter Subject or Subject Matter(서신의 제목)

Subject line은 본문의 내용을 개략적으로 파악할 수 있는 주제(main theme)를 나타낸다. 보통 Salutation 2줄 밑에 또는 중앙에 타자한다.

Salutation
Subject : Sale of Traveller's Check
RE : Your L/C NO. MO63511NS0004
Our Order No. 1234. of March 1,

Re는 라틴어의 전치사로서 concerning, in the matter of '관하여'를 의미한다. 최근에는 Subject나 Re의 사용을 피하고 제목 밑에 underlining하는 경향이 있다.

3. Attention Line or Particular Address(특정수신자 표시)

상대방 회사 내의 특정부서나 특정인 앞으로 서신이 도달되는 것을 원하는 경우에 Inside address와 Salutation 사이에 다음과 같이 표시한다.

Attention : Mr. J. H. KOH
Attention of Mr. M. C. Hammer, President
Attn : International Department

4. Identification Marks or Dictation Initials(서신관계자 표시)

서신작성의 책임소재를 명백히 하기 위하여 Signature의 마지막 줄과 같은 줄 또는 1~2줄 밑에 left margin부터 서신관계자의 두문자(Initial)를 타자한다. 이때 구술인과 서명인은 대문자로, 타자원은 소문자로 표시한다.

> MGK/HYC/jh(Dictator, Signer, Typist or Stenographer)
> MGK/jh(Dictator, Typist or Stenographer)

5. Enclosure Notation(동봉물 표시)

Identification Marks 아래 1~2줄 밑에 Enclosure, Encl. Enclosures, Encls 라 기재하고 동봉물의 내용 및 동봉물을 표시한다.

> Encl : Order Form No. 123
> Encls : 3
> 4 Enclosures

동봉물을 stapler나 clip으로 서신에 직접 첨부할 경우에는 Enclosure 대신에 Attachment나 Attach를 쓴다. 그러나 가능하면 (paper) clip를 사용하지 않는 것이 좋다.

6. Postscript(추신)

서신의 본문에 중요한 사항을 누락했거나 강조하는 경우에 Identification Marks 2줄 아래 P.S.라 표시하고 추가로 타자하거나 수기한다.

P.S.는 라틴어 postscriptum의 약어로서 'written-after' 이며 'after-thought' 를 의미한다. 만약 추신이 2가지인 경우 2번째 추신은 P.P.S.(post postscriptum)로 표시한다.

P.S. The prices remain in force for 45 days only.
P.P.S. The newest models in our lines are also priced surprisingly low.

7. Carbon Copy or Copy Notation(사본배부처)

서신의 작성자가 수취인 이외의 제3자에게 사본을 배부했음을 표시하고자 할 때에 Identification Marks 1~2줄 밑에 타자한다. 서신을 다른 사람에게 보낸 사실을 통보는 하되 누군지를 밝히고 싶지 않을 경우에는 BCC(Blind Carbon Copy to…)로 쓴다.

C.C. Mr. Thomas K. Jefferson
C.C. Credit Department
Copy to Mr. T. J. Kim
Copies to : Mrs. S. H. Chung
Mr. K. D. Hong
BCC.

8. Additional Sheet(추가면)

무역서신이 한 페이지로 끝날 때는 문제가 없으나 two-page letter인 경우 추가면을 사용하여야 한다. 다른 서신과 혼동되지 않도록 다음과 같이 표시하여야 한다.

제1면 하단 :
-To be continued-
-Continued-
-Page 1-

페이지의 뒷면을 계속 사용할 때는 P.T.O(Please turn over)나 TSVP (Tournez s' il vous plait)로 표시하나 무역통신문에 사용하는 것은 바람직하지 않다.

제2면에서는 Letterhead가 없는 것을 사용하며 다음과 같이 표시한다.

제2면 표시 예(1)

Good Friends Company-2-	May 5, 20××

제2면 표시 예(2)

Good Friends Company
Page 2
May 5, 20××

제3절 무역서한의 배치(Letter Layout)

1. Pure Block Style(완전 수직식)

본 형식에서 모든 구성요소는 왼쪽 여백을 수직으로 일정하게 남기고 타자한다. Open Punctuation이 사용되며 미국에서 가장 유행하는 초현대적이고 진보적인 형식이다. Full or Extreme Block Style이라고도 한다.

2. Block Style(수직식)

발신일자(Date), 결미인사(Complimentary Close), 즉 서명란(Signature Area)

을 제외하고 모든 요소가 수직식으로 오늘날 많이 쓰는 형식 중의 하나이다.

3. Semi-Block Style(반 수직식)

본문만을 Indentation시키고 그 밖의 Heading, Inside Address, Complimentary 등은 Block Style로 쓰는 절충형식이다.

4. AMS · Simplified Style(간이식)

Salutation과 Complimentary Close를 생략하고 완전수직식과 같이 왼편에 편중되어 있다. 미국사무관리협회(National Office Management Association/Administrative Management Society)에서 권장하는 형식이다.

5. Indented Style(사선식)

보수적인 British Style로서 Inside Address, The Body of the Letter, Complimentary Close와 Signature Area는 사선식이며 그 밖의 모든 부분은 수직식으로 되어 있다.

6. Over-hanging Style(현수식)

Inside Address는 구두점 개방식이고 본문의 각 절 및 줄만 Left Margin에 두고 나머지 줄은 다섯자 정도 앞으로 들여서 배열한다.

일반 통신문보다는 상품판매 광고 및 권유장에 주로 쓰인다.

제4절 Punctuation(구두점)

1. Open Punctuation(구두점 개방식)

본문을 제외한 모든 서신요소에 comma나 period를 사용하지 않는다. 필요한 경우 약어에는 period를 찍는다.

2. Closed Punctuation(구두점 폐쇄식)

Date, Attention, Subject Line 뒤에는 Period를 찍고 Inside Address 끝에는 comma, 마지막 줄은 period를 사용한다.

Salutation 뒤에는 colon, complimentary close와 회사명 뒤에는 comma를 찍고, 서신 작성자의 이름과 직위에는 period를 찍는다.

3. Mixed Punctuation(구두점 절충식)

일반적으로 많이 사용하는 형식으로 Salutation 뒤에는 colon, complimentary close 뒤에는 comma를 찍는다. 그러나 date와 inside address 뒤에는 구두점을 찍지 않는다.

| 표 2-5 | Pure block style, block date, open punctuation

HIGH POINT FURNITURE CO.

November 18, 20--

Winslow, Body & Jones
175 Eastbourne Parkway
Providence, RI 02919

Gentlemen :

The sketch of the desks and chairs you forwarded to us yesterday is now in the hands of our furniture designers. They have already begun work on planning and estimating the construction details. Thank you for sending it so promptly.

Within a week we should be able to offer you the price and delivery estimates for the furniture in a variety of finishes. These figures will be computed to compete favorably with any other manufacture of similar quality. Please keep in mind that the chairs and desks will be made to last. We are glad you so wisely included details of your decor. It will help greatly in saving time.

Our regional salesman suggested that you might wish to see a similar custom order which we completed last month for another business office in your area. He has already ascertained that you would be most welcome there to see the charm and serviceability of our desks and chairs add to this modern office. Should you desire this opportunity, please communicate with me at once.

Sincerely,

(Ms.)* Carol Powers
Executive Vice President

mq

| 표 2-6 | Indented style, pivoted date, mixed punctuation. archaic

November 18, 20--

Winslow, Body & Jones
175 Eastbourne Parkway
Providence, RI 02919

Gentlemen :

The sketch of the desks and chairs you forwarded to us yesterday is now in the hands of our furniture designers. They have already begun work on planning and estimating the construction details. Thank you for sending it so promtly.

Within a week we should be able to offer you the price and delivery estimates for the furniture in a variety of finishes. These figures will be computed to compete favorably with any other manufacture of similar quality. Please keep in mind that the chairs and desks will be made to last. We are glad you so wisely included details of your decor. It will help greatly in saving time.

Our regional salesman suggested that you might wish to see a similar custom order which we completed last month for another business office in your area. He has already ascertained that you would be most welcome there to see the charm and serviceability our desks and chairs add to this modern office. Should you desire this opportunity, please communicate with me at once.

Sincerely,

HIGH POINT FURNITURE CO.

Carl W. Powers
Executive
Vice President

| 표 2-7 | Hanging paragraph, or inverted indent style, centered date, mixed punctuation

HIGH POINT FURNITURE CO.

November 18, 20--

Winslow, Body & Jones
175 Eastbourne Parkway
Providence, RI 02919

Gentlemen :

The sketch of the desks and chairs you forwarded to us yesterday is now in the hands of our furniture designers. They have already begun work on planning and estimating the construction details. Thank you for sending it so promtly.

Within a week we should be able to offer you the price and delivery estimates for the furniture in a variety of finishes. These figures will be computed to compete favorably with any other manufacture of similar quality. Please keep in mind that the chairs and desks will be made to last. We are glad you so wisely included details of your decor. It will help greatly in saving time.

Our regional salesman suggested that you might wish to see a similar custom order which we completed last month for another business office in your area. He has already ascertained that you would be most welcome there to see the charm and serviceability of our desks and chairs add to this modern office. Should you desire this opportunity, please communicate with me at once.

Sincerely,

CWP/MQ

Ms. Carol Powers
Executive Vice President

| 표 2-8 | Semi-block style, pivoted date, open punctuation

HIGH POINT FURNITURE CO.

November 18, 20--

Winslow, Body & Jones
175 Eastbourne Parkway
Providence, RI 02919

Gentlemen

The sketch of the desks and chairs you forwarded to us yesterday is now in the hands of our furniture designers. They have already begun work on planning and estimating the construction details. Thank you for sending it so promtly.

Within a week we should be able to offer you the price and delivery estimates for the furniture in a variety of finishes. These figures will be computed to compete favorably with any other manufacture of similar quality. Please keep in mind that the chairs and desks will be made to last. We are glad you so wisely included details of your decor. It will help greatly in saving time.

Our regional salesman suggested that you might wish to see a similar custom order which we completed last month for another business office in your area. He has already ascertained that you would be most welcome there to see the charm and serviceability of our desks and chairs add to this modern office.Should you desire this opportunity, please communicate with me at once.

Sincerely,

HIGH POINT FURNITURE CO.

CWP/MQ

Ms. Carol Powers
Executive Vice President

| 표 2-9 | Block style, pivoted date, mixed punctuation

HIGH POINT FURNITURE CO.

November 18, 20--

Winslow, Body & Jones
175 Eastbourne Parkway
Providence, RI 02919

Gentlemen :

The sketch of the desks and chairs you forwarded to us yesterday is now in the hands of our furniture designers. They have already begun work on planning and estimating the construction details. Thank you for sending it so promtly.

Within a week we should be able to offer you the price and delivery estimates for the furniture in a variety of finishes. These figures will be computed to compete favorably with any other manufacture of similar quality. Please keep in mind that the chairs and desks will be made to last. We are glad you so wisely included details of your decor. It will help greatly in saving time.

Our regional salesman suggested that you might wish to see a similar custom order which we completed last month for another business office in your area. He has already ascertained that you would be most welcome there to see the charm and serviceability of our desks and chairs add to this modern office.Should you desire this opportunity, please communicate with me at once.

Sincerely,

Ms. Carol Powers
Executive Vice President

CWP/MQ
CC: Charles Renault
Harrion Thomas

제5절 The Addressing of Envelopes(봉투주소의 기재법)

봉투주소를 Outside Address 또는 Envelope Address라고 부른다. Inside Address와 같은 style로 작성하되 double spacing으로 하는 것이 좋다. 단 판매 촉진 시에 효과적인 Window Envelope/Outlook Envelope(투명봉투/유창봉투)를 사용하는 경우 Outside Address를 별도로 기재할 필요가 없다.

1. Return Address(발신회사의 주소)

국제무역에 사용되는 봉투 좌측상단 또는 뒷뚜껑에 Letterhead와 같은 형태의 발신인 주소와 상호를 인쇄해 둔다. Sender's Address라고도 한다.

2. Addressee's Address(수취인의 주소)

수취인의 주소 · 성명(Receiver's Address)을 아래와 같이 배열한다.

a. Topline-Name of Recipient
b. Next 1 or 2 lines-Information(Name of company, agency, department, or other identifying information) and attention line.
c. Line above last-delivery address
d. Last line-Post office/state/zip code

| 표 2-10 | Large business envelope($9\frac{1}{2}$ by $4\frac{1}{8}$ inches) properly addressed for Optical Character Recognition.

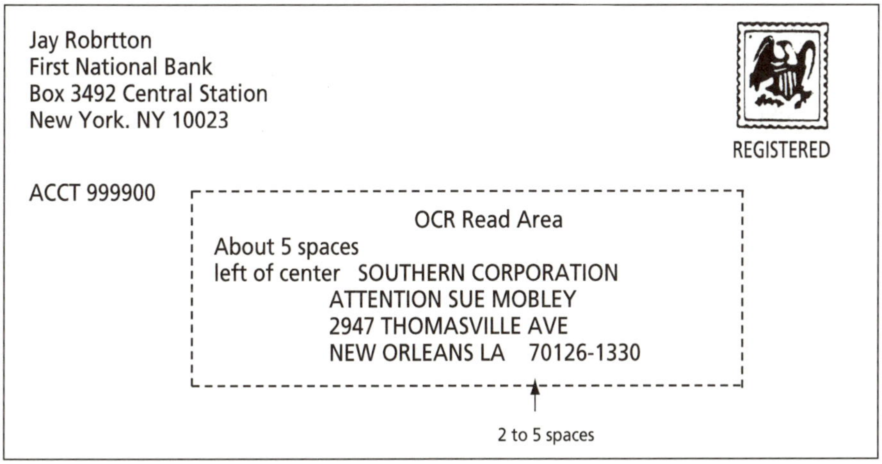

3. Mail Notation(우편지정사항)

Stamp position(소인위치) 밑에 우송편 및 그 밖의 지정사항을 항상 대문자로 타자한다. Mail Classifications이라고도 한다.

a. VIA AIRMAIL, BY AIRMAIL, AIRMAIL, PAR AVION(항공우편)

b. VIA SEATTLE(시애틀 경유)

c. BY M/S "NEW KOREA"(뉴코리아호 적재)

M/S=Motorship(S.S=Steamship, M/V=Motor Vessel)

d. MAIL FOR THE BLIND(맹인용 우편물)

e. REGISTERED, REGISTERED MAIL(등기우편), CERTIFIED MAIL(배달증명우편)

f. SPECIAL DELIVERY(미) or EXPRESS DELIVERY(영 : 속달우편)

g. BY SURFACE MAIL(일반우편, 육로나 해상으로)

4. On-Arrival Instructions(특수우편물지시)

우편물 취급에 대한 특기사항으로 Address의 하부좌측에 모두 대문자로 타자한다.

a. PERSONAL, PRIVATE & CONFIDENTIAL – '친전'

b. URGENT, IMMEDIATE – '지급'

c. PRINTED MATTER – '인쇄물'

d. PHOTO ONLY – '사진재중'

e. SAMPLE OF NO VALUE – '무료견본'

f. INTRODUCING MR. – '~씨를 소개함'

g. PLEASE FORWARD TO – '~에게 전송을 바람'

h. ACCOUNT NUMBERS – '계좌번호'

i. HOLD FOR ARRIVAL – '수신인이 도착할 때까지 보관 후 전달요망'

Humor Parade

At the Restaurant

Waiter : What would you like to have?

Guest : …….

Waiter : Beef or Pork?

Guest : …….

Waiter : Are you a vegetarian?

Guest : No, I am a Korean.

Part Ⅲ

모범무역서한
Sample Business Letters

Global
Business
English

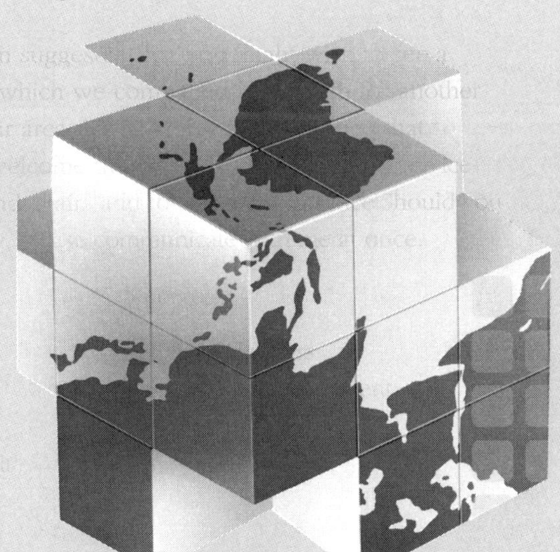

Global Business English

Chapter 01

거래제의
Proposal of Business

1. 거래처의 선정

무역상사가 외국시장에서 신규 무역거래관계를 맺는 데 있어서 우선적으로 고려해야 할 사항은 지리경제학(geonomics) 및 시장분석(market analysis)을 통해서 목표시장(target market)을 선정하고 그 시장에서 우량기업을 탐색하는 것이다. 시장조사 및 거래처 개척의 실제 수단으로 다음과 같은 거래알선 기관을 이용하여 유수한 적격업체를 선정해야 한다.

① 무역업자 자신이 목표시장에서 현지조사, 민간무역사절단 파견 또는 자사의 해외지사, 출장소, 판매순회원(Travelling Representative) 활용

② 대한상공회의소(KCCI : Korea Chamber of Commerce and Industry)나 국제상업회의소(ICC : International Chamber of Commerce)를 통하여 목표시장에서 신규거래처의 소개를 의뢰

③ 한국무역협회(Korea International Trade Association : KITA), 대한무역투자진흥공사(KOTRA : The Korea Trade-Investment Promotion Agency), 일본무역진흥회(Japan External Promotion Trade Organization : JETRO) 등을 활용

④ 국내외 정부기관 이용(산업통상자원부, 재외한국대사관 · 영사관, 재한외국대사관, 외국상무성 등)

⑤ 거래외국환은행(Foreign Exchange Bank)을 이용
대부분의 외국환은행은 국제금융의 중심지에 소재하고 있는 해외의 유수은행들과 예치환 및 무예치환 거래계약(Depositary Correspondent &

Non-depositary Correspondent Arrangement)을 체결하고 있다.

⑥ 정기간행물(Periodical)이나 무역관계단체의 회보(Bulletin) 참고

⑦ 상공인명부(Directory)

- Korea Trade Directory(Seoul)
- Kelly's Directory of Merchants, Manufacturers and Shippers(London)
- Dun & Bradstreet Reference Book(New York)
- Register of Merchants, Manufacturers and Shippers(Tokyo)

⑧ 무역박람회(Trade Fair), 세계박람회(World Fair, International Exhibition) 등의 참가

우리나라 경제 6단체

• 전국경제인연합회	The Federation of Korean Industries (FKI)
• 대한상공회의소	The Korea Chamber of Commerce & Industry (KCCI)
• 한국무역협회	The Korea International Trade Association (KITA)
• 중소기업협동조합중앙회	The Korea Federation of Small and Medium Business(KFSB)
• 한국경영자총협회	The Korea Employers Federation (KEF)
• 전국은행연합회	The Korea Federation of Banks (KFBS)

2. 거래제의문의 구성요소

거래제의 서신은 동일시장에서 동일한 품목으로 여러 외국회사와 경쟁해야 되므로 AIDA Model(Attention, Interest, Desire, Action)에 의거하여 논리적으로 다음과 같은 사항을 간단명료하게 작성하여야 한다.

① 상대방을 알게 된 동기, 경로 및 거래관계 개설의 희망

② 자기소개－업계에서 자사의 지위, 영업종목, 거래능력 및 연혁

③ 참고자료－견품, 가격표, 상품목록, 소개장

④ 거래조건, 특히 가격 및 결제조건의 개요

⑤ 거래제의회사의 신용조회처(Reference)

⑥ 결문－회답을 기대한다는 것과 좋은 거래관계의 수립희망

Sample Letter 1

Gentlemen :

We have learned from the Korea Buyers Guide that you are interested in importing Korean antique furniture.

We are one of the leading exporters of Korean-made antique furniture and we would like to form a business relationship with you. Our goods are well received by people throughout the world because of their exquisite workmanship.

Enclosed are our illustrated catalog and price list for all the products we are handling.

Prices on the list are all F.O.B. Busan basis in U.S. dollars.

In regards to our financial standing, please refer to the Seoul First Bank in Seoul.

We look forward to your prompt reply.

Yours truly,

* 요약

우리는 귀사가 한국고가구제품을 수입하는 데 관심이 있다는 것을 KOREA BUYERS GUIDE를 통해서 알게 되었습니다.

당사는 국산고가구 제품의 주요 수출업체의 하나이며 귀사와 거래관계를 맺고자 합니다.

당사 제품은 정교한 솜씨 때문에 전 세계 사람들로부터 환영받고 있습니다.

동봉한 것은 당사가 취급하는 모든 제품에 대한 도해 상품목록과 가격표입니다.

가격표에 있는 가격은 모두 미화 · 부산항본선인도조건입니다.

당사의 재정상태에 대해서는 서울에 있는 서울제일은행에 조회하시기 바랍니다. 귀사의 신속한 회신을 기대합니다.

강의노트

① leading '주요한, 으뜸가는, 가장 중요한' ; chief ; the most important, the ~ men of the day : 당대의 인물. '일류의, 유력한, 유능한' 은 leading 외에 first-class ; first-rate ; A1[eiwʌ́n] ; prime, influential ; prominent ;

qualified ; competent가 있다.

② exquisite '절묘한, 정교한'

~ workmanship : 절묘한 솜씨. ~design : 정교한 도안

③ form a business relationship with '~와 거래관계를 맺다'

establish(enter into, initiate, start, commence) a business relationship with~, open an account with ~.

※ Business의 정적인 면(static sense)은 기업이고 동적인 면(doing sense)은 무역 · 경영을 의미한다.

④ refer '~을 보내다, 언급하다, 조회하다, 참고로 하다'

The speaker often ~red to his notes.

(연사는 종종 자기의 메모를 참조했다)

For any information as to our credit standing, please ~ to the ABC Bank, Seoul branch.

(당사의 신용상태에 대한 자료는 ABC은행 서울지점에 조회하십시오)

⑤ illustrated catalog '도해 상품목록'

illustrate 예해하다, 책 등에 그림 사진을 넣다, 여기서 catalog는 미국식 철자이고 catalogue는 영국식 철자이다.

영 · 미에서 철자가 다른 주요 단어는 아래와 같다.

◈ 영국 영어와 미국 영어 철자의 차이 ◈

영 국		미 국		뜻
learnt spelt	-t	learned spelled	-ed	배우다 철자를 쓰다
centre theatre	-re	center theater	-er	중앙 극장
travelling labelled	-ll	traveling labeled	-l	여행중인 레이블을 달다
dulness skilful	-l	dullness skillful	-ll	무딘 재치있는
programme kilogramme	-mme	program kilogram	m	프로그램 킬로그램
colour honourable	-our	color honorable	-or	빛깔 명예로운
defence offence	-ce	defense offense	-se	방위 위법 행위

analyse criticise	-se	analyze criticize	-ze	분석하다 비평
aeroplane cheque grey gaol		airplane check gray jail		비행기 검사 회색 교도소

⑥ F.O.B.

Free on Board '본선인도가격' FOB ; f.o.b.

Sample Letter 2

London Chamber of Commerce　　May 15, 20××
London, England

Dear Sirs,

We are a well-established exporter of all kinds of electronic goods and have extensive relationships with local prime manufacturers in Korea.

We now desire to extend our business activities to your market and we would be most appreciative if you could introduce us to some reliable firms who are interested in importing the merchandise we handle.

For information related to our standing and reputation, we are permitted to refer you to our bankers "Seoul First Bank" and/or the local Chamber of Commerce and Industry.

If there is anything we can do for you, please do not hesitate to ask.

Very truly yours,
New Korea Electronic Co., Ltd.

＊ 요약

당사는 각종 전자제품을 취급하는 명성이 높은 수출업체이며 한국에서 국내일류 제조업체들과 폭넓은 거래관계를 유지하고 있습니다.

당사는 이제 귀시장으로 사업의 확장을 갈망하고 있으며 당사의 제품을 수입하는데 관심이 있는 신뢰할 만한 회사들을 귀소에서 소개하여 주시면 감사하겠습니다.

당사의 신용상태나 평판에 관한 자료는 거래은행인 서울제일은행이나 이곳 상공회의소에 조회하시기 바랍니다.

귀 상업회의소를 위해 무엇이든지 더 해드릴 것이 있으면 주저하지 마시고 요청하십시오.

강의노트

① well-established '확고한, 명성이 높은'

cf. long-established : 창업된 지 오래된

We are long-established manufacturers of chemical products and our goods enjoy a high reputation for their excellent quality.

(당사는 창업된 지 오래된 화학제품 제조업체이며 우리 제품은 뛰어난 품질로 훌륭한 평판을 향유하고 있습니다.)

② local prime manufacturers '국내일류제조업체들'

local : 국내의, 지방의 ~credit : 내국신용장, ~standard time : 현지표준시간, ~employee : 현지고용인, ~customs : 지방풍습

prime : 일류의(first-rate), 기본적인, ~cost : 원가, ~lending(loan) rate : 미국의 우량기업대출금리. ~minister : 국무총리

③ reliable firms '신뢰할 만한 회사'

reliable : 믿을 수 있는. ~information : 믿을 수 있는 정보. reliability : 신빙성, 확실성

회사를 company, concern, house라고도 한다.

holding company : 지주회사, wholly-owned subsidiary : 100% 지분을 갖고 있는 자회사, subsidiary : 자회사, parent company : 모회사, sister company : 자매회사, listed company : 상장기업, conglomerate : 기업집단

④ our standing/reputation

여기서 standing은 credit standing '신용상태'를 의미한다.

영업상태는 business standing(commercial standing), 재정상태는 financial standing이라 하고, reputation은 '세평, 평판'

⑤ We are permitted to refer you to our bankers.

우리의 거래은행으로부터 동 은행을 귀 상업회의소에 신용조회처로 제공해도

좋다는 양해를 받고 있으며 우리의 신용상태와 평판에 관하여는 서울제일은행에 조회하라는 뜻.

We refer you by permission to our bankers.라고 해도 좋다.

We refer you to ~, You may refer to ~, Please refer to~ '~에 조회하십시오'

⑥ and/or

A and/or B는 'A and B 또는 A or B' 의 뜻이며 or만 사용해도 무방하다.

⑦ please do not hesitate to ~ '주저하지 말고 ~하십시오'

장황한 표현이므로 생략하는 것이 간결하다.

(Poor) If we can be of further assistance, please do not hesitate to contact us.

(Better) If we can be of further assistance, please contact us.

⑧ proposal : an offer to be accepted or rejected.

proposition : an offer of terms for a transactions.

Useful Sentences(거래제의관계)

1. We have learned of your name and address from the trade magazine, "The Business World".

   업계지인 "The Business World"에서 귀사명과 주소를 알게 되었습니다.

2. Your name and address have been given to us by the Korea Chamber of Commerce and Industry.

   대한상공회의소가 귀사를 소개해 주었습니다.

3. We have obtained(acquired) your name and address from KOTRA's trade directory.

   당사는 대한무역투자진흥공사의 무역인명부에서 귀사명과 주소를 입수하였습니다.

4. We found your name and address from the Korea Chamber of Commerce and Industry.

   당사는 대한상공회의소를 통해서 귀사명과 주소를 알았습니다.

5. Mr. K.D. Hong, Korean consul in Los Angeles provided us with your name and address.

   로스앤젤레스 한국영사인 Mr. K.D. Hong이 귀사명과 주소를 우리에게 제공하여 주었습니다.

6. We obtained your address through the courtesy of the American Embassy in Seoul and take this opportunity to contact you for the following purposes :
귀사의 주소를 주한미국대사관의 호의로 알게 되었으며 다음과 같은 목적으로 귀사에 연락할 기회를 갖게 되었습니다.
7. It has come to our attention through the Electronic Journal that you are a large importer of electrical home appliances.
Electronic Journal을 통해서 귀사가 가정전기용품의 대규모 수입업체라는 것을 알게 되었습니다.
8. Your firm has been recommended to us by the Korean Consul in your city as large exporters of computers.
귀도시에 있는 한국영사가 귀사를 컴퓨터 대규모 수출업체로 추천했습니다.
9. Our sales representative covering the East Coast region of your country says you are interested in importing Korean Ginseng products.
귀국에 있는 당사 동해안지역 판매대리점이 귀사가 한국산 인삼제품의 수입에 관심이 있다는 것을 알려주었습니다.
10. We are enclosing our latest illustrated catalog together with the price list.
가격표와 함께 당사의 최신 도해 상품목록을 동봉합니다.
11. Enclosed are our catalog and price list covering the complete line of our goods.
동봉한 것은 당사의 전상품에 대한 가격표와 상품목록입니다.
12. We are sending you our patternbook and some samples separately.
당사의 견본과 견본장을 별도로 송부해드립니다.
13. Our latest price list will be sent to you upon request.
귀사에서 요청하면 당사의 최근 가격표를 보내드리겠습니다.
14. The enclosed catalog will give you a good understanding of the complete range of products we are handling.
동봉한 상품목록은 당사가 취급하는 전상품에 대한 충분한 지식을 귀사에게 제공해 줄 것입니다.
15. The list prices are all FOB Pusan basis, but CIF terms are also available

upon [your] request.
정가표가격은 모두 부산항본선인도가격조건이지만 귀사에서 요청하면 운임보험료포함가격도 제공할 수 있습니다.

Maxim

You cannot see the wood for the trees.
나무만 보고 숲을 못 본다.

Chapter **02**

신용조회 및 신용보고
Credit Inquiry and Credit Information

해외 목표시장에서 신뢰할 만한 신규거래처를 발굴하려면 해당업체의 신용도(reliability)를 일반적인 측정요소인 3C'S에 의거해서 신용조사를 실시해야 향후 거래에서 발생할 수 있는 위험이나 손해를 예방할 수 있다.

신용조회처에는 은행조회처(bank reference), 동업자조회(trade reference), 상업흥신소(mercantile agency ; commercial credit agency) 및 신용보증기금 등이 있다.

3C'S of Credit Inquiry

1 Capital(자본)

: 수권자본금(authorized capital), 납입자본금(paid-in capital), 유동자산(current or liquid assets)과 고정자산(fixed assets)의 비율(ratio), 재무제표분석(analysis of financial statements)

2 Capacity(능력)

: 연혁(history), 업종(line of business), 취급상품(products), 매출액(volume of business), 거래처(business connection), 거래조건(terms of business)

3 Character(상도덕)

: 성실성(integrity), 경험, 평판, 영업방식, 계약 또는 채무이행 (business commitments ; business engagements) 및 대금결제에 대한 확실성

Sample Letter 3

Security Pacific National Bank March 29, 20 —
50 Raffles Place, #02-03 Shell Tower
Singapore 0104

Gentlemen :

As a valued customer of this bank, Korea Trading Co., Ltd., Seoul is particularly interested in developing an export market for electronic goods to your country.

We would be very grateful if you could initiate the necessary inquiries on our behalf, and advise us of reliable importers, together with their complete financial information. For your confidential use, we are enclosing our customer information file which is given without responsibility on our part.

We thank you and anticipate your cooperation. Please be assured of our willingness to reciprocate at any time.

Sincerely yours,

＊ 요약

당행거래처인 고려무역은 귀국에 전자제품 수출시장을 개척하는 데 특별히 관심을 가지고 있습니다.

당행을 대신해서 필요한 조회를 하여 주시고 귀행에서 제공하고자 하는 신뢰할

만한 수입상의 이름을 완전한 재정상태내역과 함께 통보하여 주시면 대단히 고맙겠습니다. 당행 측에서는 아무런 책임짐이 없이 제공되는 고객정보파일을 귀행에서의 극비취급을 위해 동봉합니다.

귀행의 협조에 미리 감사드리고 당행은 항상 상호교환할 의사가 있음을 확신합니다.

강의노트

① electronic goods '전자제품'

goods=movable property ; '동산, 물건' durable/non-durable~ 내구재/비내구재. consumer~ 소비재 intangible economic~ 무형의 경제재. industrial~ 공산품

product= '생산품과 공업제품' local~ 토산품, farm~ 농산품, chief~ 주산품

commodity=편리한 물품, 필수품, 특히 일용품(useful thing)

merchandise=상품의 총칭(goods bought and sold), 불가산명사(uncountable noun)로서 항상 단수로 사용

article : 특정종류의 물품 또는 가격표나 상품목록에 기재되어 있는 개개의 품목

item : 품목, 항목. article과 같은 의미

line : 품종 a new line of products(신종제품)

② On one's behalf '~를 대신해서, ~를 대표해서'

First of all, on our behalf, I would like to thank you for the very warm reception you have given my colleague Mr. S.K.Kim and myself last Oct 8.

(우선 당사를 대신해서 지난 10월 8일 본인과 동료인 Mr. S.K.Kim에게 보여준 따뜻한 환대에 감사드립니다).

③ On our part '우리 측의, 우리 쪽에'

Please note that this information is given(furnished) without any responsibility on our part.

(이 자료는 폐사가 일체의 책임을 지지 않고 제공하는 것임을 주의하시기 바랍니다)

We advise this letter of credit without any responsibility on our part.

(이 신용장을 우리 쪽에 일체의 책임없이 통지해 드립니다)

④ assure one of '~에게 ~을 확신시키다', assure ; 보장하다, 확신시키다.

(say positively, with confidence) stand behind, guarantee, promise.

Rest ~ed(that)~이라고 확신하다. 명사는 assurance

We assure you of our desire to cooperate with your company at all times.

(우리는 항상 귀사와 협조할 의사가 있음을 확신합니다)

⑤ reciprocate [ricíprəkiet] '교환하다, 보답하다, 답례하다'

reciprocal 상호의, 호혜적인, ~contract 쌍무계약, ~duties [tariff] 호혜관세(율), ~treaty 상호조약, reciprocal L/C 상쇄신용장(Back-to-Back L/C), ~gift 답례품, ~help 상부상조

We hope to have an early opportunity to reciprocate the service.

(우리는 서비스를 교환할 수 있는 조속한 기회가 있기를 희망합니다)

You can be assured (or You can rest assured) of our best attention to your order.

(귀사의 주문에 대해서 우리가 세심하게 주의할 것을 믿어도 좋습니다)

We shall be happy at any time to reciprocate the courtesy(favor/service).

(우리는 언제나 후의(호의, 서비스)에 기꺼이 보답하겠습니다)

Sample Letter 4

Re : Chung-Ang Corporation

Dear Sirs,

In reply to your inquiry of July 29, 20××, the following information of the captioned company is given to you in strict confidence, for your private use only without the responsibility on the part of this bank or its officials. We hope this will be of assistance to you.

1) Date of establishment : Dec. 27, 20××.

2) Paid-up Capital : 21MM in Korean Won

3) President : Jae Hyun Koh

4) Line of Business : Manufacturing Industry (Glass Articles)

5) Financial Standing(As of Dec. 31, 20××)

Total Assets : 192MM in Korean Won

Total Liabilities : 132MM in Korean Won

Annual Turnover : 529MM in Korean Won

Net Profit : 24MM in Korean Won

6) General Information :

We have extended credit facilities to them in the moderate eight-

figure range, which have been conducted satisfactorily.
They are considered a sound company for normal business engagement.

＊ 요약

20××년 7월 29일자 귀 조회를 회신함에 있어서 상기 회사에 대한 아래와 같은 자료를 당행 측이나 임직원의 아무런 책임 없이 오직 비공개사용을 위해 극비로 제공해 드립니다.

이 자료가 귀사에 도움이 되기를 희망합니다.

1) 설립년도 : 20××. 12. 27.
2) 납입자본금 : 이천일백만원
3) 회사대표 : 고재현
4) 업종 : 제조업(유리제품)
5) 재정상태(20××년 12월 31일 현재)
   총자산 : 일억구천이백만원
   총부채 : 일억삼천이백만원
   연간매출액 : 오억이천구백만원
   순이익 : 이천사백만원
6) 종합의견
   당행은 3~4천만 정도의 여신을 동사에 지원하고 있으며 그 결과 만족할 만한 정도로 이행하고 있음. 정상적으로 채무이행을 하는 건실한 회사로 사료됨.

강의노트

① annual turnover '연간매출액'
annual 해마다의, 1년의(=yearly) ~income 연간수입, ~event 연례행사, ~turnover 일정기간이나(일정거래에 대한) 매상고, 거래액, the annual production 연간생산고

② normal business engagements '정상적인 채무이행'(=normal business commitments)

③ moderate eight-figure(=eight figures, eight digits) '3/4천만 정도'
신용보고를 할 때 여신이나 수신계정을 막론하고 피조사자의 계정잔고를 정확하게 공개하지 않는 것이 미국형 신용조사의 관례이다.

low-1, 2	moderate-3, 4
medium-5, 6	high-7, 8, 9
five figure :	만단위 수
six figure :	십만단위 수
seven figure :	백만단위 수
eight figure :	천만단위 수
nine figure :	억단위 수

④ MM : million의 약어. MIO로 쓰기도 한다.

⑤ Information

무역영어에서는 정보라기보다는 '통지, 내용, 자료, 참고사항' 의 의미로 많이 쓰인다.

For your information, we are enclosing a booklet which will explain all about our trade.

(귀사 참고용으로 당사의 사업전반을 설명하고 있는 소책자를 동봉합니다)

Data(자료) – 숫자나 수량 혹은 사건 등 분석되지 않는 사실

Information(정보) – 어떤 상황을 정확하게 도움이 되게 하는 '정리된 자료'

다시 Data와 Information을 정의하면 :

Data is something used as a basis for discussing, decision-making, calculating or measuring.

Information is processed data or meaningful data.

⑥ Credit facilities '신용 편의'

facilities는 복수로 사용하며 편의, 시설, 설비의 뜻이다. facilitate 조정하다. 용이하게 하다. 촉진하다.

We would like to point out that the aforementioned credit facilities are granted at the discretion of the Bankers Trust Company, New York.

(상기에서 언급한 신용편의는 BTC New York의 재량으로 공여된 것임을 알려드립니다).

⑦ paid-up capital '납입자본금'

즉, 주식의 발행으로 조달된 자본금이고 나머지는 미납입자본금(unpaid or uncalled capital)이라 한다.

⑧ net profit '순이익'

profit(net income) – 기업의 영업결과에 대하여 일체의 부채와 경비를 제외한 순이익

revenue(gross income) – 국가나 개인의 소득총액

Sample Letter 5

Gentlemen :

Re : Seoul Trading Co., Ltd., Seoul

In response to your letter of June 20, 20××, we are pleased to furnish you with the following information regarding the subject.

Seoul Trading Co., Ltd. is a corporation chartered in 20×× having succeeded a partnership that commenced operation about 10 years ago. Ownership is divided between Mr. Young Deok Kim and his brother Mr. Yong Shin Kim. This company imports plywood and veneer principally for domestic distribution via wholesalers and manufacturers.

Our bank has extended credit to the above company for over 10 years. We presently extend a low nine-figure line of credit. Deposit balance in 20×× averaged medium seven-digit(figure).

If we can be of further assistance, please do not hesitate to contact us.

Yours very truly,

* 요약

20××년 6월 20일자 귀 서신에 대한 회신으로 상기 회사에 대해서 아래와 같이 신용조회자료를 제공해 드립니다.

서울무역주식회사는 10년 전에 영업을 시작한 합명회사를 승계해서 20××년에 법인등기된 회사입니다. 소유권은 김영덕 씨와 그의 형제인 김영신 씨로 양분되어 있습니다. 동사는 제조업자와 도매업자를 경유하여 국내유통을 위해서 주로 합판을 수입하고 있습니다.

당행은 십여 년간 동사에 여신지원을 하고 있으며 현재 여신지원 규모는 1~3억 정도이며 예금평잔은 5~6백만 정도입니다.

당행에서 더 도울 일이 있으면 주저하지 마시고 연락하여 주십시오.

강의노트

① chartered in '허가를 받은' charter 선언, 허가
charter party 용선계약(agreement between a shipowner and merchant for the use of a ship)

② furnish ~ with '~에게 ~을 제공하다' (extend, favor, supply, provide ~with)
We would appreciate it very much if you review your file on this matter and furnish us with the status of this item.
(이 일에 대해서 귀사의 기록을 검토하시고 이 문제의 상태를 폐사에 제공하여 주시면 감사하겠습니다)

③ in response to '~의 회답으로, ~을 회신함에 있어' (in answer to, in reply to ~)
In response to your inquiry of June 1, 20-, we take pleasure in offering you as follows :
(20×× 6월 1일자 귀 문의에 대한 회답으로 아래와 같이 오퍼합니다)
In reply to your inquiry about Mr. Smith as a credit standing, we would advise you to supply on a cash basis only.
(스미스 씨의 신용상태에 대한 회답으로 우리는 귀사가 단지 현금조건으로만 공급해 줄 것을 권합니다)

④ domestic distribution '국내유통'
domestic 국내(of the home, not foreign), ~goods(manufacture, make) 내국품, ~market 국내시장, ~exchange 내국환

⑤ commence '시작하다, 개시하다'
commencement 학위수여식, 시작, 개시

⑥ corporation '법인, 주식회사'
Profit~ 영리법인, Non-profit~ 비영리법인, Incorporate 삽입하다, 통합하다, 주식회사로 하다

> 주식회사
> 미국 : Corporation, Company, Inc.(Incorporated)
> 영국 : ~Company, Ltd.(Limited)
> 독일 : A.G.(Aktiengesllschaft),
> G.m.b.H.(Geselschaft mit beschraenkter Haftung)
> 프랑스 : S.A.(Societe Anonyme)
> 호주, 남아연방 : Pty. Co.(Proprietary Company)

⑦ line of credit '신용공여한도, 신용대부, 외상판매의 한도'
금융기관이 일정기간을 정하여 환거래은행 또는 고객에 대하여 미리 설정해 둔

신용공여의 종류 및 최고한도로서 운영자금대출, L/C 개설, 당좌대월, 지급보증 등의 신용을 회전사용기준(revolving basis)으로 제공하는 것이다. 신용공여한도를 다 써버린 경우 out of stock이나 exhaust 대신 'full up' 이라 한다.

⑧ deposit '~을 예금하다, ~을 놓다, ~착수금으로 주다'
current~ 당좌예금, time~ 정기예금
trust~ 신탁예금, oil~ 석유매장량
depositor 예금자, 위탁자

Sample Letter 6

International Banking Department　　March 27, 20××
Bankers Trust Company
280 Park Avenue, New York
Gentlemen :

One of our customers is interested in a commercial transaction and we wish to develop details regarding :

American Trading Co., Inc.
New York, New York

We would appreciate your conducting an investigation on our behalf. We are particularly interested in the amount and type of credit extended and the manner of payments. We would also like to know the type of business, financial structure, and responsibility of the company. Your impressions of the management would likewise be helpful.

Any information which you give us will be used discreetly and we shall welcome an opportunity to be of similar service to you at any time.

Please reply by airmail.

Very truly yours,

*** 요약**

당행거래처의 하나가 무역거래에 관심이 있고 American Trading Co., Inc.에 대해 상세한 것을 알고자 합니다.

당행을 대신하여 귀행에서 조사를 실시하여 주시면 감사하겠습니다. 당행은 지급방법, 여신지원형태 및 금액에 대해서 특히 관심이 있습니다.

당행은 또한 동사의 책임감, 재무구조 및 영업방법에 대해서도 관심이 있습니다. 경영진에 대한 귀행의 인상은 더욱이 도움이 될 것입니다.

귀행에서 제공한 일체의 조사내용은 신중하게 사용할 것이며 우리는 언제나 유사한 서비스를 제공할 기회가 있으면 환영합니다.

우편으로 회신하여 주시기 바랍니다.

강의노트

① Details '세부사항' (=particulars, description)

Please give us all the ~.

(모든 세부사항을 폐사에 알려주십시오)

Please furnish us with our reference number or other ~.

(당사의 참조번호 혹은 기타 세부사항을 제공하여 주십시오)

② management '경영, 관리, 운영, 경영진'

라틴어 manus(hand)에서 유래됨

MBO(Management by Object) 목표관리

MIS(Management Information System) 경영정보시스템

Management(or Managing) is the process of getting things done by and through others.

(경영은 다른 사람들을 통해서 어떤 것을 성취하는 과정이다)

③ likewise '역시, 더욱이' moreover

【Sample Letter 6】에서는 독자가 쉽게 이해할 수 있도록 likewise, and, also, particularly라는 연결어(transitional word and phrases)를 사용하였다. 따라서 접속사(conjunctions)를 활용하면 각 문장을 연결시키는 데 도움이 되며 논리적 전개가 가능하다.

〈Transitional Words and Phrases to Help Tie Sentences Together〉

- **Addition**

again	equally important	in addition	next
also	finally	last	others
and	first	lastly	secondly

and then	further	likewise	thirdly
besides	furthermore	moreover	too

- **Cause and Result**

accordingly	because of	hence	thus
as a result	consequently	therefore	unless
assuming	for this reason	thereupon	

- **Comparison**

better yet	in like manner	similarly	an even greater sum…
here again	likewise	still worse	even more important

- **Contrast**

although, even though		however	on the other hand
and yet		in contrast	on the contrary
at the same time	nevertheless	still	
but		notwithstanding	yet

- **Instances, Lists, Explanations**

in particular	for example	for instance	to illustrate

- **Place**

adjacent to	here	on the opposite side
beyond	nearby	opposite to

- **Summary**

as has been stated	for instance	in short	to be sure
as I have said	in brief	in summary	to sum up
	in other words	on the whole	

- **Time Sequence**

afterward	during	in the meantime	soon
at the same time	following	meanwhile	then
before	immediately	previously	while

④ discreetly '신중하게, 분별있게'

discretion 신중, 사려분별, 재량

discreet 분별있는, 신중한 discretionary 임의의, 자유재량의

You must show more discretion in choosing your trading partner.

(교역상대자를 선택하는 데 더 신중해야 한다)

⑤ similar [símilər] '유사한, 동종의' similarity 유사점

It would give us great pleasure to be able to render you a similar service should the opportunity occur.

(혹시 기회가 있어서 이번 일과 유사한 서비스로 보답할 수 있으면 매우 기쁘겠습니다)

Useful Sentences(신용조회관계)

1. For our financial standing, we would refer you to the ABC Bank, Chicago Agency.
   당사의 재정상태에 대해서는 ABC은행 시카고 지점에 조회해 주십시오.
2. The ABC Bank of your city will give you any information concerning our credit standing.
   귀 도시에 있는 ABC은행이 폐사의 신용상태에 대한 일체의 자료를 제공해 줄 것입니다.
3. As for our means and business standing, we are permitted to mention the XYZ Bank, New York branch.
   폐사의 재정 및 영업상태에 대해서는 XYZ은행 뉴욕지점에 조회하시기 바랍니다.
4. Our bankers are the Seoul First Bank, Myungdong branch.
   당사의 거래은행은 서울제일은행 명동지점입니다.
5. All answers will be treated(held, kept, dealt) with the utmost confidence. If we can ever be of a similar service to you, please call on us.
   모든 회답은 최대한 비밀로 취급될 것입니다. 만일 귀사를 위해 유사한 서비스를 제공할 일이 있으면 연락하여 주시기 바랍니다.
6. Although the above concerns are of good repute, we do not assume any responsibility for their credit.
   비록 상기회사들의 세평은 좋습니다만 우리는 그들의 신용에 대하여 책임을 지지 않습니다.
7. Accounts are conducted in immaculate fashion.
   계정들이 흠없이(연체나 부실없이) 운영되고 있습니다.
8. On receipt of your general terms and conditions, we can give you firstclass references.
   폐사는 귀사의 일반거래조건을 받는 즉시 일류조회처를 제공하겠습니다.
9. Please inform us in private confidence of your opinion about their financial standing(status).
   동사의 재정상태에 대해서 극비로 귀사의 의견을 통지하여 주시기 바랍니다.

10. The concern enjoys a good reputation in the business circle here.
    그 회사는 이곳 실업계에서 훌륭한 평판을 향유하고 있습니다.
11. Please let us know your frank and objective opinion of the financial status concerning their company.
    그들의 재정상태에 대해서 귀사의 객관적이고 솔직한 의견을 알려주십시오.

Maxim

Do not like to sleep or you will grow poor ; stay awake and you will have food to spare.

잠자기를 좋아하면 가난하게 된다. 눈을 뜨고 열심히 일하라. 그러면 먹을 것이 풍족할 것이다.

Chapter 03

조회 및 그 회답

Inquiries and Replies to Inquiries

거래관계의 권유를 받은 자가 그 물품에 대한 관심 또는 구매할 의사가 있게 되면 그에 대한 조회(inquiry)를 하게 하는데, 이를 문의라고도 한다.

일반적으로 조회는 조회서(letter of inquiry) 또는 전신으로 행해지는데, 그 내용은 ① 가격표(price list), 상품목록(catalogue) 또는 견본(sample)의 송부를 요청하는 경우, ② 해외 수입상이 수입의사표시로서 무역계약조건(품명, 수량, 선적시기, 가격 및 기타 조건)을 문의하는 경우, ③ 구체적인 offer의 발행을 요청하는 경우 등이 있다. 조회는 매도인이 하는 selling inquiry와 매수인이 하는 buying inquiry로 구분하여 selling inquiry는 sales letter의 성격을 내포하는 것이고 보통 inquiry는 buyer가 상품을 매입하기 위해 문의하는 것을 말한다. 매도인은 해외의 매수인으로부터 조회를 받으면 감사의 표시를 하면서 신속하게 회답하여야 한다. 구체적인 회답의 방법으로는 견적서(estimate), 견적송장(proforma invoice), 가격표(price list) 및 견본(sample)을 보내면서 주문을 권유한다.

Sample Letter 7

Dear Sirs,

We refer to your advertisement in the May 8, 20×× of "The International Trade News" concerning the newly developed Toaster Model TR2000.

Please send us your catalogue and the best terms for this new product. It would also be appreciated if you could give us some idea of the time required between order and delivery.

For your information, we are one of the largest importers of electrical appliances in Hong Kong and are trying to import the newly developed Toasters from Korea. If your prices are competitive, we plan to place a large initial order with you.

Your prompt attention to this matter would be appreciated.

Yours faithfully,

* 요약

당사는 신규개발품인 Toaster Model TR2000에 대해서 국제무역뉴스 5월 8일자 귀사광고를 참조했습니다.

신제품에 대한 귀사의 상품목록과 최상의 거래조건을 송부해 주십시오. 또한 주문 후 인도 시까지 필요한 기간을 알려주시면 감사하겠습니다. 귀사의 참고를 위해 당사는 홍콩에서 전기기구의 최대수입업자의 하나이며 한국으로부터 새로 개발한 Toaster를 수입하고자 합니다.

귀사의 가격이 저렴하면 당사는 대량의 첫 주문을 할 예정입니다. 이 일에 대해서 귀사에서 신속히 배려하여 주시면 감사하겠습니다.

강의노트

① advertisement '광고'

구체적인 뜻은 Advertising의 하위개념으로서 광고물이나 광고메시지를 의미하며 Advertising은 광고행위 또는 광고과정 전체를 말한다. Commercial은 상업광고방송의 메시지를 지칭할 때 사용한다.

Advertisement는 라틴어의 'Adverter' 라는 말에서 나온 것으로 '돌아보게 하다' (ad → to, verter → turn)의 뜻이다.

Our best advertisement is a satisfied customer.

(당사의 최상의 광고는 만족한 고객이다)

We are interested in your advertisement in the "Trade Journal" of May 1.

(당사는 5월 1일자 Trade Journal에 게재된 귀사광고에 관심을 갖고 있습니다)

② If your prices are competitive '귀사가격이 경쟁적이면(저렴하면)'

reasonable (moderate) price '저렴한 가격'

We can handle considerable quantities of your products if they suit our trade and your prices are competitive enough.

(귀사의 상품이 당사의 영업에 적합하고 가격이 저렴하면 귀사상품을 상당 수량 취급할 수 있습니다)

③ place a large initial order with ~ '~에게 대량으로 첫 주문을 하다'

initial 처음의, 최초의, 시작인 ~expenditure 창업비, ~deposit 초임금, ~fee 가입비(학회, 클럽 등의) initial order 첫 주문(=first order)

If your prices are reasonable, we shall place a large initial order with you in the near future.

(귀사 가격이 저렴하면 가까운 장래에 대량의 첫 주문을 하겠습니다)

Sample Letter 8

Dear Sirs,

Thank you very much for your inquiry of May 1, 20×× for our Toaster Model TR2000.

Today we have separately sent you our latest illustrated catalogue and price list covering our entire line of goods. You may find in them a minute illustration of our Toaster and its FOB Busan price.

You may be sure that we can effect shipment within one month after receipt of your order.

We are glad to know that you are considering importing a large number of the newly developed Toasters from Korea, depending on our prices.

You may rest assured that our prices are lower than those of any other competitors.

We do hope to hear from you soon.

Yours faithfully,

＊ 요약

당사 Toaster Model TR2000에 대한 5월 1일자 귀사의 조회에 감사합니다.

금일 별도의 우편으로 당사 전상품에 대한 최신 도해 상품목록과 가격표를 귀사로 보냈습니다.

당사의 Toaster에 대한 상세한 설명과 FOB 부산가격조건을 알게 될 것입니다.

주문 수령 후 1개월 이내에 선적이 가능함을 확신합니다.

동 제품의 가격조건이 맞으면 귀사가 한국으로부터 신규개발품인 Toaster를 대량수입할 것인지를 알고자 합니다.

당사가격이 다른 경쟁업체보다 저렴하다는 것을 믿어도 좋습니다.

조속한 회신을 희망합니다.

강의노트

① under separate cover '별도의 우편으로'

under separate mail이라고도 한다.

separately로 쓰는 것이 간결하다.

(wordy) We wish to inform you that we have today sent you under separate cover our catalog and price list.

(concise) Today we have separately sent you our catalog and price list.

② You may be assured~ (=You may rest assured) '~하리라는 것 믿어도 좋습니다, 틀림없이 ~하겠습니다.'

You may be assured of our willingness to reciprocate your favor.

(귀사의 호의에 보답할 의사가 있음을 믿어도 좋습니다)

③ receipt [risi:t] '수령, 수취, 영수증'

upon(on) receipt of ~을 받는 즉시.

We shall be glad to submit our offer upon receipt of your request.

(귀사의 요청을 받자마자 오퍼를 제출하겠습니다)

As to the establishment of account, we should gladly open such an account upon receipt of your initial funds in dollars.

(계좌개설에 대해서는 귀사로부터 미국 달러로 초입금을 받는 즉시 개설하겠습니다)
Shipment can be made upon receipt of your L/C.
(귀사로부터 신용장을 받자마자 선적이 이루어질 것입니다)
④ minute '(시간의) 분, 미소한, 상세한'
up to the~ 최신의, ~description 상세한 묘사, the~st details 가장 정밀한 세목

Sample Letter 9 Price List(가격표)

KOREA TRADING INTERNATIONAL INC.

PHONE : (02)551-3114
F A X : (02)551-3100

11TH FLOOR, TRADE TOWER,
159, SAMSUNG-DONG, KANGNAM-KU,
SEOUL, KOREA

DATE : Jan. 10, 20××
YOUR REF
OUR REF :

Messrs. Fairbros Trade, (Ltd.)
London, England

PRICE LIST NO. 12

Prices are subject to change due to market fluctuation.

1. RAWHIDE DOG CHEWS

ITEM NO.	F.O.B. KOREA(USD)	ITEM NO.	F.O.B. KOREA(USD)
301	11.04/doz	600	13.20/doz
303	10.30/doz	804	1.98/doz
306	3.13/doz	805	2.62/doz
309	4.62/doz	806	3.63/doz
309B	1.98/100pcs	808	5.71/doz
310	3.05/doz	808H	6.72/doz
315	5.28/doz	810	10.29/doz
400	19.25/100pcs	907	5.55/doz
402	5.50/100pcs	909	9.90/doz

2. STAINLESS STEEL DOG DISH

3100	0.82/pc	3400	2.00/pc

3200	1.13/pc	3500	2.80/pc
3300	1.61/pc	3600	3.90/pc

3. CAT COLLARS & LEADS

011	0.42/pc	017	0.74/pc
012	0.52/pc	018	0.99/pc
013	0.64/pc	019	1.38/pc
014	0.88/pc		

4. CAT. TOYS(POLYBAG W/HEADER)

101	4.51/doz	177	3.49/doz
120	3.33/doz	179	3.30/doz
132	3.48/doz	180	3.65/doz
139	3.36/doz	181	3.30/doz
154	3.17/doz	184	4.40/doz
166	4.14/doz	198	3.86/doz

E & OE

Korea Trading International Inc.

＊ 요약.

고려무역이 London 소재 Fairbros 무역회사 앞으로 발행한 가격표

강의노트

① Prices are subject to change due to market fluctuation. '가격은 시가변동조건입니다.'

② price list '가격표'

일반적으로 가격표에 기재된 가격을 list price라고 한다.
price '값, 가격, 대가'의 뜻이며 다음과 같은 수식어가 붙는다. charge 부과된 가격(요금, 수수료, 부담금)
best price (매도인에게는) 최상가격, (매수인에게는) 최하가격
ceiling price 최고가격, floor price 최저가격
sticker price 생산자 표시가격

excessive (extravagant, fancy, unreasonable, exorbitant) price 과도한 가격 : cost an arm and a leg
reduced price 할인가격
competitive price 경쟁(싼) 가격
rock-bottom[bedrock, close, closely calculated] price(더이상 깎아 줄 수 없는) 결착가격
moderate[reasonable, affordable] price 적당한 가격, 저렴한 가격
current[prevailing, ruling, market] price 시가
cost[prime, first] price 원가(생산에 필요한)
fixed[set, regular] price 정가
asked[quoted] price (매도인이) 부른 가격
bid price 매수인이 붙인 가격, 입찰가격
abate[reduce, shade, lower, lessen, cheapen, bring down, cut down] a price 감가하다
raise[advance, increase, harden, put up, bring up] a price 가격을 올리다
prices advance[go up, rise, mount, rally] 가격이 오르다
prices[jump, shoot up, soar, sky-rocket, rise suddenly] 가격이 급등하다.
prices slump[drop suddenly, fall suddenly, decline heavily, toboggan] 가격이 급락하다.

Sample Letter 10

KOREA TRADING INTERNATIONAL INC.

PHONE : (02)551-3114	11TH FLOOR, TRADE TOWER,	DATE : May 18, 20××
F A X : (02)551-3100	159, SAMSUNG-DONG, KANGNAM-KU,	YOUR REF :
	SEOUL, KOREA	
	TRADE CENTER P.O.BOX	OUR REF : EX-20-25

PROFORMA INVOICE

To : Good Friends Co., Ltd.
Shipment: WITHIN 30 DAYS AFTER RECEIPT OF YOUR L/C
Payment: BY AN IRREVOCABLE SIGHT L/C IN OUR FAVOR

Origin: R.O.K.
Destination: ATHENS, GREECE
Packing: EXPORT STANDARD PACKING
Quality: EXPORT STANDARD QUALITY
Inspection: MAKER' S TO BE FINAL
Validity: JANUARY 15, 20××
Remarks:

Description	Quantity	Unit Price	Amount	Remarks
			F.O.B. KOREA	
MEAT TENDERIZER FM-1002(NEW TYPE)	70PCS	@S350.-	US24,500.-	

-subject to our final confirmation-

Korea Trading International Inc.

K. D. Hong

K. D. Hong

Manager
General Merchandise Dept.

E. & O. E.

N. B. The prices are open for 6 weeks only.
All quotations are subject to change without notice.

＊ 요약

고려무역이 그리스 Good Friends Co., Ltd.로 보내는 견적송장이다.

강의노트

① Proforma Invoice '견적송장'

proforma는 라틴어의 pro forma로서 as a formality only '형식상의, 견적의' 뜻이다.

Invoice는 불어의 envoyer(send)에서 유래된 것이다. 견적송장이란 수출상이 거래를 유발촉진하기 위한 수단으로, 또는 수입허가, 외화배정 등을 받기 위한 수입상의 요청에 의해 수입상에게 장차 그가 매입할 화물에 대해서 시산적으로 작성발송하는 송장으로 송장상에 표시된 물품가격 등에 대해 법적구속력이 없는 일종의 free offer이다.

② maker' s(inspection is) to be final '제조자의 검사를 최종적인 것으로 함'

③ E. & O.E. - Errors and omission are excepted의 약어 '오류와 누락분은 제외'

④ N.B. - note well이라는 뜻의 라틴어 nota bene의 약어로서 '주의, 비고'

⑤ Subject to our final confirmation '당사의 최종확인조건'

Maxim

A prudent man keeps his knowledge to himself, but the heart of fools blurts out folly.

슬기로운 사람은 자기가 아는 것을 나타내지 않지만 미련한 사람은 어리석음을 떠벌이고 다닌다.

Useful Sentences(조회에 관한 문례)

1. Thank you for your inquiry of February 21, 20×× for our new Word Processor IT200.
   당사의 신형 워드프로세서 IT200에 대한 20×× 2월 21일자 귀사 문의에 감사드립니다.
2. We received your inquiry of July 1 and are pleased to reply as follows:
   당사는 7월 1일자 귀사 문의를 받았으며 아래와 같이 회신하여 드립니다.
3. We received your letter of March 20th and we are happy to send you a catalog of our product.
   3월 20일자 귀 서신을 잘 받았고 당사의 상품목록을 보냅니다.
4. As requested, we have sent you 2 copies of our latest catalog by separate airmail today.
   요청한 대로, 당사의 최신상품목록 2부를 별도의 항공우편으로 금일 보냈습니다.
5. Our revised price list will be ready by the end of this month. We will

send it to you as soon as it is ready.
당사의 개정 가격표는 금월 말까지 준비될 것입니다. 준비되는 대로 귀사로 보내겠습니다.

6. Two copies of our estimate you requested in your letter of April 15th will be sent to you in a few days.
4월 15일자 귀 서신에서 요구한 당사 견적서 2통을 2, 3일 내에 송부하겠습니다.
7. The enclosed brochure lists an assortment of electrical appliances with their FOB Incheon prices.
동봉한 소책자는 인천본선인도가격조건의 각종 전기기구 제품 일람표입니다.
8. All the items listed in our catalog are now in stock and are ready for immediate shipment.
당사의 상품목록에 기재된 모든 품목은 현재 재고가 있으며 즉시 선적할 준비가 되어 있습니다.
9. Please take the time to study the catalog we sent you and inform us of your requirements.
당사에서 보내준 상품목록을 검토하시고 귀사의 필요품목을 알려주시기 바랍니다.
10. Of the sample we sent[to] you, we believe No. 6 will suit your trade best.
당사가 송부한 견본 중에서 제6호가 귀사가 영업하는 데 가장 적합하리라고 믿습니다.
11. Enclosed are quotations, which are available for two weeks only.
동봉한 것은 단지 2주간 유효한 견적가격입니다.
12. We would be pleased to grant you a discount of 3% from our list prices for an order of 100 dozen or more.
100다스 이상의 주문에 대해서는 정가표의 3퍼센트의 할인을 허용합니다.
13. Our goods are of the finest materials and highest workmanship, and are second to none in design and durability.
당사제품은 최상의 재료와 솜씨로 만들어졌고 디자인이나 내구성도 아무에게도 지지 않습니다.

14. The model CB300 you inquired about is out of stock now, but the improved Model CB301 can be supplied immediately.
귀사가 문의한 Model CB300은 현재 재고가 없습니다. 그러나 개량형 CB301은 즉시 공급할 수 있습니다.

15. The price of this article must be revised soon on account of the recent rise in the cost of raw materials.
이 제품에 대한 가격은 최근 원재료 비용의 상승으로 곧 개정되어야 합니다.

16. The export prices of kitchen utensils are going up, so it is almost certain that we will not be able to quote the same price next month.
주방용품의 수출가격이 상승하고 있으므로 다음달에는 똑같은 가격으로는 견적할 수 없을 것이 거의 확실합니다.

17. As we want to expand our sales to you, we have quoted you very low prices this time.
당사판매를 귀사에 확장키로 했기 때문에 이번에는 아주 저렴한 가격을 제공했습니다.

18. The prices have gone up steadily since January this year, but we have not yet raised our quotations.
가격이 금년 1월 이후 꾸준히 상승하고 있지만 당사는 아직 가격을 인상하지 않았습니다.

19. We trust that this information will be of help to you and we welcome any further inquiries and comments from you.
이 자료가 귀사에 도움이 되리라고 믿고 귀사의 의견과 추가문의를 환영합니다.

20. We are looking forward to your first order.
귀사의 첫 주문을 기대합니다.

Chapter **04**

오퍼 및 오퍼의 승낙
Offer and Acceptance

1. Offer(청약)

무역거래에서 매도인이 매수인으로부터 조회를 받으면 일반적으로 오퍼를 발행하는 것이 순서이다.

Offer(청약)란 그에 응하는 acceptance(승낙)와 결합하여 계약을 성립시키는 일방적 의사표시로서 무역에서는 보통 수출자가 상대방인 수입자에게 일정한 물품을 일정한 가격, 품질, 선적, 결제조건 등으로 매도하겠다는 의사표시를 말한다.

거래처를 선정하고 거래처와 거래교섭(circular inquiry, free offer, counter offer 등) 후 거래당사자 일방(offeror)의 확정의사표시인 firm offer를 전신이나 서신으로 다른편 당사자에게 보내고 타방(offeree)은 동의하는 확정적 의사표시(acceptance)를 전신이나 서신으로 보냄으로써 법률상 서면계약서(written contract)의 효력을 갖게 된다.

2. Offer의 종류

① 오퍼의 주체를 기준
- selling offer
- buying offer

② 오퍼의 확정력을 기준
- firm offer
- free offer

③ 오퍼의 특수한 상황을 기준 : condtional offer

④ 오퍼의 발행지를 기준 { 국내 발행 offer / 국외 발행 offer }

(1) Firm offer(확정오퍼)

청약자가 승낙기간을 지정하고 그 기간 내에 수락회답할 것을 조건으로 하는 오퍼 또는 이러한 승낙기간을 정하지 아니한 경우에는 그 오퍼가 확정적(firm), 철회불능(irrevocable)이라는 것을 표시한 오퍼를 말한다.

(2) Free offer(불확정오퍼)

확정오퍼와는 달리 승낙기간을 정하거나 기타의 방법으로 확정적임을 표시하지 아니한 오퍼로서 상당한 기간 효력을 가지나 상대방이 승낙의 통지를 발송하기 전까지는 청약자가 일방적으로 철회 또는 변경할 수 있다. 다만, 이 경우 신의와 성실의 원칙에 위배되어서는 아니 된다.

(3) Counter offer(반대오퍼)

매도인의 오퍼에 대하여 매수인이 가격, 수량, 선적조건 등에 관해 오퍼내용의 일부 변경 또는 추가를 제의해 오는 경우가 있다. 이를 counter offer라 하는데, 원 오퍼(original offer)에 대한 거절이고 동시에 새로운 오퍼이다. 그리고 원청약자는 흔히 새로운 오퍼에 대해서 다시 매도인으로서의 counter offer를 하게 되는데, 큰 무역거래에서는 counter offer가 몇 차례 반복되다가 일방의 최종적인 승낙으로 계약이 성립되는 것이 보통이다.

(4) Offer subject to prior sale(선착순 매도조건오퍼)

매수 희망자의 승낙이 매도했을 때 해당 물품이 판매되지 않고 재고가 있어야만 계약이 성립된다는 것을 조건으로 하는 오퍼로서 offer subject to being unsold라고도 한다. 물품을 빨리 처분하기 위하여 여러 곳에 동시에 오퍼할 때 이용된다.

(5) Offer on approval(승인오퍼)

오퍼와 함께 현품을 보내서 상대방이 실험 또는 사용해 보아 만족할 조건으로 발행하는 오퍼로서, 상대방이 만족하지 아니하면 일정기간 내에 반품할 수 있다. 이와 비슷한 조건으로서 그 현품을 일정기간 판매하다가 남으면 반품할 것을 조건으로 하는 offer on sale or return은 있으나, 이들은 보통무역에서는 거의 이용되지 아니한다.

(6) Offer subject to confirmation(확인조건오퍼)

이것은 "subject to our final confirmation"이라는 단서가 붙은 오퍼로서 청약자에 대한 구속력이 없고 따라서 엄밀한 의미에서는 오퍼가 아니다. offer without engagement 또는 offer subject to change without notice와 마찬가지로 상대방의 승낙만으로 계약이 성립되는 것이 아니고 다시 청약자의 최종확인이 있어야 계약이 성립된다.

Sample Letter 11

Gentlemen :

We are pleased to make a firm offer subject to your reply reaching here by June 20 as follows :

Article : Shoes
Quality : UCLA brand No. 5
Quantity : 100 pairs
Price : US$30 a pair F.O.B. Tokyo
Shipment : July-August
Terms : Draft at 60 d/s under irrevocable letter of credit

We are confident that this is the best offer we can make and that no other firms can offer you better terms than these. At present, we are receiving a lot of orders from all over the world and there is a possibility of us running out of stock in the near future. Therefore, it would be in your best interest to place an order as soon as possible.

We look forward to your early order.

Yours very truly,

* 요약

귀사의 회답이 6월 20일까지 당지에 도착하는 조건으로 아래와 같이 확정오퍼합니다.

품목 : 신발
품질 : UCLA 제5번
수량 : 100족(켤레)
가격 : 동경본선인도가격 1켤레에 미화 30불
선적 : 7~8월
결제조건 : 취소불능신용장에 의거 일람후 60일 출급 환어음에 의함.

동 청약은 당사에서 최상의 조건으로 작성된 것이며 어느 업체도 이보다 나은 조건을 제공할 수 없다는 것을 확신합니다.

현재 당사는 세계도처에서 많은 주문을 받고 있으며 가까운 시일에 재고가 품절될 가능성이 있습니다.

그러므로 즉시 주문을 하는 것이 귀사에 이익이 되리라고 생각합니다.

조속한 주문을 기대합니다.

강의노트

① Shipment : July-August '7월 1일부터 8월 31일 사이에 선적'
Due to the very brisk demand for this article, we can accept orders only for a July-August shipment.
(동 제품에 대한 활발한 수요로 인해서 당사에서는 단지 7~8월 선적을 위한 주문만 승낙합니다)

② Draft at 60 d/s '일람후 60일 출급어음'
60 d/s=60 days after sight

③ running out of '물품 따위가 바닥이 나다, 다 써버리다'
reach an end of(stocks, supplies).
We are running out(short) of stock in this line.
=Our stock in this line is running low.
(이 품목에서 폐사의 재고가 달립니다)
'품절입니다. 다 팔렸습니다'를 다음과 같이 다양하게 표현할 수 있다.
I' ve just sold the last one.
(=We just ran out completely)
(=I' m afraid we' re out)

(=We are sold out for today)
(=We are out until tomorrow)
(=That' s all for today)
(Sorry, they' re all sold out)

Sample Letter 12

Gentlemen :

We would like to provide you with a sample of a new type of fountain pen we have recently developed.

This innovative fountain pen has been designed so that you can write with different tip width simply by adjusting it.

The price is US$480 per dozen and the minimum order is 200 dozen. You will be granted a 5% discount for an order of 500 dozen or more.

A sample will arrive separately by airmail.

We hope you will examine the sample and place an order soon.

Yours truly,

* 요약

당사에서 최근 개발한 신형 만년필 견본을 제공합니다.

이 혁신적인 만년필은 간단히 조정하면 여러 가지 폭으로 쓸 수 있도록 고안되었습니다.

가격은 1다스에 미화 480불이고, 최저주문량은 200다스입니다. 500다스 이상의 주문에 대해서는 5% 할인을 허용합니다.

견본은 별도의 항공우편으로 송부했습니다.

동 견본을 조사하시고 조속히 주문해 주시기를 희망합니다.

강의노트

① sample '표본, 견본'

견본에는 원견본(original sample), 비치견본(duplicate, keep, file, reference sample), 제3견본(triplicate sample) 등이 있으며, 이것을 1조(one set)라고 하고, 동일한 견본번호(sample number)를 붙인다.

매수인이 매도인에게 제시하는 견본, 즉 매수인 견본(buyer' s sample)으로 품질을 결정하는 경우 매도인은 유사견본(similar sample)을 만들어 이것을 반대견본(counter sample)으로서 매수인에게 보내어, 매수인은 승낙을 얻어야 되고, 또한 견본을 우송할 때는 비치견본(duplicate sample)이나 제3견본(triplicate sample)을 보관하는 것이 바람직하다.

'견품' 의 영어로서는 sample : pattern : swatch : specimen 등이 있는데 다음과 같이 구별해서 쓴다.

- **Sample** : 대량에서 취한 일부분으로서 그 대량의 품질을 보이는 것. 원료품(raw materials)에서 반조제품(semi-manufactures), 제조품(manufactures)에 이르기까지 모든 상품에 사용한다.
- **Pattern** : 직물류에 대해서 사용된다. Pattern card '견품 카드'
- **Swatch, Cutting** : 직물류, 가죽의 견품 조각을 말한다.
- **Specimen** : 전체의 한 예로 보이는 것으로서 동 · 식 · 광물 기타의 '표본' 에 대하여 사용된다.

  Specimen Page '서적의 견본페이지'

  Specimen of Signature '서명견본'

  Specimen of Check '수표 견양'

② discount '물건에 대한 할인액, 할부가 아닌 현찰지불에 대한 할인액, 만기 전의 어음에 대한 할인'

~broker 매매중개인, ~house 어음할인소

We will grant/give a 5 percent discount of the list price if you place an order for 30 dozen or more of this article.

(동 제품을 30다스 이상 주문하면 정가의 5% 할인을 허용하겠습니다)

③ offer는 '준다', '바친다' 는 뜻이다. 비즈니스에서는 거래 때 조건을 제안한다는 의미로 쓰인다. '앞으로' 란 의미의 ob와 '들고 가다', '나르다' 란 뜻의 라틴어 ferre의 합성어다. 물건과 사람을 동시에 나르는 배인 ferry 등과 사촌단어다.

Sample Letter 13 Sample Letter 11에 대한 회신

Gentlemen :

Thank you for your June 1st offer for 100 pairs of UCLA brand shoes No. 5 at US$30 a pair F.O.B. Tokyo.

While we appreciate your kind offer, we feel that US$30 a pair is too high. Shoes of a similar quality are being retailed at department stores here at much lower prices.

We wonder if you would kindly consider reducing the price to US$20 a pair. If you could come down to this price level, we might be able to order 300 pairs.

Your consideration of this matter and immediate reply would be greatly appreciated.

Yours truly,

* 요약

UCLA브랜드신발 No. 5 FOB동경 1켤레당 미화 30불 100켤레에 대한 6월 1일자 귀사오퍼에 감사드립니다.

귀사의 친절한 오퍼에 감사드리는 한편 한 켤레에 미화 30불은 너무 비싸다는 것을 말씀드립니다. 귀사제품과 유사한 품질의 신발이 이곳 백화점에서 대단히 저렴한 가격으로 소매되고 있습니다.

귀사에서 1켤레에 미화 20불까지 가격을 깎아주는 것을 고려할 수 있는지 궁금합니다. 귀사에서 그러한 가격수준으로 삭감하여 주신다면 당사에서는 300켤레까지 주문할 수 있습니다.

이 일에 대해서 귀사의 배려와 조속한 회신을 하여 주시면 감사하겠습니다.

강의노트

① brand '상표, (상표가 붙은)품질, 품종'

brand new 신품의, 최신의(=novelty), ~preference 제품선호성

VISA is the fastest growing Traveler's Check in the world, selling at the rate of US$8 billion annually, as well as being one of the largest brands sold with over 20 percent of the world market share.

(VISA는 연간 80억 달러 정도를 판매하는 세계에서 가장 급성장하고 있는 여행자수표일뿐 아니라 세계 시장점유율의 20퍼센트를 상회하고 있는 최대상표의 하나입니다)

② retail '소매, 물건을 소매하다'

③ appreciating '감사의, 인식하고 있는, 감상할 줄 아는, 인정하고 있는' (=appreciative)

appreciate (가치를)정당하게 평가하다, 감상하다, 감사하다, (땅, 물건)값이 오르다.

appreciation : 감사, 인식, 지식, a letter(plaque) of~ 감사장(패)

Your kind cooperation in this matter will be appreciated.

(이 일에 대해서 귀사에서 협조해주시면 감사하겠습니다)

You can' t appreciate English poetry unless you understand its rhythm.

(운율을 모르고는 영시를 감상할 수 없다)

Our products are receiving a growing appreciation from our overseas customers.

(당사 제품에 대한 해외고객들의 인식이 날로 높아가고 있습니다)

Sample Letter 14 Sample Letter 13에 대한 회신

Gentlemen :

Your counter offer of June 10th has been received.

However, the suggested price of US$20 a pair is too much of a reduction. You say you can get shoes of the same quality at much lower prices, but we are quite sure that our UCLA brand No. 5 are far superior in quality to any other shoes at the same price level.

It is hard for us to accept your counter offer of US$20 a pair, but considering you are a good customer, we think we may concede to US$25 a pair provided you give us minimum order of 300 pairs.

Your earliest possible reply would be appreciated.

Yours truly,

＊ 요약

6월 10일자 귀사 반대청약을 받아보았습니다.

그러나 귀사가 제시한 한 켤레당 미화 20불은 너무 많이 삭감했습니다. 귀사에서는 대단히 저렴한 동질의 신발을 구매할 수 있다고 언급했지만 당사의 UCLA브랜드 No. 5는 똑같은 가격수준의 다른 신발보다는 품질이 훨씬 우수하다는 것을 확신합니다.

귀사의 한 켤레에 미화 20불의 반대청약은 당사로서는 승낙하기가 어렵습니다만 귀사가 당사의 우량고객임을 감안하여 귀사가 최저주문량인 300켤레를 주문한다면 한 켤레에 미화 25불까지 양보할 수 있다고 생각합니다.

가능하면 귀사에서 조속히 회신을 하여 주시면 감사하겠습니다.

강의노트

① counter offer '반대청약, 카운터오퍼'

As for the suggested 2% discount, we regret we cannot accept your counter offer.

(제안한 2%의 할인에 대해서 귀사의 반대청약을 승낙할 수 없음을 유감으로 생각합니다)

(Your) PRICE (is) TOO HIGH (WE) COUNTEROFFER (at) 9.70

(가격이 너무 높습니다. 9달러 70센트 카운터오퍼함)

Our BEST (Price is) 11.20(Your) COUNTEROFFER (is) IMPOSSIBLE

(당사 최저가격 11.20 반대청약 수리불능)

counter에는 '반대의, 역의, 대응하는 ; (짝진 것의)한쪽의, 부의' 의 뜻이다.

counteract 반작용하다, 중화시키다, 약화시키다.

counterattack 반격, 역습

counterclaim 반소, 맞고소

counterpart 쌍을 이루는 것, (짝진 것의)한쪽

(2통으로 작성한 증서의 1통 대응부)

countersign 연서, 부서

countervailing duties [tariff] 상쇄관세, 상계관세

② superior[su:piəriə] '보통보다 나은, 우수한', ~to 보다 나은 (better than)

better than the average 평균보다 수적으로 많은

※ 라틴어 비교급(Latin comparative)은 비교급 다음에 than 대신에 to를 사용한다.

be superior to ~보다 월등한
be inferior to ~보다 열등한

interior to ~보다 안쪽의
exterior to ~보다 바깥쪽의
anterior to ~보다 앞선
posterior to ~보다 늦은
senior to~ 보다(나이가) 위인
junior to ~보다(나이가) 어린
prefer~to 보다 ~를 더 좋아하다

③ concede[kənsi:d] '양보하다, 주다, 양도하다, 허용하다'
admit : grant : allow
concession 양보, 허용, 양보된 것
concessive (문법) 양보를 나타내는

Sample Letter 15 Sample Letter 14에 대한 회신

Gentlemen :

We are glad to accept your offer of June 20th for 300 pairs of UCLA Brand No. 5 at US$25 a pair, CIF San Francisco for August shipment.

Enclosed is our Purchase Note No. 10 to confirm this transaction.

In order to cover the amount of this purchase, we have arranged with our bankers for an irrevocable letter of credit amounting to US$7,500 to be opened in your favor.

Your prompt execution of this order will be very much appreciated.

Yours truly,

＊ 요약

6월 20일자 UCLA브랜드 제5호 한 켤레에 미화 25불인 8월 선적을 위한 샌프란시스코 착 운임보험료 포함가격으로 300켤레에 대한 귀사 오퍼를 승낙합니다.

동봉한 것은 동 거래를 확인하기 위한 당사의 매입계약서 제10호입니다.

동 매입대전의 결제를 위해서 당사에서는 귀사를 수익자로 해서 미화 7,500불에 달하는 취소불능 신용장을 개설할 것을 거래은행에 의뢰했습니다.
이 주문에 대해서 귀사에서 신속히 실행해주면 대단히 감사하겠습니다.

강의노트

① cover '자금준비, 대금상환' (=protection)
It seems you debited our A/C for US$6,000 instead of US$5,000 on July 1, 20×× to cover said remittance.
(귀사는 상기 송금을 결제하기 위해서 20××년 7월 1일 미화 5,000불 대신 미화 6,000불을 당사 계좌에서 차기한 것 같습니다)
The cover has not been made yet through XYZ Bank.
(자금상환이 아직까지 XYZ은행을 통해서 이루어지지 않았습니다)
Cover는 '덮개, 표지, 피난처, 담보, 보증금, 상품명세' 의 의미로도 사용된다.

② in your favor '귀사를 수익자로, 귀사를 수취인으로' favoring, F/O
To cover this purchase, we have arranged an L/C to be opened in your favor.
(동 매입을 결제하기 위해서 귀사를 수익자로 해서 신용장을 개설할 것을 의뢰했습니다)

③ Purchase Note '매입계약서'
purchase[pə:tʃə́s] 구입, 매입, 사다, 구입하다
 ~ money 매입금액(대금, 계약금)
purchasing agent 구매담당원/중개인
purchasing power 구매력

④ execution '실행, 집행, 수행'
execute 실행, 수행하다
Please look into your records and execute payment immediately.
(귀사의 기록을 조사하시고 즉시 지급하여 주십시오)

Sample Letter 16

Gentlemen :

We confirm having accepted your counter offer via e-mail for 100 units of Video Cassette Recorder XYZ at US$2,500 per unit CIF

New York for September shipment. Our e-mail reads as follows : RYE FIFTEENTH BOOKED SHIPMENT SEPTEMBER WRITING.

We are enclosing our Sales Note No. 10 to confirm this contract. We would appreciate it if you would immediately arrange with your bankers to open an irrevocable L/C in our favor to ensure September shipment as agreed upon.

We thank you very much for this order and assure you of our best attention to its execution.

Yours truly,

*** 요약**

VCR XYZ 10대, 뉴욕착 운임보험료 포함가격으로 1대당 미화 2,500불 9월 선적을 위한 귀사 이메일 반대청약 '귀사 이메일 15일자 수락함. 선적 9월 가능. 세부사항 추후우송예정' 을 승낙했음을 확인합니다.

본 계약을 확인하기 위해서 당사판매계약서 제10호를 동봉합니다. 약정한 대로 9월 선적을 확보하기 위해서 당사를 수익자로 취소불능신용장을 개설할 것을 귀사 거래은행에 즉시 의뢰해 주시면 감사하겠습니다.

동 주문에 감사드리며 실행을 위해서 당사에서는 최선의 배려를 할 것을 확신합니다.

강의노트

① RYE FIFTEENTH BOOKED SHIPMENT SEPTEMBER WRITING

RYE는 Re Your E-mail의 약어이며 여기서 BOOKED는 (수주장)에 기장한다. 즉 (주문)수락하다의 뜻으로 to book an order는 to accept an order의 뜻이 된다. book 외에 accept, confirm, acknowledge도 주문을 승인하는 경우에 사용한다.

WRITING은 We will write to you in detail by airmail의 뜻이다.

② We would appreciate it if '~하여 주시면 감사하겠습니다.'

(=It will be appreciated if ~)

We would appreciate it if you send us a copy of L/C immediately.

(신용장의 사본을 당사로 즉시 송부하여 주시면 감사하겠습니다.)

③ assure ~ of '~할 것을 ~에게 확신하다' guarantee ; stand behind.

We assure you of our desire to work more closely with your company in the many years to come.
(앞으로도 귀사와 더욱 긴밀하게 일할 의사가 있음을 확신합니다)
assurance 자신, 확신, 약속, 보증

④ ensure '확실하게 하다, 보증하다, 안전하게 하다' ; make sure

Sample Letter 17

KOREA TRADING CORP.

"Kanam B/D, 1464-10, Seocho-dong, Seocho-ku Seoul Korea ☎:82-2-2278-3543 Fax:82-2-2273-9632 e-mail: kft@korea.com"

OFFER SHEET

MESSRS: ABC Publishing Co., Ltd. Offer No. : KFT-0806-306
105-67 Gongduk1-dong, Mapo-gu, Seoul, Korea 121-801 REF. NO. : 061708
Tel: 82-2-7075-100, Fax: 82-2-7075-160 DATE: June 17, 20××

We are pleased to order the under-mentioned articles as per conditions and details described as follows.

Code	Name	Q'ty	Unit	Unit Price	Amount
87767	Xeikon 6000 5/5 @ 1200 dpi	1	set		
63970	Jumbo Reel Unwinder (Kern)	1	set		
63972	Airshaft 76 mm	2	set		
104770	Paper stacker Xeikon 4000/5000plus/6000	1	set		
60800	Print Protector	1	set	£520,000.00	£520,000.00
83462	Starterkit Xeikon 4000/5000plus/6000	1	set		
	Installation	1			
5655	Tool Calibration Wrench DVL	1	set		
5748	Tool Distance Calibration Bar 500mm DVL	1	set		
1779	Tool Distance Calibration Clock 500mm DVL	1	set		
	Operator & productivity training				
	Sea freight and etc.				
	Total				£520,000.00

1. Origin:	Belgium
2. Latest shipping date:	Aug. 15, 20××
3. Payment:	By an at sight and irrevocable letter of credit to be opened in favour of Punch Graphix International nv at Duwijckstraat 17, 2500 Lier, Belgium. Advising bank: ABN AMRO at Regentlaan 53, BE-1000 Brussel, Belgium, SWIFT Code: ABNABEBRANT, Account No.: BE85 7215 2076 5406
4. Account & Consignee:	ABC Publishing Co., Ltd., 105-67, Gongduk1-dong, Mapo-gu, Seoul, Korea 121-801 Tel: 82-2-7075-100, Fax 82-2-7075-160
5. Notify Party:	Korea Trading Corp., Kanam B/D, Seocho-dong, Seocho-ku, Seoul, Korea 137-073 Tel: 82-2-2278-3543, Fax: 82-2-2273-9632, Email: kft@korea.com"
6. Delivery	By sea
7. Shipping Port	European Port
8. Destination Port	"Pusan Port, Korea"
9. Price:	CIF Pusan
10. Packing:	Export Standard Package
11. Remarks:	Insurance policy will be covered 100% of Invoice value.

Very truly yours,

* 요약

한국의 고려무역이 발행한 물품매도확약서(offer sheet)의 실례이다.

강의노트

① offer의 형식

특정한 방식이 없으며 구두로 행하여도 무방하지만 무역에서는 보통 서신이나 Fax에 의하거나 일정한 서식을 갖춘 offer sheet(청약서, 대외무역법에서는 물품매도확약서라고 한다)

② 유효기간(validity)

offer의 종류에 관계없이 offer에는 유효기간이 명시되어 있다.

※ 유효기간 표현방법

i) 기일에 의한 표현

We look forward to your reply within seven days.

ii) 기간에 의한 표현

We would like a firm offer in your reply reaching us by the July 20, 20××.

iii) 단기임을 표시하는 표현

We would like a firm offer in your reply reaching us by tomorrow (within 24 hours).

또한 유효기간을 연장할 때는 extention of offer 혹은 extention of validity of offer라 한다.

③ 단위(unit price)

offer에서 가장 중요한 요소로서 나라마다 화폐단위가 다르므로 사용화폐를 분명히 명시해야 한다.

특히 dollar 표시는 사용국가별로 가치평가에 현저한 차이가 있다.

Dollar(U.S.dollar, Australian dollar, Hong Kong dollar, Canadian dollar 등).

일반적으로 통화결정은 안전성, 교환성, 유통성을 고려하는데 우리나라는 외환관리상 대외결제 시에 사용할 수 있는 현행 지정통화(designated currency)를 원칙으로 하고 있다.

지정영수통화는 IMF 8조국통화, 유럽통화단위 및 홍콩통화이고 지정지급통화는 모든 외국통화를 말한다.

한편 단가는 가격조건, 결제통화를 결정하여 제시한다.

예) US$2.40 per piece F.O.B. Busan

◈ 각국 통화단위 및 CODE ◈

지역	국명	CODE	단위	보조단위
아시아	말레이시아	MYR	링기트(Ringgit)	센(Sen)
	사우디아라비아	SAR	리얄(Riyal)	쿠르쉬(Qursh) 할라라(Hallalah)
	싱가포르	SGD	달러(S$)	센트(Cent)
	요르단		디나르(Dinar)	필(Fil)
	인도	IDR	루피(Rupi)	파이사(Paisa)
	일본	JPY	100엔(Yen)	–
	중국	CNY	위안(Yuan)	지아오(Jiao)
	쿠웨이트	KWD	디나르(Dinar)	필(Fil)
	레바논		풍(Poung)	피아스트(Piastres)

아시아	아랍에미레이트	AED	디르함(Dirham)	
	이집트	EGP	파운드(Pound)	피아스트(Piastres)
	바레인	BHD	디나르(Dinar)	필스(Fils)
	홍콩	HKD	달러(Dollar)	센트(Cent)
	네팔		루피(Rupee)	피스(Pice)
	대만	TWD	달러(Dollar)	센트(Cent)
	스리랑카	LKR	루피(Rupee)	센트(Cent)
	태국	THB	바트(Baht)	사탕(Satang)
	필리핀	PHP	페소(Peso)	센타보(Centavo)
	인도네시아	IDR	루피아(Rupiah)	
	베트남		동(Dong)	
오세아니아	뉴질랜드	NZD	달러(Dollar)	센트(Cent)
	오스트레일리아	AUD	달러(Dollar)	센트(Cent)
유럽	유럽단일 통화	XEU	유로(Euro)	
	노르웨이	NOK	크로네(Krone)	오레(Ore)
	덴마크	DKK	크로네(Krone)	오레(Ore)
	스웨덴	SEK	크로나(Krona)	오레(Ore)
	스위스	CHF	프랑(Franc)	상팀(Centime)
	영국	GBP	파운드(Pound)	펜스(Pence)
아메리카	미국	USD	달러(Dollar)	센트(Cent)
	캐나다	CAD	달러(Dollar)	센트(Cent)
	브라질		크루제이로(Cruzeiro)	센타보(Centavo)
	멕시코		페소(Peso)	센타보(Centavo)
	아르헨티나		페소(Peso)	센타보(Centavo)
	파나마		발보아(B)	센타시모(Centesimo)

* **유로화에 통합된 국가의 통화** : 독일, 프랑스, 벨기에, 룩셈브르크, 네덜란드, 오스트리아, 아일랜드, 이탈리아, 스페인, 포르투갈, 핀란드, 그리스 등 모두 19개국

Useful Sentences(오퍼 및 승낙)

1. We thank you for your inquiry of March 10th and are pleased to offer you as follows subject to our final confirmation.
   3월 10일자 귀 문의에 감사드리며 당사 최종확인조건부로 아래와 같이 오퍼를 합니다.
2. A trial order will convince you of the excellent quality of our product.
   시험주문이 당사제품의 품질이 우수하다는 것을 확신시켜 줄 것입니다.
3. These goods have been specially made to meet your requirements.
   이 제품들은 귀사의 요구에 부응하여 특별히 제조되었습니다.

4. We believe these prices can compete well with those of other firms.
우리는 이 가격으로 타사 가격과 충분히 경쟁할 수 있다고 믿습니다.
5. We are clearing our stock now, so these prices are 20 percent lower than those of other manufacturers.
현재 재고품을 정리하고 있으므로 이 가격은 다른 제조업자의 가격보다 20%가 저렴합니다.
6. Please note that the prices will inevitably be raised in the near future because of low stock and increasing demand.
소규모의 재고와 증가하는 수요 때문에 가까운 장래에 가격이 불가피하게 상승하게 될 것이라는 것에 유의하시기 바랍니다.
7. As this is our first transaction with you, we are prepared to reduce our price to US$25 per set instead of the US$30 per set you suggested.
이번이 귀사와는 첫 거래이므로 귀사가 제안한 미화 30불 대신 미화 25불까지 깎아드릴 용의가 있습니다.
8. You requested us to give you the terms of a draft at 60 d/s, but we regret that we cannot comply with your request. Would 30 d/s terms be agreeable?
귀사에서 일람후 60일 출급어음조건을 요청했습니다만 당사에서는 귀사의 요청에 응할 수 없음을 유감으로 생각합니다. 일람후 30일 조건으로 하면 어떻겠습니까?
9. We are sending you our Contract No. 27 in duplicate. If you find them correct, please sign one and return it to us.
계약서 제27호 2부를 송부합니다. 정확하다고 판단되면 서명후 1부를 당사로 회송하여 주십시오.
10. Please let us know the Letter of Credit number as soon as the credit has been opened.
신용장이 개설되자마자 신용장번호를 당사에 알려 주십시오.
11. We are pleased to accept your offer of April 10th as we are satisfied with your price as well as with the time of shipment.
귀사의 선적시기뿐만 아니라 가격에 만족하므로 4월 10일자 귀사 오퍼를 승낙합니다.

12. We will persuade our suppliers to make a further price reduction if you place an order of more than 1,000 yards.
귀사에서 1,000야드 이상을 주문하신다면 공급업자에게 추가할인(감액)을 설득하겠습니다.
13. We feel that your counter offer is not acceptable because the price for such material is on the rise at present.
현재 재료가격이 상승 중에 있기 때문에 귀사의 반대청약을 승낙할 수 없다고 생각합니다.
14. The price we suggested is far lower than that in the average market.
우리가 제안한 가격은 평균시장가격보다 훨씬 저렴합니다.
15. We are prepared to provide you with a trial order of 100 dozen if you guarantee delivery on or before October 30.
귀사가 10월 30일 전에 선적(인도)을 보증한다면 100다스의 시험주문을 할 용의가 있습니다.
16. Large orders are now rushing in from your country and the market here is very strong.
현재 귀국으로부터 대량주문이 쇄도하고 있으며 이곳 시장은 호황입니다.
17. This is the best offer we can make at present and we trust that you will accept it at once.
이것은 현재 당사가 발행할 수 있는 최선의 오퍼입니다. 귀사에서 즉시 그것을 승낙하리라 믿습니다.
18. After carefully examining your sample, we have found that your quality is rather inferior to that of other suppliers.
귀사 견본을 정밀조사한 결과 귀사제품이 다른 공급업체의 제품보다 다소 열등한 것을 발견했습니다.
19. We will execute your order in strict accordance with your instructions.
귀사의 지시에 따라서 귀사 주문을 엄격히 이행하겠습니다.
20. This is our rock-bottom price and there is a possibility of our raising it in the near future because of a rise in the labor cost.
이것은 당사의 결착가격입니다. 그리고 노동임금의 상승으로 인해서 가까운 장래에 가격을 인상할 가능성이 있습니다.

Chapter 05

주문 및 계약
Orders and Contract

매매계약이 성립되는 경우는 ① 수출자가 먼저 offer하여 수입자가 이를 수락(accept)할 때와, 그 반대로 ② 수입자가 먼저 주문(order)을 하고 수출자가 이를 승낙(acknowledge)하는 것이다.

무역거래는 절대적 통일형식이 존재하지 않지만 대체로 다음과 같은 과정을 경유하여 이루어진다.

Market research→Credit inquiry→Circular letter/Business proposal →Trade inquiry→Offer/Order→Acceptance/Acknowledgement→ Sales contract→Opening L/C

이러한 일련의 과정 가운데 무역계약에서 그 중핵이라 할 수 있는 매매계약은 흔히 전신의 교환으로 이루어지지만 다시 문서로 상호 확인하는 것이 매매계약의 원활한 이행과 또 계약조건의 오해에 의한 분쟁을 예방하기 위하여 판매계약서(Sales Note), 구매계약서(Purchase Note), 주문확인서(Confirmation of Order), 매매계약서(Sales Contract) 등의 문서로 사용하는 것이 일반적이다.

주문서(Order Sheet; Order Form; Order Blank)의 기재사항은 다음과 같다.

(1) 매매상품의 명세(Description of Article) · 품질(Quality)

(2) 수량(Quantity)

(3) 매매가격(Price)

(4) 선적시기(Time of Shipment ; Delivery)

(5) 대금결제조건(Terms of Payment)
(6) 포장 및 화인(Packing and Marking)
(7) 보험조항(Insurance Clauses)
(8) 운송서류(Transport Document)
(9) 기타 필요한 사항

Sample Letter 18

Gentlemen :

We are pleased to give you the following order, based on the catalog and price list you sent us on August 1 :

Quantity	Description	Price per Unit (FOB Tokyo)
20	Portable Radio Set A102	US$ 50.00
10	Cassette Tape Recorder B84	US$ 150.00
10	Microphone C59	US$ 100.00

Please acknowledge this order by return and let us know the earliest possible time of shipment. Upon receipt of your confirmation we will open a letter of credit in your favor.

As the goods are urgently needed, we hope you will try to send them on the first available vessel.

As for the payment, you may draw a draft at sight when you have effected shipment.

Your prompt attention to this matter will be appreciated.

Yours truly,

＊ 요약

8월 1일자로 귀사에서 송부한 상품목록과 가격표를 기초로 해서 당사는 아래와 같이 주문합니다.

수량	명 세	단가(FOB 동경)
20	휴대용 라디오 세트 A102	미화 50불
10	카세트 테이프 녹음기 B84	미화 150불
10	마이크 C59	미화 100불

회신 시에 동 주문을 승낙하여 주시고 가능한 조속한 선적시기를 알려주십시오. 귀사로부터 확인을 받자마자 귀사를 수익자로 하여 신용장을 개설하겠습니다.

모든 상품이 긴급히 필요하므로 가능한 첫 번째 이용할 수 있는 선박으로 선적하여 주시기 바랍니다.

결제조건에 대해서는 귀사에서 선적이 이루어지면 일람출급 환어음을 발행하여 주십시오.

이 일에 대해서 신속히 배려하여 주시면 감사하겠습니다.

강의노트

① order '순서, 질서, 지시, 명령, 주문'

out of~ (기계가)고장나서, (몸이)좋지 않아서,

repeat ~재주문, trial ~ 시험주문, minimum~ 최저 인수가능 주문량.

'주문하다' 는 to order, to place an order with somebody for something : to give an order to somebody나 to favor somebody with an order for something.

This is a trial order. If the quality proves satisfactory, we will give you large orders in the future.

(이번에는 시험주문입니다. 품질이 만족스럽게 판명되면 당사에서는 장차 대량 주문을 하겠습니다)

(We favor repeat orders : 재주문을 받습니다. 재주문을 주십시오)

② draw a draft at sight : '일람출급 환어음을 발행하다'.

draw만으로도 '환어음을 발행하다' 의 뜻으로 a draft '환어음' 을 생략하여 쓰기도 한다.

Draw at sight ; draw at 60 days after sight '일람 후 60일급 출급 환어음을 발행하다' drawer 발행인, drawee 피발행인.

무역거래 내용에 따라서 매도인과 매수인의 명칭이 아래와 같이 여러 가지로 사용된다.

◈ 거래별 매도인 및 매수인 명칭 ◈

거래내용	매도인	매수인
매매관계	Seller	Buyer
수출입관계	Exporter	Importer
신용장거래	Beneficiary	The Applicant (for the Credit)
☆D/A, D/P거래	Customer	Drawee
계정책임관계	Accounter	Accountee
화물관계	Consignor	Consignee
신용공여관계	Accreditee	Accreditor (=Accredited Buyer)
어음관계	Drawer/Payee	Drawee/Payer

☆D/A는 Documents Against Acceptance '인수도조건'
수출상이 발행한 일람정기 또는 확정출급 화환어음을 일람지급없이 인수함으로써 관계 운송서류가 인도되는 것을 말한다.
☆D/P는 Documents Against Payment '지급도조건'
화환어음의 지급인(수입상)은 수출상이 발행한 일람출급환어음 대금을 결제하여야만 관계 운송서류가 인도되는 것을 말한다.

③ based on '~에 근거를 둔, ~기초로 해서'
Direct taxation is usually based on income. (직접세는 보통 수입에 근거한다)
basis '기초, 근거, 원칙, 방식'
We are sending you the following trial order on the basis of your estimate of May 1.
당사는 5월 1일자 귀사 견적을 근거로 해서 아래와 같이 시험주문서를 송부합니다.
All sales are conducted on a small profit and quick return basis.
(모든 판매는 박리다매 조건으로 하고 있습니다)

Sample Letter 19

Gentlemen :

Thank you for your order of September 1st for 20 units of portable radio set A102, 10 units of cassette tape recorder B84 and 10 units of microphone C59.

Enclosed is our Sales Note No. 58 in duplicate, which we hope you will find correct.

All the goods ordered are in stock and can be shipped to you by October 15 at the latest, provided you open a letter of credit in our favor immediately.

As soon as your L/C reaches us, we will start arranging shipment.

Thank you again for this order.

Yours very truly,

* 요약

마이크 C59 10대, 카세트테이프 녹음기 B84 10대, 휴대용 라디오세트 A102 20대에 관한 9월 1일자 귀 주문에 감사드립니다.

당사의 매출계약서 제58호 2통을 동봉합니다. 그것이 정확하다는 것을 알게 되기를 바랍니다.

주문한 모든 제품은 재고가 있으며 귀사가 당사를 수익자로 하여 즉시 신용장을 개설한다면 늦어도 10월 15일까지 선적할 수 있습니다.

신용장이 내도하자마자 당사에서는 선적을 준비하겠습니다.

이번 주문에 다시 한 번 감사드립니다.

강의노트

① be in stock '재고가 있다'

out of ~품절이다.

stock 재고품, 가축, 주식, ~holder 주주(미)=shareholder(영)

◆ 동일한 사물 · 관념의 의미가 미국과 영국에서 다른 어구로 사용되는 예를 들면 아래와 같다.

	미 국	영 국
지폐	Bill	Note
변호사	Attorney	Solicitor
수화물	Baggage	Luggage
시가의 일구획	Block	Row
연쇄점	Chain store	Multiple shop
당좌계정	Checking Account	Current Account
주식회사	Corporation	Limited Liability Company
1 [2] 층	First [second] floor	Ground [first] floor
화물차	Freight train	Goods train
주유소	Gas Station	Filling Station
본사	Head office	Home office
할부구매	Installment Buying	Hire-purchase
(방 등을)예약하다	Make a reservation	Book a room
왕복표	Round trip ticket	Return ticket
편도표	One-way ticket	Single ticket
소작농	Sharecropper	Tenant farmer
지하철도	Sub(way)	Underground ; tube
화물자동차	Truck	Lorry
지하도	Underpass	Subway
항상	Always	At all times
자동차 천장	Top	Hood
자동차 뚜껑	Hood	Bonnet
조심하세요	Watch your step	Mind the gap
학교중퇴생	School dropout	School leaver
지우개	Eraser	Rubber

② in duplicate '정 · 부 2통으로 된'

duplicate 중복의, 이중의, 두 배의, 정본에 대한 부본, 복사, 복사하다, 두 배로 하다.

avoid duplication 중복을 피하다

Please use this letter as our authorization to you to effect the payment, avoiding possible duplication.

(중복을 피하면서 이 서신을 귀사가 지급을 이행하라는 수권서로 사용하시기 바랍니다)

◆ 무역관련 서류 작성 시에 빈번하게 사용하는 통수는 다음과 같다.

1통 : 1 copy	1-fold	
2통 2 copies	2-fold	duplicate
3통 3 copies	3-fold	triplicate
4통 4 copies	4-fold	quadruplicate
5통 5 copies	5-fold	quintuplicate
6통 6 copies	6-fold	sextuplicate
7통 7 copies	7-fold	septuplicate
8통 8 copies	8-fold	octuplicate
9통 9 copies	9-fold	nonuplicate
10통 10 copies	10-fold	decuplicate

Sample Letter 20

Sample Letter 18에 대한 주문거절
(Decline of order)

Gentlemen :

Thank you for your order of September 1 for 20 units of Portable Radio Set A102, 10 units of Cassette Tape Recorder B84 and 10 units of Microphone C59.

We have in stock Portable Radio Set A102 and Cassette Tape Recorder B84, but regret to say Microphone C59 is out of stock. This article is no longer manufactured because it has become outdated. Our new model C60 has recently been launched and enjoys wide popularity. We would like you to consider this model instead of C59.

The other two items will be shipped to you as soon as possible.

Your prompt reply by email concerning C60 would be appreciated.

Yours very truly,

* 요약

마이크 C59 10대, 카세트테이프 녹음기 B84 10대 그리고 휴대용 라디오세트 A102 20대에 대한 9월 1일자 귀 주문에 감사드립니다.

카세트테이프 녹음기 B84와 휴대용 라디오 A102는 재고가 있습니다만 마이크

C59는 품절임을 유감으로 생각합니다. 동 제품은 다소 구식이기 때문에 더 이상 제조하지 않고 있습니다. 최근에는 새로운 모델 C60이 개발되어 폭넓은 인기를 누리고 있습니다. 당사는 귀사가 C59 대신 이 모델의 구입을 고려할 것을 요청합니다.

다른 2가지 품목들은 조속히 선적할 수 있습니다.

C60에 대해서 귀사에서 이메일로 조속히 회신하여 주시면 대단히 감사하겠습니다.

강의노트

① launch '(배를)진수시키다, (사업 등을) 착수하다, 시작하다'
He is launching a new business. (그는 새로운 사업을 시작하고 있다)

② outdated '구식의, 진부한', stick-in-the-mud
We found that the agency arrangement between our firms was outdated.
(양사 간의 대행 약정서가 구식이라는 것을 알았습니다)
This model has become outdated and is now substituted by the new model SC70.
(이 모델은 구식이 되어가고 새로운 모델 SC70으로 거의 대체되고 있습니다)

③ instead of '~의 대신에', in place of
Destination should read Busan instead of Incheon.
(목적항은 인천 대신에 부산으로 정정해야 됩니다)
Commodity size should now read 20″×25″ instead of 8″×10″
(상품규격을 8″×10″ 대신 20″×25″로 고쳐야 합니다)

④ refuse to do A : A하는 것을 단호히 거절하다.
decline to do A : A하는 것을 완곡히 거절하다.

Useful Sentences(주문, 주문수락 및 거절, 대체품추천)

1. We are pleased to enclose our official order sheet No. 123 for your electric refrigerator CD-21.
귀사 전기냉장고 CD-21에 대한 당사 정식주문서 제123호를 동봉합니다.
2. We have tested your sample and found it very satisfactory. Please supply 1,000 dozen as per our enclosed Order Form No. 124.
귀사 견본품을 시험한 결과 대단히 만족스러웠습니다. 동봉한 당사 주문서

제124호와 같이 1,000다스를 공급해 주십시오.

3. We may reject the goods if there are any marks or blemishes on the surface.
   만일 표면에 어떤 표시나 흠이 있으면 물품의 인수를 거절하겠습니다.
4. Please follow our shipping instructions when you pack the order.
   주문품을 포장할 때 당사의 선적지시사항을 따르십시오.
5. Our customers require the goods for summer vacation, so please send the goods by the end of July.
   당사 고객들이 하기휴가용으로 그 제품을 필요로 합니다. 그러므로 7월 말까지 그 제품을 보내주십시오.
6. If this order is satisfactorily executed, you may expect further business with us.
   만약 이 주문이 만족스럽게 이행된다면 귀사는 당사와의 추가거래를 기대해도 좋습니다.
7. We acknowledge (with thanks) your order of February 3 for 500 dozen silk scarves.
   실크 스카프 500다스에 대한 2월 3일자 귀사 주문을 감사한 마음으로 승낙합니다.
8. We will do all we can to fill your order so that the goods will be shipped before October 15.
   상품이 10월 15일 전에 선적될 수 있도록 당사에서는 귀 주문품을 조달하는데 최선을 다하겠습니다.
9. The goods will be packed in strict accordance to your instructions.
   상품은 귀사 지시에 따라서 철저히 포장할 것입니다.
10. We have received your letter of credit for your order No.123 and are now proceeding with shipment in accordance to the terms agreed upon.
    귀사 주문 제123호에 대한 신용장을 받았습니다. 그리고 협정한 조건대로 현재 선적을 준비하고 있습니다.
11. It is our hope that this order will be the first step in a long and pleasant business relationship between us.
    이 주문이 양사 간에 오랫동안 그리고 유쾌한 거래관계의 첫걸음이 되기를 희망합니다.

12. Your order of October 1st for our eel skin wallet is appreciated, but much to our regret, we are unable to fill it at present.
당사 뱀장어 가죽지갑에 대한 10월 1일자 귀사 주문에 감사드립니다. 그러나 현재로서는 대단히 유감스럽게도 그 주문을 이행할 수 없습니다.
13. The goods you requested are no longer in stock due to the recent increase in orders.
최근 주문이 쇄도함에 따라 귀사에서 요구한 제품은 품절입니다.
14. As there is no demand for the article, we have stopped manufacturing it.
이 제품에 대한 수요가 전혀 없기 때문에 당사에서는 그 제품의 제조를 중지했습니다.
15. Unfortunately the articles you ordered in your letter of October 11 are out of stock.
불행히도 10월 11일자 귀 서신에서 주문한 그 제품은 품절입니다.
16. However, we can offer a very similar product model No. 77 instead, which is perhaps more suitable for your needs.
그러나 대신 대단히 유사한 제품인 제77형을 제의합니다. 그것은 귀사의 목적에 오히려 더 적합하다고 생각합니다.
17. We regret that production of AB121 you ordered has been discontinued for some time, so we would like to recommend CD 125 which is available now.
귀사가 주문한 AB121의 생산이 당분간 중지되었음을 유감으로 생각합니다. 그러므로 현재 입수가능한 CD125를 추천합니다.
18. As our factory is at present fully occupied with orders, we regret having to decline your order.
당사 공장은 현재 주문품으로 완전가동되고 있어 귀사 주문을 거절하게 됨을 유감으로 생각합니다.
19. We cannot fill your order now because the raw materials have recently become hard to obtain.
최근 원재료를 입수하는 데 어려움이 있어 현재 귀사 주문을 이행할 수 없습니다.

20. Because of a serious shortage in shipping space, we cannot deliver your order before July 20th.
선복이 심각하게 부족하기 때문에 7월 20일 전에 귀 주문을 인도할 수 없습니다.

21. As soon as conditions return to normal, we will be pleased to contact you.
상황이 정상적으로 돌아가자마자 귀사에 연락하겠습니다.

22. We regret we have not been able to serve you this time, but hope to do business with you again.
이번에 귀사에 봉사할 수 없음을 유감으로 생각합니다. 그러나 다시 귀사와 거래를 맺기를 희망합니다.

Sample Letter 21

Memorandum of Terms and Conditions of Business

This memorandum made and entered into between Korea Trading Co., Ltd, Seoul(hereinafter called the Sellers) and World Trading Co., New York(hereinafter called the Buyers) witnesses as follows :

(1) Business :

Business is to be transacted between Sellers and Buyers as principals to principals, on their own account and responsibility for the sale of the sellers' sporting shoes in New York.

(2) Quality :

The Sellers are to supply the Buyers with samples free of charge and the quality of the goods to be shipped be fully equal to that of the sample on which an order is given.

(3) Quantity :

The minimum quantity for an order is to be the standard contents of one package. Assortment of various articles is to be accepted so long as the total quantity exceeds the minimum just explained.

(4) Prices :

Prices are to be quoted in U.S. dollars on the basis of C.I.F. New

York unless otherwise specified.

(5) Firm Offer :

Firm offers are to remain effective for forty-eight hours after the time of dispatch, excluding Sundays and national holidays.

(6) Orders :

Except in cases where firm offers are accepted all orders are to be subject to the Seller's final confirmation.

(7) Discount :

The special discount of 3 percent from the contract price is to be accorded on an order exceeding 1,000 pairs in quantity.

(8) Packing :

Proper export wooden case packing is to be used, each case bearing the mark <A_1> with port mark, running case number, and the country of origin.

(9) Shipment :

Shipment is to be made within the time stipulated in each contract, except in circumstances beyond the Sellers' control. The date of bills of lading shall be taken as conclusive proof of the date of shipment. Unless expressly agreed upon, the port of shipment shall be at the Sellers' option.

(10) Force Majeure :

The Sellers shall not be responsible for the delay in shipment due directly or indirectly to force majeure including mobilization, war, riots, civil commotions, hostilities, blockades, requisition of vessels, prohibition of export, fires, floods, earthquakes, tempests, strikes, lockouts and any other contingencies, which prevent shipment within the period stipulated. In the event of any of the aforesaid causes arising, documents proving its occurrence or existence shall be submitted by the Sellers to the Buyers without delay.

(11) Delayed Shipment :

In all cases of force majeures stipulated in Article 10, the period of shipment stipulated shall be extended for a period of twenty-one days. In case shipment within the extended period should still be prevented by a continuance or the consequences any of the causes mentioned in Article 10, it shall be at the Buyers' option either to allow the shipment of late goods or to cancel the order by giving the Sellers a notice of cancellation by e-mail or facsimile.

(12) Insurance :

All shipments are to be covered on ICC(B) including War Risks for the invoice amount plus ten percent; and the insurance policy is to be made out in U.S. Dollars and the claims are payable in New York.

(13) Payment :

Draft is to be drawn at 60 d/s under Irrevocable Letter of Credit which should be opened in favor of the Sellers immediately upon contract, for the corresponding value of an order, with full set of shipping documents, viz. Bill of Lading, Insurance Policy, Commercial Invoice and other documents which each contract requires.

(14) Credit :

The letter of credit shall be established in favor of the Sellers by cable or mail, as the case may be, immediately upon contract for the corresponding value of an order and shall be maintained for fourteen days beyond the latest date set forth for shipment for negotiation of relative drafts. If the Buyers fail to establish the letter of credit as specified above, the Sellers shall reserve the right to cancel the contract.

(15) Claims :

Any claim exceeding 10 percent of the invoice amount is to be cabled within 10 days from the date of final discharge of goods at destination. Any claim beyond the amicable adjustment between Sellers and Buyers is to be settled by arbitration at destination.

(16) Arbitration :

Claims and disputes, failing amicable settlement between the Sellers and the Buyers, shall be submitted to two arbitrators appointed by each party, and should they be unable to agree, the decision of an umpire selected by the arbitrators, including the apportionment of the expenses of the arbitration, shall be final. Arbitration under this provision shall be carried out in the U.S.A.

This agreement shall be valid on and after December 1, 20××.

(Buyers)	(Sellers)
World Trading Co.	Korea Trading Co., Ltd.
Samuel Clark	*J. H. Kim*
Samuel A. Clark	J. H. Kim
President	Managing Director

* 요약

일반거래조건 협정서

본 협정서는 서울에 있는 고려무역 주식회사(이하 매도인이라 칭함)와 뉴욕소재 세계무역주식회사(이하 매수인이라 칭함) 간에 작성 및 체결되어 다음과 같이 합의하였음을 입증한다.

(1) 거래 : 거래는 New York에서 매도인의 스포츠화(운동화) 판매를 위해 자신의 계산과 책임으로 본인 대 본인으로서 매도인과 매수인 간에 행한다.

(2) 품질 : 매도인은 매수인에게 무료로 견본을 제공하여야 하며, 선적품의 품질은 주문성립의 근거가 된 견본의 품질과 완전히 일치하여야 한다.

(3) 수량 : 1회 주문에 대한 최저수량은 한 상자의 표준적인 내용물이어야 한다. 각종 품목을 혼합했을 때는 합계수량이 방금 설명한 최저수량을 초과하는 한 인수한다.

(4) 가격 : 가격은 별도 명시가 없는 한 New York까지의 운임 · 보험료 포함 조건에 의하여 미국 달러로 견적한다.

(5) 확정청약 : 확정청약은 일요일과 국경일을 제외하고 타전한 시각 이후 48시간 동안 유효하다.

(6) 주문 : 확정청약이 승낙되는 경우를 제외하고 모든 주문은 매도인의 최종 확인을 조건으로 한다.

(7) 할인 : 주문수량이 1천 켤레를 초과할 때는 계약금액에서 3%의 특별할인을 부여한다.

(8) 포장 : 적합한 수출용 목재상자로 포장하여야 하며, 각 상자에는 항구명, 상자 일련번호 및 원산지 표시와 함께 <A_1> 표시를 한다.

(9) 선적 : 선적은 매도인의 불가항력인 경우를 제외하고 각 계약서에 정해진 기일 이내에 하여야 한다. 선화증권의 일자는 선적일의 최종적 증거로 간주한다. 명시적 합의가 없는 한 선적항은 매도인이 선택한다.

(10) 불가항력 : 매도인은 동원, 전쟁, 폭동, 소요, 교전, 봉쇄, 선박징발, 수출금지, 화재, 홍수, 지진, 폭풍우, 파업, 폐쇄 및 약정된 기간 내의 선적을 방해하는 기타 일체의 우발사고를 포함하는 불가항력에 직접 또는 간접으로 기인하는 선적지연에 대해서는 책임을 지지 아니한다. 위에 언급한 어떠한 사유가 발생하는 경우에는 그 발생 또는 존재를 증명하는 서류를 매도인이 지체없이 매수인에게 보내야 한다.

(11) 선적지연 : 제10조에 규정한 모든 불가항력의 경우에는 규정된 선적기간을 21일간 연장한다. 만약 제10조에 언급한 사유의 어떤 것의 계속 또는 결과로 인해 연장된 기간 내에도 선적을 하지 못하는 경우에는, 늦어진 상품의 선적을 허용하든지 또는 매도인에게 전자우편이나 팩시밀리로 취소통지를

하여 주문을 취소하든지는 매수인이 선택한다.

(12) 보험 : 모든 선적품은 송장금액에 10%를 가산한 보험금액에 대해 전쟁위험 포함 협회적화약관 (B)조건으로 부보하여야 한다. 또한 보험증권은 미국 달러로 작성하고, 보험금은 뉴욕에서 지급한다.

(13) 결제 : 환어음은 선적서류 전통, 예컨대 선화증권, 보험증권, 상업송장, 기타 각 계약서에서 요구하는 서류를 첨부하여 주문에 상당하는 금액에 대해 계약 즉시, 매도인을 수익자로 개설되는 취소불능신용장에 의거 일람후 60일 출급으로 발행하여 한다.

(14) 신용장 : 신용장은 주문에 해당하는 금액에 대해 계약 즉시, 경우에 따라 전신 또는 우편으로 매도인을 수익자로 하여 개설하고, 관련된 환어음의 매도를 위하여 규정된 최종 선적기일 후 14일간 유효하게 된다. 만일 매수인이 위에 명시된 대로 신용장을 개설하지 못하면 매도인은 계약을 취소할 권리를 갖는다.

(15) 손해배상청구 : 송장금액의 10%를 초과하는 모든 손해배상청구는 목적지에 상품의 최종양륙일자로부터 10일 이내에 타전되어야 한다. 매도인 및 매수인 간에 원만히 조정할 수 없는 손해배상청구는 목적지에서의 중재로 해결하여야 한다.

(16) 중재 : 클레임과 분쟁이 매도인과 매수인 간에 우호적으로 해결되지 아니하면 각 당사자가 임명하는 두 명의 중재인에게 넘기고 만일 중재인들이 합의를 하지 못하면 중재비용의 할당을 포함하여 중재인들이 선정하는 심판인의 결정을 최종적인 것으로 한다. 이 규정에 의한 중재는 미국에서 실시한다.

본 협정서는 20×× 년 12월 1일부터 발효한다.

(매수인) 세계무역주식회사	(매도인) 고려무역주식회사
사뮤엘 클라크	김 재 현
대표이사	전무이사

강의노트

① Memorandum of Terms and Conditions of Business '거래조건 각서'

유상계약에 있어서의 유효한 계약서는 반드시 첨인증서이어야 할 필요는 없으므로 계약내용에 기재한 서면에 당사자가 서명만하면 충분하다. 따라서 'Contract' 라든가 'Agreement' 라는 표제가 있는 문서만 유효한 것은 아니다. 표제가 'Memorandum' 'Letter of Intent' 'Side Letter' 로 표시되는 문서라 하더라도 내용에 법률상의 구속력을 갖는 합의이고 당사자의 서명이 있으면 이것

또한 계약서임을 유의할 필요가 있다.

- **Contract** : 두 사람 이상의 당사자 간에 체결된 법률상 강제 가능한(enforceable at law) 합의(agreement)이다.
- **Agreement** : 법률상 구속력을 갖고 있지 않은 합의도 포함되기 때문에 엄격히 말하면 계약(contract)보다 넓은 개념이다.
  그러나 실무에서는 양자를 구별하고 있지 않기 때문에 agreement와 contract는 동의어로 사용하더라도 상관없다.
- **Memorandum** : Letter of Intent와 같이 장래 계약을 체결할 것을 약속하는 계약인 경우와 본 계약 중의 특정조항의 세부적 사항이나 구체적 내용 등에 관하여 당사자 간에 약정하고 서명한 종된 계약인 경우 등이 있다.
- **Letter of Intent** : 장래에 계약을 체결할 것을 약속하고 계약체결시의 계약내용의 대략을 기재하여 양 당사자가 서명한 문서이며, 계약체결을 약속한 계약임.
- **Side Letter** : 본 계약에 있는 특정조항에 관하여 구체적 내용을 당사자의 일방이 타방에 대하여 편지의 형식으로 2통 작성하여 송부한 후 타방이 그 편지의 끝에 '상기 승낙하며 동의한다'(accepted and agreed)라고 문언을 붙여 서명하여 1통을 상대방에게 반송하는 경우이며, 종된 계약의 일종임.

위에서 memorandum은 '비망록, 약식상업서신, 계약서, 각서'의 뜻을 가지고 있으며 복수는 memoranda 또는 memorandums. Memo는 memorandum의 약자이며 어원은 라틴어로 "반드시 기억해야 되는 것"이란 뜻이다. 영어는 여러 언어가 혼합된 것(an amalgam of many tongues)이므로 다음과 같이 어려운 외래복수형(Foreign Plural)을 미리 숙지하여야 한다.

Singular	Plural
addendum	addenda
alumna(fem.)	alumnae
alumnus(masc.)	alumni(also mixed)
analysis	analyses
appendix	appendixes, appendices
attorney general	attorneys general
bacillus	bacilli
bacterium	bacteria
basis	bases
cactus	cacti
crisis	crises
curriculum	curriculums, curricula
datum	data
deer	deer

fish	fish(same kind)
focus	focuses, foci
formula	formulas, formulae
genus	genera
gladiolus	gladioluses, gladioli
hypothesis	hypotheses
iris	irises
larva	larvae
maidservant	maidservants
madam	mesdames
manservant	menservants
memorandum	memorandums, memoranda
moose	moose
mother-in-law	mothers-in-law
nebula	nebulae
oasis	oases
parenthesis	parenthese
phenomenon	phenomena
radius	radiuses, radii
secretary general	secretaries general
secretary of state	secretaries of state
stimulus	stimuli
stratum	strata
synopsis	synopses
terminus	termina
thesis	theses
vortex	vortices

② made and entered into '작성된, 체결된'

이러한 동의어의 중복사용(parallelism)은 각종 계약서 법률문서에서 흔히 보는 표현이다. 각각 and/or의 앞 또는 뒤만으로 번역해도 무방하다. 이러한 특수한 표현을 하면 계약서를 난해하게 하므로 가능한 한 이러한 중복된 표현은 피하는 것이 좋다.

alter or change	final and conclusive
assume and agree	finish and complete
authorize and empower	full force and effect
bind and obligate	furnish and supply
cease and come to an end	kept and performed
chargeable or accountable	kind and character
convey, transfer, and set over	kind and nature
deemed and considered	known and described as

due and owing
each and all
each and every
null and of no effect
order and direct
over and above
perform and discharge
perform or observe
power and authority
relieve and discharge
remise, release, and forever quitclaim
made and entered into
mentioned or referred to
null and void
shall and will
shall have and exercise(the power)
sole and exclusive
true and correct
type and kind
under and subject to
understood and agreed
within and under the terms of

다음과 같이 한쪽이 다른 한쪽을 포함하는 의미를 가지고 있는 용어의 중복사용도 무의미하기 때문에 유의하여야 한다.

all and every
any and all
authorize and direct
authorize and require
by and between
by and under
desire and require
from and after
have and obtain
may have access to and examine
means and includes
request and demand

③ as principals to principals '본인 대 본인으로'

거래형태에 대한 규정으로서 거래당사자 모두 '본인' 이며 as principal to agent '본인 대 대리인으로' 거래하는 것이 아니라는 것이다. 즉, Both sellers and buyers [both parties] shall act as principals to principals and not as agents.

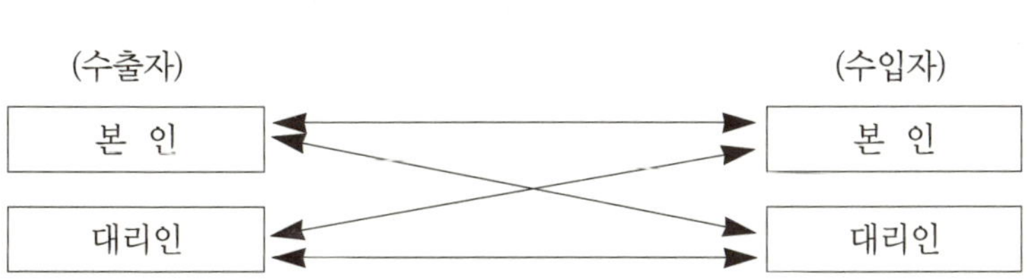

여기서 본인(principal)이란 '거래로부터 발생하는 권리 의무의 주체로서, 자기의 계산과 위험(for account and risk)으로 거래하는 자' 를 말한다.

반면 대리인(Agent)이란 '거래의 권리 · 주체가 타인으로서, 타인의 계산과 위험으로 거래하는 자' 이다.

즉, 거래로부터 발생하는 손익은 본인에 귀속되며, 대리인은 본인을 위해 제공된 서비스에 대한 보수로서 수수료를 받는 것이다.

④ on their own account '각자의 계산으로'
for one's own purposes and profit ; at one's own risk '자기들 자신의 이익을 위하여 또 자기들 자신의 위험으로'

⑤ to be quoted '제시될(가격이나 수량)'

⑥ assortment '분류, 종별, 구색을 갖춘 것, 여러 가지 섞은 것'
동사는 assort '여러 가지 갖추다, 여러 가지를 섞다'
assorted '여러 종류의, 혼합의'
This shop has a good assortment of goods to choose from.
(이 상점은 물건의 구색이 좋다)

⑦ Excluding Sundays and national holidays '일요일과 공휴일은 제외하고'
미국에서는 national holidays 대신에 bank holidays를 사용하여 은행이 영업을 하지 않는다는 뜻이고, 영국에서는 법정휴일인 Good Friday, Easter Monday, Whit Monday, The first Monday in August, Christmas Day, Boxing Day 등 6일을 제외한다는 뜻이다.
해운에서는 사용하는 SHEX [ʃeks]는 Sundays and holidays are Excepted의 용선계약(Contract by Charter Party)에서 화물의 적재를 위해서 허용하기로 정하는 본선의 정박기간(lay days)에 일요일과 공휴일은 포함시키지 않는다는 뜻이다.

⑧ Packing '포장. 짐꾸리기'
곡물류나 광물류 등의 bulky goods나 자동차, 선박 등의 일부 비포장 개체물품(unpacked individual items)을 제외하고는 대부분의 물품은 포장을 요한다.
물품의 포장(packing)은 '화물꾸밈'은 물론 '화물만들기', 즉 하조(packaging, package)를 포함하는 개념이다.
Buyer 또는 운송관계인이 당해 거래목적물임을 쉽게 확인할 수 있게 하거나 화물의 운송목적지의 판별과 Cargo dealing을 정확하고 용이하게 할 수 있게 하기 위하여 외장(outer packing)에 특정한 기호나 문자 따위를 표기하는 것을 화인 혹은 화표(Shipping Marks, Case Marks, Cargo Marks)라 한다.

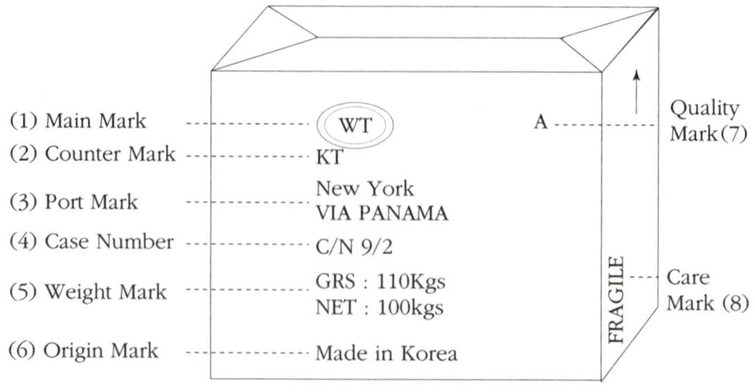

(1) 주화인(Main mark) : 다른 화물과의 식별을 용이하게 하기 위하여 특정한 기호(Symbol)를 표시하고 그 안에 상호 등의 약자를 삽입한다.
화인을 아래와 같이 전문으로도 통지할 수 있다.
TEN CASES SPORTING SHOES SHIPPED ARIRANGHO TODAY MARKED KT IN CIRCLE OVER NEW YORK
'스포츠화 10상자 금일 아리랑호로 선적, 화인은 아래와 같다.

KT

New York

(2) 부화인(Counter Mark ; sub-mark) : Main mark만으로 타 화물과의 구별이 어려울 때 생산자 또는 공급자의 약자를 Main mark 아래에 보조적으로 표시한다.
(3) 착항표시(Port mark ; Destination Mark) : 화물의 Loading이나 Unloading (discharge)을 명확히 하고 오송을 사전에 방지할 수 있게 하기 위하여 목적항 및 목적지를 표시한다.
복수항로의 경우 – 'New York Via Panama' 'New York overland Via Seattle' ect.
(4) 화번(Case Number) : 각 화물을 송장(Invoice)이나 적화목록(MF : Manifest) 또는 기타 운송서류(Transport Documents)와 대조하여 식별 · 확인하기 위하여 외장 1개에 한 번호씩 일련번호(consecutive number ; serial number ; running number)로 표시한다. 통신문에서는 with number 1(and) up ; No.[또는 #] 1/30 ; 1-30 등으로 표기한다.
(5) 중량표시(Weight Mark) : 운임계산, 통관, 하역작업 등을 용이하게 할 수 있도록 순중량(Net Weight)과 총중량(Gross Weight)을 표시
(6) 원산지표시(Origin mark) : 당해물품의 생산국을 외장의 맨 아래에 표시
(7) 품질표시(Quality Mark) : 물품의 등급 또는 품질수준이나 공인기관의 품질검사 합격 등을 표시
(8) 주의표시(Care mark, Side mark, Caution mark) : Cargo dealing(Cargo handling)에 있어서의 특히 주의할 점을 경계적으로 표시하는 것으로 외장의 측면에 표시하는 것이 일반적이다. 다음은 그러한 문구들이다.
- 서늘한 곳에 둘 것 : Keep Cool
- 깨어지기 쉬움 : Fragile
- 거꾸로 들지 말 것 : Right Side Up
- 취급주의 : Handle With Care

- 건조한 곳에 보관할 것 : Keep Dry
- 직사광선은 피할 것 : Keep Out Of Sun
- 평적 : Keep Flat
- 평적하지 말 것 : Never Lay Flat
- 세워둘 것 : To Be Kept Upright
- 쇠갈고리 사용말 것 : No Hooks
- 갑판적 : On Deck
- 통관수속필 : Examined
- 운임지불필 : Freight Paid
- 운임미불 : Freight Unpaid
- 현금인환 : C.O.D.(Cash On Delivery)
- 이면을 윗쪽으로(상단) : This End up
- 습기조심 : Guard Against Dampness
- 열기주의 : Keep Away From Heat
- 부패성 상품 : Perishable Goods
- 폭발성 : Explosive
- 인화성 : Inflammable

이상에서 열거한 화인의 내용은 모두 표시해야 하는 것은 아니지만 이들 가운데 Main mark와 Port mark 및 Case number는 반드시 표시해야 하는 필수적인 것들이다. Case number가 없는, 특히 port mark가 누락된 화물을 무인화물(NM : No Mark Cargo)이라 하는바, 이 경우는 화주에게 손해를 가져다 주는 사례가 빈번하므로 화인의 내용이나 형태는 Sales note나 Purchase note 등에 게시하는 것이 보통이다.

⑨ option '선택권'
right or power of choosing
optional 임의의, 강제적이 아닌, ~subject 선택과목

⑩ Force Majeure [fó:rsməʒə́:r] '불가항력' (=superior force)
이와 유사한 표현으로 Act of God [providence] '천재 · 불가항력적 사고', Accident beyond Control(미) '불가항력적 사고'

⑪ Contingencies [kəntíndʒənsiz] '우발적 사건, 부수사건'
contingent '불확실한, 우연의, ~upon 여하에 달린, 의존적인'

⑫ stipulated
stipulate(계약서, 조항 등이) 규정하다, 명기하다.
stipulation 약정, 규정, 조항

⑬ ICC(B) Including War Risks '전쟁위험을 포함한 협회적화약관 B조건'
협회적화약관(Institute Cargo Clause : ICC)은 1983년부터 개정된 ICC(A) (B)

▣ 마크모양의 명칭 ▣

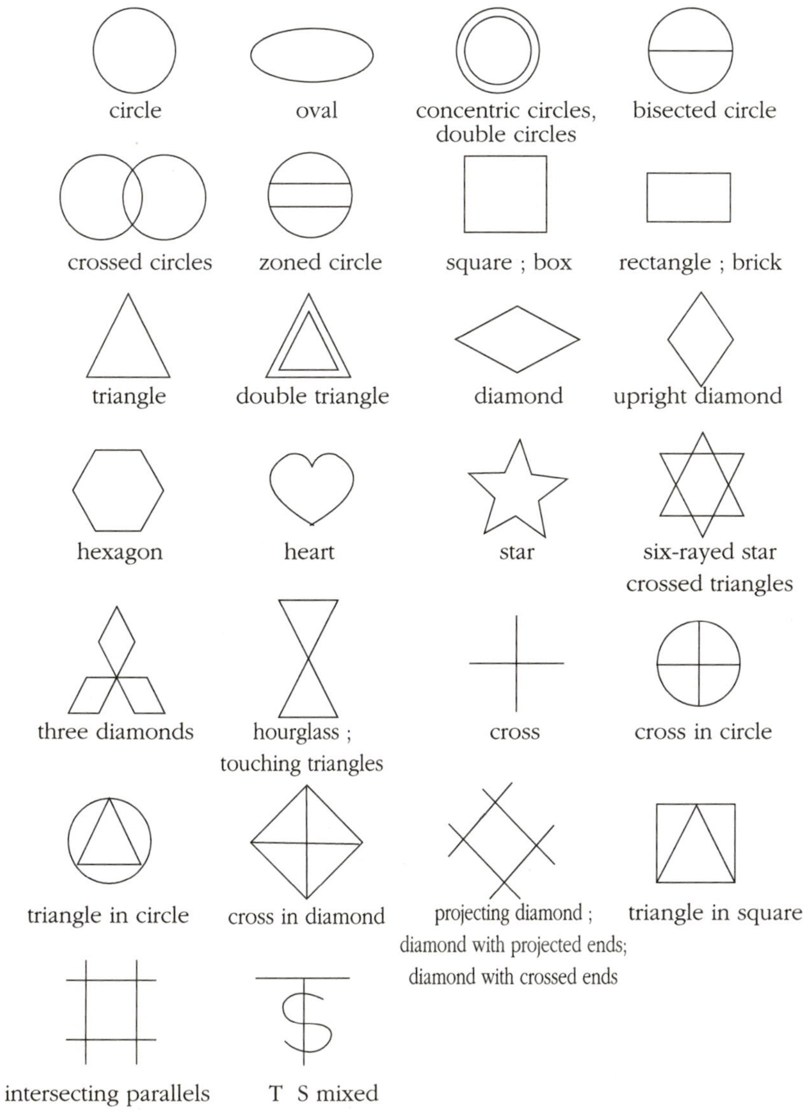

(C) 조건이 시행되고 있다. ICC(A)는 종전의 A/R(all risks 전위험 담보조건), ICC(B)는 종전의 WA(with average 분손담보조건), 그리고 ICC(C)는 종전의 FPA(free from particular average, 단독해손부담보조건)에 해당된다.

다음의 위험들은 피보험자(insured)가 특별약관(special clauses)을 맺어야 보험자(insurer)가 담보한다.

한편, 위의 기본조건에 수반되는 주요 부대조건은 다음과 같은 것들이 있다.

(1) TPND(Theft, Pilferage and Non-Delivery) : 도난, 좀도둑 및 포장 단위당 화물이 도착지에 송두리째 도착 안한 경우를 담보하며, ICC(A)에서는 담보가 안 된다.
(2) JWOB(Jettison, Washing Over Board) : 갑판적재 화물의 경우 투화 또는 갑판유실이 되면 그 손해를 담보하며, 보험자는 On-deck Clause(갑판적재 약관)를 첨부하여 인수한다.
(3) RFWD(Rain, Fresh Water Damage) : 빗물 또는 담수에 의한 손해를 보상하는 조건이며, ICC(C) 조건에서는 담보되지 않는 손해이다.
(4) COOC(Contact with Oil and Other Cargo) : 유류 또는 다른 화물과 접촉되어 입은 손해를 담보해 주는 조건이다.
(5) SRCC(Strikes, Riots and Civil Commotions) : 파업, 폭동 및 소요로 인해 화물에 입은 손해를 담보해 주는 조건이다.
(6) ISE(Inland Storage Extension) : 화물이 도착항에서 담보기간(60일)을 초과해서 보관될 경우 발생되는 손해를 담보하는 조건이다.
(7) ITE(Inland Transit Extension) : 화물을 도착항 행정구역을 벗어나 최종 창고까지 운송할 경우 발생되는 손해를 담보하는 조건이다.
(8) T/S(Transhipment) : 화물의 환적 시 발생하는 손해를 담보하는 조건이며 할증보험료가 부과된다.
(9) Shortage 부족위험담보
(10) Leakage 누손담보
(11) Breakage 파손담보
(12) Hook 갈고리 손상담보
(13) Breakage, Bending and Denting 파손, 굴곡, 눌린 자국 손해담보
(14) Sweat and Heat 땀 및 열증발 손해담보

⑭ made out '작성된'

협회적하보험약관[Institute Cargo Clause, 協會積荷保險約款]

1912년 런던보험업자협회(ILU : Institute of London Underwriters)가 채택한 적하약관이다. 협회약관 또는 협회적하보험약관이라고도 하며, 'institute cargo clause'의 머리글자를 따서 'ICC'라고도 한다. 1982년을 기준으로 이전의 약관을 구약관, 이후의 약관을 신약관이라고 한다.

런던보험업자협회(ILU)에서는 1981년 이전까지는 협회화물약관을 다음과 같이 구분하였었다.

① 협회적하보험약관(전위험담보) : Institute Cargo Clause(A/R) ② 협회적하보험약관(분손담보) : Institute Cargo Clause(W.A.) ③ 협회적하보험약관(단독해손담보)

: Institute Cargo Clause(F.P.A.).

그러나 약관의 내용이 지나치게 고어체와 난해한 문장으로 되어 있고, 전위험담보약관의 담보범위가 불명확하기 때문에 분쟁이 발생하는 경우가 많았을 뿐만 아니라 분손담보약관과 단독해손부담보약관의 담보범위가 어떻게 다른 것인지 분명하지 못한 점이 많았다.

그러므로 1978년에 UNCTAD(UN Conference on Trade and Development)에서 작성된 해상보험에 대한 보고서에 따라서 협회적하보험약관을 개정하지 않으면 안 되었다.

1981년 7월 1일에 새로 개정된 협회적하보험약관의 초안을 영국과 기타 국가의 보험회사에게 공람시켜 검토하도록 하였으며, 이 해에 확정되었다.

보상범위의 명칭도 A/R을 ICC(A), WA를 ICC(B), FPA를 ICC(C)로 바꾸었다.

① 협회적하보험약관(A) : Institute Cargo Clause(A)

② 협회적하보험약관(B) : Institute Cargo Clause(B)

③ 협회적하보험약관(C) : Institute Cargo Clause(C).

적하보험약관 (A)에서는 제4조, 제5조 및 제6조에 규정된 면책위험 외에 모든 위험을 담보한다는 포괄 책임주의를 채택하고 있다.

신약관은 구약관의 전위험담보(A/R), 분손담보(W/A), 분손부담보(FPA)를 ICC(A), ICC(B), ICC(C)로 표시하여 명칭을 간소화하고 내용도 획일성을 갖추었다. 그러나 보험자의 보상범위나 기타의 담보에 대한 근본적인 조항은 거의 변동이 없다.

ICC(B)와 ICC(C)는 ICC(A)에 비하여 부보하지 않는 위험이 많으므로, 화물의 종류에 따라서 부가위험을 특약으로 약정해야 한다. 부가위험으로는 도난 · 발화 · 불착손(TPND), 갑판유실(WOB), 좌초 · 침몰 · 화재 · 충돌(SSBC) 등이 있으며, 추가보험료를 지급하고 부보해야 이들 위험에 의한 손해를 보장받을 수 있다. 우리나라는 1983년 3월 1일부터 신약관을 시행하고 있다.

⑮ viz. [viz] 라틴어 videlicet의 abbreviation으로 '즉' namely의 뜻이다.
Your bill of exchange shows two different amounts, viz. US$50,000 in figure and U.S. dollars forty thousand in wording.
(환어음에 2개의 상이한 금액을 나타내고 있습니다. 즉, 숫자는 US$50,000이고 문자는 US$40,000입니다)

⑯ be maintained for '동안 유지되다'
be made available for '동안 이용 가능할 수 있게 만들어지다'
be valid for '동안 유효하다' 라고도 하는데, 신용장의 유효기간(validity)을 여기서는 최종선적일보다 14일 동안 더 길게 잡은 것이다. 그 이유는 수출업자가 선적후 운송서류를 준비해서 거래외국환은행에 매도(negotiation)하는 데 걸리는 시간을 참작한 것이다.

⑰ provision '공급, 조항, 규정'
provisions 양식, 식량공급
provisional 임시의, 잠정적인
A ~ government/contract 임시정부/가계약
⑱ arbitration '중재, 조정'
arbitrate '중재/조정하다'
arbitrator '중재자, 조정자'
⑲ apportionment '배분, 배당'
⑳ conditions '장래에 발생하여야 할 불확실한 조건'
terms '현재로부터 확실하게 발생하여야 할 조건'

Sample Letter 22

AGENCY AGREEMENT

AGREEMENT has been reached between Korea Trading Co., Ltd., of Seoul, Korea(hereinafter called the 'Company') and Sun Enterprizes, Ltd., New York, U.S.A.(hereinafter called the 'Agents') to do business on the following terms and conditions :

1. The Company name Messrs.Sun Enterprizes, Ltd. as their Exclusive Selling Agents for sale in the U.S.A. of such goods as are enumerated in the attached sheet(hereinafter called the 'Commodities')

2. The present agreement is signed with the understanding that it will be effective for a period of two years starting from January 1, 20××, and that, if neither of the parties to the contract indicates their desire to rescind the contract with a two month written notice, the contract upon its expiration date will be automatically renewed for another period of two years.

3. The Company pledge themselves to effect all business in the U.S.A. in the Commodities through the Agents and not to execute any commercial transactions through other persons or organizations in addition to the Agents.

4. The Agents bind themselves not to represent any other Korean firms for the Commodities without first getting the Company's

consent to do so.

5. The Agents will be in charge of promoting and developing sales in U.S.A. of the Commodities, and the Company will supply manufactures of their own and other Korean manufacturers.

The advertisements in U.S.A. will be effected at the expense of the Agents, and the Company will give all possible help to the Agents, free of charge, with samples, printed matters, sales ideas and technical reports, et cetera.

6. The Company either will pay or credit the Agents with commissions for all orders at the following rates, unless otherwise arranged at the time of accepting orders ; 3%(three percent) for Sweater and Socks and 5%(five percent) for sundry goods, on the total value of all invoices, irrespective of whether the orders have come through the Agents or direct from buyers in U.S.A.

7. In case any orders are obtained by the Agents at higher prices than those quoted by the Company, the said overprice or excess will be equally divided between the Company and the Agents, that is to say, 50% to each party.

8. In case the Agents purchase the Commodities for their own account, the percentage corresponding to the commissions will be deducted from the total value of the invoice or invoices. The corresponding discount will be included on the invoices as "special discount" (but in no circumstances as commissions). This method will allow the Agents to receive the goods for their own stock at slightly lower rates.

9. The Company will quote prices in US Dollars C.I.F. New York, unless otherwise stated, including commission for the Agents as specified in Article 6.

10. The Company will draw drafts on indentors 30d/s D/P, with shipping documents attached, and send copies of invoices and all other shipping documents to the Agents.

11. All the commissions and overprices due to the Agents will be credited by the Company to the Special Account of the Agents by means of Credit Notes. The amounts thus accumulated will be liquidated by the Company approximately every six months and

only when the indentors' accounts have been fully settled.

12. In the event of any draft or drafts drawn by the Company on indentors being dishonored, the Agents will either accept and pay such drafts instead and take the goods covered by such drafts for their own account, or will do their utmost to dispose of the goods shipped on behalf of the Company as quickly and profitably as possible, and the commission in respect of the said goods will only be payable when the proceeds are not less than the original amount of draft.

13. All orders will be subject to confirmation of the Company, that is to say, they are not considered as contracts until the Company approves and confirms them by cable.

14. Each party will bear their own cabling and other expenses.

15. The Agents will not assign this Agreement or any part hereof or any right accruing to the hereunder without their prior written consent of the Company.

16. Any dispute or difference arising from or relating to this agreement will be settled by arbitration in the U.S.A. by the American Commercial Arbitration Association under the commercial arbitration rules of the said association.

17. This Ageement contains the entire and only agreement between the Company and the Agents in respect to the agency about the Commodities. Therefore this Agreement wholly cancels, terminates and supersedes any agreement or agreements, formal or informal, oral or written, heretofore entered into between the Company and the Agents in respect to the agency about the Commodities.

No change, modification and amendment of this Agreement is binding upon the parties hereto unless made in writing and signed by the Company and the Agents.

18. The parties hereto further mutually agree that any breach of the stipulations of this Agreement will, at the option of the party aggrieved, terminate this Agreement by giving the other party sixty days notice in writing.

This agreement has been prepared by Sun Enterprizes, Ltd.,

under date of December 5, 20××. in two copies and signed and sent to Korea Trading Co., Ltd. in Seoul by registered mail. The duplicate is to be returned to the Agents, duly signed by the principals as token of approval and agreement.

New York, December 5, 20××.
Sun Enterprizes, Ltd.,
Manuel G. Serapio, Jr.
President

We certify that the above statement bears the true and genuine signature of Mr. Manuel G. Serapio, Jr. of Sun Enterprizes, Ltd. New York.

December 10, 20××.
The New York Chamber of Commerce
Lawrence Au
Secretary General

* 요약

대리점계약

한국 서울 소재 고려무역주식회사(이하 '회사' 라 칭함)와 미국 뉴욕주의 썬엔터프라이즈주식회사(이하 '대리점' 이라 칭함) 간에 아래 조건으로 거래할 합의가 이루어졌다.

1. 회사는 썬주식회사를 별지에 열거된 상품(이하 '상품' 이라 칭함)의 미국에서의 판매를 위한 총판대리점으로 지명한다.
2. 본 계약은 20××년 1월 1일부터 시작하여 2년간 효력을 가지며 본 계약당사자의 어느 편도 본 계약을 폐기할 의사를 2개월의 서면예고로 표시하지 아니하면 본 계약이 그 만기일에 다시 2년간 자동적으로 갱신되리라는 양해하에 서명한다.
3. 회사는 상품에 있어서는 미국과의 일체거래를 대리점을 통하여 행하고 대리점 이외의 다른 개인이나 단체를 통하여는 여하한 상거래도 하지 않을 것을 서약한다.
4. 대리점은 상품에 대하여 먼저 회사의 그렇게 하라는 동의를 얻지 않고는 여하한 다른 한국 상사도 대리하지 않을 것을 맹세한다.
5. 대리점은 미국에 있어서의 상품의 판매를 촉진하고 발전시키는 책임을 지고

회사는 자기 또는 다른 한국제조업자의 제품을 공급한다.

미국에서의 광고는 대리점의 비용으로 행하고 회사는 견품, 인쇄물, 판매착상, 기술보고서 등 가능한 모든 원조를 무료로 제공한다.

6. 회사는 주문을 수락할 때 달리 약정이 되지 아니하면 모든 주문에 대하여 대리점에게 하기요율로 구전을 지급하든가 대기한다.

   주문이 대리점을 통해서 왔는가 또는 미국의 구매자로부터 직접 왔는가를 불문하고 모든 송장의 총액에서 스웨터와 양말은 3분, 잡화에 대하여는 5분.
7. 대리점이 여하한 주문이든지 회사가 제시한 가격보다 비싼 가격으로 얻는 경우 동 초과가격, 즉 초과분은 회사와 대리점이 등분, 즉 각 당사자에게 5할씩 분배한다.
8. 대리점이 자기자신의 계정을 위하여 상품을 구매하는 경우에는 송장 또는 송장들의 총액으로부터 구전에 해당되는 금액을 감한다. 이 해당할인은 송장면에서는 '특별할인' 에 포함시킨다(여하한 경우에도 구전으로는 계산되지 않는다). 이 방법은 대리점이 자기자신의 재고를 위한 물품을 약간 저렴한 가격으로 받을 수 있게 한다.
9. 회사는 제6조에 명시된 대로 대리점 구전을 포함하여 별도의 명시가 없는 한 미국달러 C.I.F. 뉴욕조건으로 가격을 제시한다.
10. 회사는 대리점경유주문자 앞으로 선적서류를 첨부하여 일람후 30일 출급 D/P조건으로 환어음을 발행하고 송장 및 기타 모든 선적서류의 사본을 대리점에 보낸다.
11. 대리점이 받을 모든 구전과 초과가격은 회사가 대변표에 의하여 대리점의 특별계좌에 대기한다. 이와 같이 누적된 금액은 회사가 6개월마다 그리고 대리점경유주문자의 계좌가 완결되어야만 청산한다.
12. 회사가 대리점경유주문자 앞으로 발행한 여하한 환어음 또는 환어음들이건 부도가 되는 경우에는 대리점은 이러한 환어음을 대신 인수지급하고 이러한 환어음의 대상물품을 자기자신의 계정을 위하여 인수하든가 적송물품을 회사를 대리하여 가능한 대로 속히 유리하게 처분하기 위하여 최선을 다하되 동 물품에 관한 구전은 매출금이 원래의 환어음 금액보다 적지 아니한 때에만 지불한다.
13. 모든 주문은 회사의 확인을 조건으로 한다. 즉, 회사가 전보로 승인하고 확인하기까지는 계약으로 간주되지 않는다.
14. 각 당사자는 각자의 전보료 기타의 비용을 부담한다.
15. 대리점은 회사의 사전서면 동의 없이는 본 계약 또는 그 어느 부분 또는 본 계약하에 자기에게 생기는 여하한 권리도 양도하지 않는다.
16. 본 계약으로부터 또는 본 계약에 관련하여 발생하는 분쟁 또는 의견의 불일

치는 미국상사중재협회의 중재규칙에 의거 동 협회에 의하여 미국에서 중재로 해결한다.

17. 본 계약은 상품에 관한 대행에 관하여 회사와 대리점 사이의 모든 또는 유일한 합의를 기재하고 있는 것이다. 따라서 본 계약은 상품에 관한 대행에 관하여 지금까지 회사와 대리점 사이에 체결된 공식 또는 비공식의, 구두 또는 서면에 의한 일체의 합의를 전적으로 취소, 종료, 대체한다. 본 계약의 변경, 수정 및 정정은 서면으로 행해지고 회사와 대리점에 의하여 서명되지 아니하면 본 계약의 당사자들을 구속하지 아니한다.

18. 본 계약 당사자들은 본 계약규정의 여하한 위반도 타방에게 60일의 사전서면통고를 함으로써 피해자의 재량에 의하여 본 계약을 폐기할 것을 또한 합의한다.

본 계약은 20××년 12월 5일 썬엔터프라이즈주식회사가 2통을 작성, 서명하여 서울 소재 고려무역주식회사로 등기우편으로 송부하였다. 부본은 승낙과 합의의 표시로 본인이 정히 서명하여 대리점에 반송한다.

상기 문서에 뉴욕주 소재 썬엔터프라이즈주식회사 마누엘 세라피오의 진정한 서명이 있음을 증명함.

20××년 12월 10일
뉴욕상업회의소
사무총장 로렌스 · 오

강의노트

① Exclusive Selling Agents ‘배타적 판매 대리점, 총판매대리점’

특정지역, 특정상품(a certain territory and/ or a certain class of goods)에 대해서 본인을 독점적 · 배타적으로 대리할 권리(sole and exclusive right to represent the principal)를 가지는 대리점으로서 Sole Selling Agents라고도 한다. 반면 독점적 · 배타적 권리가 없는 대리점을 Non-Exclusive Agent라고 부른다.

② credit ‘대변에 기입하다’

‘대기하다’ 로 반의어는 debit 또는 charge ‘차변에 기입하다, 차기하다’

credit advice 대기통지서, debit advice 차기통지서

> VALUE MAY 10, 20××.
>
> DEBIT OUR A/C AND CREDIT DMARKS1,000,000 TO BANKERS TRUSTCO FOREIGN EXCHANGE A/C WITH DEUTSCHE BANK FRANKFURT MAIN QUOTING OURREF NO PWC 123.

(20××년 5월 10일을 결제일로 하고 당사계좌에서 차기하여 당사 참조번호 PWC123을 인용하면서 1,000,000마르크를 프랑크프루트에 있는 도이치은행의 BTC 외국부계좌로 입금시켜 주십시오)

We authorize you to debit our account.

(당사의 계좌에서 차기할 것을 귀사에 수권합니다)

We will credit the proceeds to your account No. 123-456 with Seoul bank at maturity.

(만기일에 대금을 서울은행 귀사계좌 123-456에 입금시키겠습니다)

③ overprice '초과가격'

'초과가격'으로 overage[óuvəridʒ]라고도 한다

overcharge 부당한 값을 청구하다

overdue (도착시간, 지불기한 등이) 지난

overdraft 당좌대월

overlap (부분적으로) 겹치다, 중복하다

oversea(s) 해외에 있는, 해외로 가는

oversight 간과, 실수

overstock 과잉공급하다

overtime 규정된 시간 외에

④ for their own stock '자기자신의 재고를 위하여'

여기서는 대리점이 자기들의 비용으로 수입하는 경우를 말한다.

⑤ rates '율'

여기서는 가격의 뜻으로 사용되고 있지만 원래는 '율, 비율, 등급, 평가'란 뜻으로 다양하게 쓰인다.

at any rate 하여튼

firstrate 일류의

letter rating 서신평가

exchange rate 환율

⑥ indentors[indéntəz] '구매위탁자'

indent 구매위탁

indent order 구매위탁주문

⑦ due to the Agents '대리점이 받을'

'대리점에게 지급되어야 하는' due to는 '~로 인하여'와 '~가 받아야 할, ~에게 귀속되는'의 뜻으로 아래와 같이 사용된다.

We have negotiated the drafts under reserve due to late presentation.

(당사는 지연제시로 인하여 그 어음을 유보하에 매도하였다)

The original credit was sent to the beneficiary directly due to a clerical

error on our part.
(원신용장이 우리측의 사무착오로 인하여 수익자에게 직접 보내졌습니다)
The first beneficiary shall have the right to claim any difference due to him.
(최초수익자(원수익자는)는 그가 받아야 할 차액을 청구할 권리를 갖는다)

⑧ In the event of~ '~하는 경우에는'
In the event of the drawee continuing to hold the documents pending, please persuade them to liquidate.
(지급인이 계속해서 그 서류를 미해결로 유보하는 경우에는 청산을 설득하여 주십시오)
In the event that the applicant refuses to pay against documents we sent on February 3, please let us know immediately by fax.
(신용장개설의뢰인이 2월 3일자로 우리가 보낸 서류의 지급(인수)을 거절하는 경우에 즉시 팩스로 당사에 알려주십시오)

⑨ hereof '본 계약의'
=of this(Agreement)
hereafter 이후
hereby 이것에 의하여
herein 이 안에
hereof 이것의 ; 이것에 관하여
hereunder (이) 아래에
hereunto 이것에
herewith 이것으로

⑩ accruing [ə́krú:iŋ] '생기는, 발생하는'
accrual 발생, 발생금액, 증가액
accrue 자연증가나 발달로 생기다.
On maturity, please transfer the principal plus its accrued interests to our a/c with the Chase Manhattan Bank, New York.
(만기일에 원금과 발생이자를 CMB 뉴욕에 있는 우리 계좌로 이체하여 주십시오)

⑪ the parties hereto '본계약의 당사자들'
hereto=to this(Agreement) '의 당사자'
Parties to a Conspiracy '공모당사자들' 과 같이 to를 사용한다. 해석은 of '의'로 한다.
Parties to a Letter of Credit : 신용장의 당사자들
Nature by Ralph Waldo Emerson : 에머슨의 자연론

Hurrah to Both the Winner and the Losers : 승자패자 모두 만세
Electronic goods from Japan : 일제전자제품
the man in a yellow shirt : 노란 셔츠 입은 사나이
a research assistant to the professor : 교수의 연구조교
a check for US$500 : 미화 500불짜리 수표
the bill for this month : 이달의 청구서
an authority on economics : 경제학의 권위자

⑫ duly '정히, 정당하게, 제때에'
=(right and proper ; punctually)
As beneficiary needs the funds very urgently, we request you to remit the proceeds duly to our a/c with ABC Bank, New York.
(수취인이 자금을 급히 필요로 하기 때문에 그 물품대금을 뉴욕에 있는 ABC은행 당사계좌로 정히 송금시킬 것을 요청합니다)
We are returning the agency arrangement form duly signed, as you requested.
(귀사에서 요청대로 정히 서명한 대행계약서를 회송합니다)

Useful Sentences(포장 및 보험관계)

1. Please arrange packing in the same way as shipped previously.
   전에 선적할 때와 똑같은 요령으로 포장을 준비하여 주십시오.
2. Your shipping and packing instructions will receive our utmost attention.
   당사에서는 귀사의 선적 및 포장지시에 대해서 최대한의 주의를 기울이겠습니다.
3. We will check the goods carefully so they will reach you in good condition.
   상품이 양호한 상태로 귀사에 도착할 수 있도록 주의깊게 상품을 점검하겠습니다.
4. All cases shall be marked "MK" in triangle.
   모든 상자에는 삼각형 안에 MK의 화인을 표시해야 합니다.
5. Each piece of chinaware is to be individually wrapped in thick paper, packed in straw, shipped in wooden crates marked #, and numbered 1

to 50.
각 도자기는 두꺼운 종이로 싸서 짚으로 채운 다음 나무상자에 포장하여 일련번호 #1-50 표시하여 선적하여 주십시오.

6. The machines must be well greased with all movable parts secured before being loaded into marked crates.
일련번호가 표시된 상자에 넣기 전에 기계의 모든 동작부품은 기름으로 칠해야만 합니다.
7. As we effect insurance on the goods we purchase from you, you will please quote us on C. & F. Busan.
당사가 귀사로부터 구입한 상품에 대해서는 당사에서 부보해야 하므로 부산항 운임포함가격을 제시하여 주십시오.
8. We shall effect insurance at this end under our open policy.
이곳에서 포괄예정보험으로 부보하겠습니다.
9. As usual, the goods have been insured on F.P.A. (Free from Particular Average) terms.
보통 물품은 단독해손부담조건으로 부보하고 있습니다.
10. Please effect insurance on our account for the amount of your invoice, plus 10% imaginary profit.
귀사 송장금액에 10%의 희망이익을 가산하여 당사 비용으로 부보하여 주십시오.
11. Please send us the insurance policy together with your receipt for the premiums paid as soon as possible.
보험료 지불 영수증과 함께 보험증권을 조속히 당사로 송부하여 주십시오.
12. We will insure these goods subject to the New I.C.C.(B).
당사에서는 상품에 대해서 개정 협회적화약관(B)조건으로 부보하겠습니다.

Maxim

A stitch in time saves nine.

제때에 한 바늘 꿰매면 나중에 아홉 바늘 꿰매는 수고를 덜게 된다.

Chapter 06

신용장
Letter of Credit

제1절 신용장의 의의

신용장(letter of credit)이란 국제무역거래에서 대금결제의 신속화 및 정확성을 위하여 수입업자(applicant)의 요청으로 수입업자의 거래은행(opening bank)이 수출업자(beneficiary)에게 신용장조건에 일치한 서류를 제시하면 수출대전을 지급하겠다고 확약하고 대신에 수입업자는 서류를 확인조사한 후에 수입대전을 상환, 물품을 확보함으로써 수출입 양당사자에게 만족을 주는 방법이다. 또한 신용장거래는 본질적으로 매매계약서라는 개별의 독립된 거래이며 서류상의 거래이다. 즉, 신용장은 분명히 매매계약 등에 근거를 두고 개설되는 것이긴 하지만 신용장거래 그 자체에 매매계약과는 별개의 독립성을 부여하고 있으며(신용장통일규칙 제4조), 은행은 서류로 거래하는 것이며 그 서류가 관계된 물품, 서비스 또는 의무이행으로 거래하는 것은 아니다(Banks deal with documents and not with goods, services or performance to which the documents may relate).

1. 신용장의 제당사자(Parties to the Letter of Credit)

(1) 개설의뢰인(Opener, Applicant for Opening)

신용장개설을 의뢰한 사람으로 수입업자를 말한다.

수입상은 최종 지급인으로서 Buyer, Accredited Buyer, Accountee, Grantee, Applicant, Consignee, Importer 등으로 불리운다.

(2) 개설은행(Opening or Issuing Bank)

신용장을 개설하는 은행으로서 대부분 수입업자의 거래은행이다.

Establishing Bank, Issurer, Credit Writing Bank, Grantor.

(3) 통지은행(Advising Bank)

신용장의 개설은행이 그 수익자에게 직접 신용장발행을 통지해주지 않고 수익자 소재지의 자행지점이나 환거래은행(correspondent bank)을 경유하여 통지할 때 이 거래은행을 통지은행이라 한다.

통지은행은 통지하는 신용장의 진위성(authenticity of the credit)을 검토하기 위해서 상당한 주의(reasonable care)를 기울여야 한다. Notifying Bank, Transmitting Bank.

(4) 수익자(Beneficiary)

신용장의 혜택을 받는 수출상인 매도인을 말하며, Accreditee, User, Addressee, Seller 등으로 불리운다.

(5) 매입은행(Negotiating Bank)

수익자가 개설은행 앞으로 환어음을 발행하고 신용장의 운송서류를 첨부하여 환어음의 매입을 의뢰하는데, 이때 환어음을 매입하는 은행을 말한다.

(6) 확인은행(Confirming Bank)

개설은행 이외의 제3은행이 신용장에 의거 발행하는 환어음을 인수, 지급 또는 매입하겠다는 확약을 하는 은행이다. 따라서 수출상인 수익자는 이중의 지급보증을 얻게되는 셈이다. 확인은행이 확인한 신용장을 확인신용장(Confirmed L/C)이라 한다.

(7) 인수은행(Accepting Bank)

개설은행이 스스로 어음의 지명인, 즉 인수인이 되지 않고 다른 거래은행으로 하여금 인수인이 되게 하는 경우 이 은행을 인수은행이라 말한다.

(8) 결제은행(Reimbursing Bank)

개설은행의 예치환거래은행(Depositary Correspondent Bank)으로 개설은행을 대신해서 개설은행계좌에서 매입은행(Negotiating Bank)에 대금을 결제해 주는 은행이다. Settling Bank라고도 한다.

〈참고〉 신용장거래의 과정

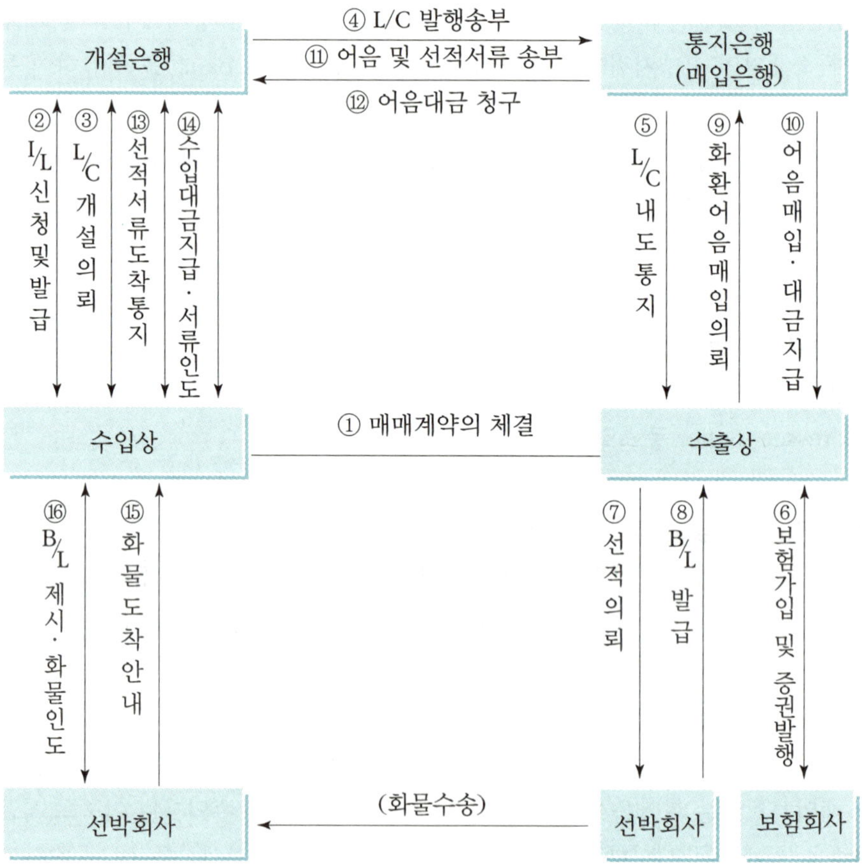

Sample Letter 23

Gentlemen :

Your Sales note No. 58 has been received. Having found it to be correct, we enclose the duplicate thereof duly signed by us.

We have instructed the Korea First Bank, Seoul to open an Irrevocable Letter of Credit in your favor for US$3,500 to cover our order for 20 units of Portable Radio Set A102, 10 units of Cassette Tape Recorder B84 and 10 units of Microphone C59. Advising bank is Korea First Bank, Tokyo branch.

We need our order urgently, so please expedite shipment.

Your attention will be appreciated.

Yours very truly,

*** 요약**

귀사 매출계약서 제58호 잘 받았으며 그 내용이 정확하므로 당사에서 정히 서명한 부본을 동봉합니다.

당사에서는 마이크 C59 10대, 카세트테이프 녹음기 B84 10대, 휴대용 라디오세트 A102 20대 주문품의 결제를 위한 미화 3,500불을 귀사를 수익자로 하여 취소불능신용장을 개설할 것을 한국제일은행에 의뢰했습니다. 통지은행은 한국제일은행 동경지점입니다.

당사는 주문품이 긴급히 필요하므로 선적을 속히 하여 주시기 바랍니다.

귀사에서 배려하여 주시면 대단히 감사하겠습니다.

강의노트

① expedite[ékspidait] 촉진하다, 신속히 처리하다
expeditious[ekspidíʃəs] 빠른, 신속하고 빠른
expedite payment 지급을 이행하다(=execute payment immediately)

② instruct 가르치다, 지시하다
instruction 교수, 지도, 지시. payment instructions 지급지시
instructional 교육상의, 교육적인(=instructive)

Sample Letter 24

Gentlemen :

Your Letter of Credit No. 1234 covering your Order No. 200 for 300 bicycles RS-5 has been received.

However, we would like to ask you if you could extend the shipping date and the credit validity for two weeks respectively.

A labor conflict has occurred in the factory for your order and the production of your goods has been stopped for the time being. Fortunately, there is a possibility that the strike will be over within two weeks. Of course, we will do our best to ship your order as soon as the conflict is over.

Your cooperation will be appreciated.

Yours very truly,

* 요약

자전거 RS-5, 300대 귀사 주문에 대한 신용장 제1234호가 내도했습니다.

그러나 귀사에서 신용장의 유효기간과 선적기일을 각각 2주간씩 연장해 줄 것을 요청합니다.

귀사 주문품을 의뢰한 공장에서 노동쟁의가 발생해서 당분간 제품생산이 중단되었기 때문입니다. 다행히도 파업은 2주 내에 끝날 전망입니다. 물론 쟁의가 끝나는 대로 가능한 빨리 귀사 주문품을 선적하도록 최선을 다하겠습니다.

귀사에서 협조해 주시면 대단히 고맙겠습니다.

강의노트

① extend the shipping date and the validity in the credit.
(신용장의 유효기일과 선적기일을 연장하다)
여기서 extend는 (공간, 시간적으로)연장하다, 넓히다, 제공하다, 제의하다 (=offer, grant, accord)
명사는 extension
Both the shipping and expiry date have been extended to Feb. 19, 20××.
(선적기일 및 유효기일은 2월 10일까지 연장되었다)

날짜 표시 앞에 'To' 'Until' 'Till' 등의 표현이 있을 때는 그날 자체도 포함되는 것으로 해석된다(신용장통일규칙 제3조).

'after' 는 해당일을 제외하고 'on or about' 는 지정일로부터 5일 전후로 이루어지는 기간을 지칭하되 전후 양말일(兩末日)을 각각 포함한다.

Validity는 '유효(성), 효력, 확실(성)' 이라는 뜻이다.

Valid 유효한(계약 따위가 법적으로), 근거가 있는, 정당한, validate[vǽlideit](정당함을) 확인하다, make~ (법적으로)유효하게 하다.

② conflict 싸움, 투쟁, (의견, 욕구 따위의)충돌, 갈등, be in ~(with)(…과) 충돌하다, 모순되다.

③ strike 파업, 치다, 때리다, 파업하다.

Sample Letter 25

Dear Sirs,

Your client, Happy Goods Co., has signed a purchase agreement with our customer, Hansung Co., to import USD25,000 of sporting goods. Happy Goods Co. stated they would issue a letter of credit through your bank. Please provide us with the information on status of issuance for the letter of credit. Please quote our Ref : BWC-01 when replying.

Yours truly,

＊ 요약 신용장개설에 관한 문의

i) 귀행의 고객인 Happy Goods Co.는 당행의 고객인 한성상사와 운동용구 25,000불을 수입하기로 구매계약을 체결하였음.

ii) Happy Goods Co.는 귀행을 이용하여 신용장을 개설하기로 함.

iii) 신용장개설 상황에 관하여 알려주기 바람.

iv) 회신 시 당사 참조번호(BWC-01)를 표시해 주기 바랍니다.

Sample Letter 26 신용장개설문의에 대한 회답

Dear Sirs,

This is a reply to your query dated Dec. 19, 20××. Your ref : BWC-01.

The letter of credit requested by Happy Goods Co. has been delayed due to problems with the import quotas. The letter of credit will be issued and sent to your institution as soon as the problem is resolved.

Yours truly,

* 요약

i) 귀사 20××. 12. 19일자 참조 : BWC-01로 문의하신 건에 대한 회신입니다.
ii) Happy Goods Co.에서 요청한 신용장은 수입쿼터 문제로 지연되고 있음.
iii) 문제가 해결되는 즉시 신용장을 발행하여 귀사로 송부하겠음.

강의노트

① query '문의(=inquiry)'
Should you have any query concerning this matter, please do not hesitate to contact us.
(이 일에 대해서 의문이 있으면 주저하지 말고 당사에 접촉하여 주십시오)

② import quota '수입쿼터' : 특정상품에 대해 정해진 수량/가격만큼만 수입될 수 있도록 하는 일종의 행정명령

③ institution '제정, 설립, 단체'
~al 제도상의, 학회(협회)의, 관례적인
~alize 관습화하다, 공공단체화하다.

Sample Letter 27

Happy Goods Co.
35 Genaldine Road
New York, NY10210

February 12, 20××

Dear Sirs,

We call your attention to the fact that the letter of credit covering your order No. 105 has not reached us in spite of our repeated requests.

We urged our suppliers to execute an early delivery of products at higher prices to meet your request, which we trust you will approve.

As we have not received your L/C, we may be forced to cancel your order. However, we would prefer you to establish your L/C by the end of February, so that we can continue our cordial business relationship.

Yours sincerely,
Hansung Company
Sundal Kim
Export Manager

＊ 요약 수출업자가 수입업자에게 신용장을 개설할 것을 독촉

i) 귀사가 주문하신 주문서 105호를 결제하기 위한 신용장이 우리가 여러 번 요청하였음에도 불구하고 아직 도착되지 않았음에 주의를 요함.

ii) 귀사의 요청에 부응하여 우리는 물품공급자에게 제품을 조기에 납품토록 하고 더 비싼 가격을 주었는바 귀사가 기꺼이 승인하리라 믿음.

iii) 아직까지 신용장을 받지 못해 귀사의 주문을 취소해야 할 처지임.

iv) 우호적인 우리의 거래관계를 유지할 수 있도록 2월말까지 신용장을 개설할 것을 권유함.

강의노트

① call your attention to '주목해 주시기 바랍니다' (=give your attention to~)
I'd like to call your attention to several discrepancies found in the documents.
(서류상에 몇 가지 하자가 발견된 사실에 주목해 주시기 바랍니다.)

② reach '도달하다, 이르다, 미치다'
We regret that your letter of February 10, 20×× has not reached us until now.
(지금까지 2월 10일자 귀 서신이 당사에 도착되지 않았음을 유감으로 생각합니다)

③ in spite of '~에도 불구하고' (=notwithstanding)
No answer has yet been received from you, in spite of our numerous inquires concerning the above matter.
(상기 문제에 대하여 수차례에 걸친 조회를 했음에도 불구하고 아직 귀사로부터 회신을 받지 못했습니다)

④ be forced to '~에게 ~강제로 하다', '억지로~시키다'
Unless you ship the goods by the end of July, we shall be forced to cancel the order.
(귀사가 상품을 7월 말까지 선적해주지 않으면 그 주문을 취소하겠습니다)

⑤ approve '승인하다' (=meet with approval), '만족하다' (=satisfy with approval)
We hope that your goods will reach you safely/on time and meet with your approval.
(우리는 상품이 안전하게/기일 내에 도착하여 귀사가 만족하기를 희망합니다)

⑥ meet '~을 만나다, ~에 잘 대응하다, ~를 채우다, 만족시키다, (부채 따위를) 지불하다'
meet debts 빚을 갚다
meet a bill 어음을 지불하다

[신용장 완성 예 I] 표준양식(매입신용장)

NAME OF ISSUING BANK-NOM DE LA BANQUE EMETTRICE

KOREA INSTITUTE BANK
cpo 8519, Seoul, Korea

Irrevocable Documentary Credit
Credit documentaire irrevocable

Number-Numero
M1901NS0017

Place and date of issue-Lieu et date d'emission
Seoul Korea On Nov. 19. 20××

Date and place of expiry-Date lieu de validite
Apr. 19. 20××. in Seoul, Korea

Applicant-Donneur D'ordre

Hansung Company, Limited
137 Ankukdong, Chongroku,
Seoul, Korea

Beneficiary-Beneficiaire
Woven Fabric Co. Ltd.,
250 North Bridge Road,
HEX 16-03 Raffles City Tower,
Singapore 0617

Advising Bank-Banque Notificatrice Ref. Nr. No. Rél

Commercial Bank of Singapore
131 South Bridge Road,
Singapore 0660

Amount-Montant USD 35, 119.72
US Dollars Thirty Five Thousand One Hundred and Nineteen and 72 Only

Partial Shipments / Expeditions partielles
☒ allowed / autorisees ☐ not allowed / non autorisees

Transhipment / Transbordement
☐ allowed / autorise ☒ not allowed / non autorise

Credit available with-Credit utilisable chez
any bank in Singapore

☐ by sight payment / par paiement a vue ☐ by acceptance / par acceptation

☐ by negotiation / par negociation ☐ by deferred Payment at / par paiement differe a

☒ and beneficiary's draft at / et la traite du beneficiaire au Sight

on / sur Korea Institute Bank, Seoul, Korea

Loading on board/dispatch/taking in charge at/from Singapore.
Port Mise a bord/expedition/prise en charge á/de

Not Later than Apr. 5, 20××
for transportation to : Busan, Korea
a destination de :

Covering : 100% silk woven Fabric Chinese origin 45 inch by 2541. 75 yards at USD 6. 70 USD 35, 119, 72 CIF Busan
Accompanied by the following documents :
- Full set of clean on board ocean bills of lading, made out to the order of Korea Institute Bank, Seoul marked "Freight Prepaid" and "Notify Accountee".
- Signed Commercial Invoice in quadruplicate.
- Marine Insurance Certificate in duplicate, endorsed in blank for 110% of the Invoice value against all risks
- Packing list in quadruplicate.

Special conditions :
- This credit is transferable.
- All banking charges including postage outside Korea are for account of the beneficiary.
- The amount of each draft must be endorsed on the reverse of this credit by the negotiating bank.
- All documents and drafts must be forwarded to Korea Institute Bank, Seoul, directly by courier service in one lot.

Documents to be presented within ☐ days after the date of issuance of the transport document(s) but within the validity of the credit.
Documents a presenter dans les ☐ jours apres la date d'emission du/des document(s) de transport mais is penode de validite du credit.

We have issued the documentary credit as detailed above. It is subject to the Uniform Customs and Practice for Documentary Credits(2007 Revision, International Chamber of Commerce, Paris, France, Publication No. 600). We request you to advise the credit to the beneficiary

Nous avons emis ce credit documentaire d'ecrit ci-dessus. il est soumis aux Regles et Usances Uniformes reletives aux Credits Documentaires (Revision) 2007 Publication No. 600 de la Chambre de Commerce Internationale. Paris, France). Nous Vous prions de notifier le credit au beneficiaire

☒ without adding your confirmation. ☐ adding your confirmation. / en ajoutant votre confirmation. ☐ and authorize you to add your confirmation / sans ajouter votre confirmation / et vous autorisons a ajouter votre confirmation.

The number and the date of the credit and the name of our bank must be quoted on all drafts required. Please acknowledge receipt.

Le numero et date du credit ainsi que le nom de notre banque devront etre mentionnes dans toute traite requise. Veuillez nous accuser reception.

Reimbursement-Remboursement
Claim Reimbursement by drawing your sight draft on Korea Institute Bank, Singapore.

This document consists of / Ce document consiste en	signed page(s) / page(s) signes(s)	SIGNATURE

[신용장 완성 예Ⅰ] 표준양식(매입신용장)

<table>
<tr><td>신용장 개설은행명칭
한국협회은행
(주소)

개설장소 및 개설일
대한민국 서울. 20××. 11. 19</td><td>취소불능화환신용장

유효기일 및 장소
20××. 4. 19 대한민국 서울</td><td>번호
M1901NS0017</td></tr>
<tr><td>개설의뢰인
한성주식회사
(주소)</td><td colspan="2">수익자
Woven Fabric(주)
(주소)</td></tr>
<tr><td>통지은행
싱가폴 상업은행
(주소)</td><td colspan="2">금액(미화 35,119.72)
미화삼만오천일백십구불칠십이선정</td></tr>
<tr><td>분할선적 환 적
☒ 허용 ☐ 불가 ☐ 허용 ☒ 불가

선적지/발행지/수화지 싱가폴항
선적기일 20××. 4. 5
도착지 대한민국 부산</td><td colspan="2">신용장 사용은행(지정)
싱가폴 어느 은행이나 가능
☐ 지급 ☐ 인수 ☐ 매입
☐ 연지급을 하기서류와 상환하여 행함. 또한,
☒ 수익자의 환어음은 일람출급조건으로 한국협회은행 (서울) 앞으로 발행할 것</td></tr>
<tr><td colspan="3">상품명세 : 중국산 100% 견직원단 폭 45인치×2541.75야드(야드당 6.70불) 계 35,119.72불(CIF 부산)
제시서류명세 :
- 한국협회은행앞 지시식으로 발행되고, "운임지급필" 및 "통지처 : 지급인"을 표시하고 있는 무고장 본선적재 해양선화증권의 전통
- 서명된 상업송장 4통
- 상업송장가액의 110%를 부보하고 백지배서를 한 전위험담보조의 해상보험증명서 2통
- 포장명세서 4통
특수조건
- 본 신용장은 양도가능함
- 대한민국 밖에서 발생하는 우편료 포함 모든 은행수수료는 수익자 부담임
- 매입은행은 매입 시 환어음의 금액을 본신용장 이면에 기입할 것
- 전서류 및 환어음은 한번에 모두 서울한국협회은행 앞으로 특사배달로 직접 송부할 것</td></tr>
<tr><td colspan="3">서류제시기일 ☐ 일(운송서류 기산일부터 기산하며, 신용장 유효기일 이내임)</td></tr>
<tr><td colspan="3">상기와 같이 화환신용장을 개설함. 본 신용장은 화한신용장통일규칙(국제 상업회의소 2007년 개정 발행번호 600)을 준수함.
본 신용장을 하기와 같이 수익자에게 통지해 주실 것.

☒ 귀행의 확인없이 ☐ 귀행이 확인하여 ☐ 귀행에 확인을 수권함.

신용장 번호와 발행일 및 당행명칭을 매 환어음상에 표기할 것
접수사실을 통보해주시기 바람
자금구상 : 귀행 일람불환어음을 당행 싱가폴지점에 제시하여 구상을 청구할 것.
본 신용장은 ①장의 서명된 원본으로 되어 있음
(서 명)</td></tr>
</table>

강의노트

① M1901NS0017
신용장번호로서 보통 우측 상단에 기재한다.
여기서 'N' 은 '수입용도' 로 'Normal' (내수용일반재)을 뜻한다.
이외에 M(Machine) : 외화획득용시설재
B(Bonded) : 보세가공용
E(Export) : 수출용
A(Army) : 군납용
G(Government) : 정부용
S(Sightseeing) : 관광용
'S' 는 '결제방법' 으로 'At sight' (일람불 방식)을 뜻한다.
U(Usance) : 연불방식
P(Document Against Payment ; D/P) : 지급도조건
A(Document Against Acceptance ; D/A) : 인수도조건
R(Remittance) : 송금방식

② Date and place of expiry '유효기일 및 유효기일 장소'
지정된 지명에서 유효기일이 끝나므로 이를 유의하여야 한다.
"Drafts must be negotiated on or before…."
"This credit expires in Korea on … 20××."
"This credit is valid until…10-for presentation of documents with the advising bank." 등으로 표시하기도 한다.

③ Amount '금액, 즉 신용장금액' 을 말한다.
보통 Amount라고 표시된 column에 숫자와 문자를 병기한다.
"up to an aggregate amount of…."
"for a sum not exceeding a total of…."
"to the extent of not exceeding a total of…."
"for a maximum amount of…". 등으로 표시된다.

④ Not later than Apr. 5, 20××. '20××년 4월 5일에 최종선적일' 이다.
최종목적지(place of final destination)는 'shipment to 혹은 for transportation to' 다음에 표시되는데 복합운송에서는 양륙항(port of discharge)과 구별되어 표시된다.
선적항(shipping port, port of loading)은 'shipment from' 이라는 문언 다음에 항구의 명칭이 표시된다. 그런데 내륙운송도 포함하는 복합운송증권(combined transport document) 등의 경우에는 발송지(place of dispatch), 수탁지(place of taking in charge at)가 되는 수도 있다.

또한 분할선적(partial shipment)과 환적(transhipment)이 허용되는 경우 'allowed, permitted, authorized' 등으로 표시하고, 불허하는 경우 'prohibited, not allowed, not permitted' 등으로 표시한다.
또한 분할선적조항으로 "September and October shipment, equally divided."
"Half in September and the balance two months later."
"Shipment : 20 c/s during September and 30 c/s during October, 20××" 등으로 표현하기도 한다.

⑤ Documents to be presented within 10 days ~.
서류제시기간(time limit for presentation)이다. 만일 아무런 표시가 없으면 21일내에 제시되어야 하므로 그 후 제시되는 서류도 수리할 의향이라면 "Documents presented later than 21 days, after the date of issuance of the transport documents is acceptable."로 표시한다.

[신용장 완성 예 Ⅱ]

Sample Letter 28 Standby-Credit

UNION BANK OF CALIFORNIA
114 Irving Street
Los Angeles, California, U.S.A.

Dec. 12, 20××.

Dear Sirs,

We hereby establish our irrevocable standby letter of credit No. STB1212 in your favor for account of Unical Co. Ltd., California, USA, up to an aggregate amount of USD 4,750,000.00(Say US Dollars Four Million Seven Hundred and Fifty Thousand Only) or the Korean Won equivalent to this amount as security for your loan plus its interest extended to Unical Co., Ltd., Seoul Branch, CPO Box 23467 Seoul, Korea("the Borrower") to purchase materials and equipment for the execution of the Seoul Skyline Project No. 12-12-20.

The interest rate of the loan extended under this credit shall not exceed the rate of zero point five percent per annum over the six months Libo rate. This credit is available against your sight draft drawn on us, accompanied by your simple receipt in duplicate, and your signed statement certifying that the Borrower has failed to repay your loan and interest effected under this credit.

This credit expires on December 12, 20××, after which date it shall become null and void.

This letter of credit is subject to Uniform Customs and Practice for Documentary Credit, 2007 Revision, International Chamber of Commerce, Publication No. 600.

Truly yours,

____

Authorized Signature

[신용장 완성 예 Ⅱ]

보증신용장(현지금융담보)

캘리포니아 유니온은행

(주소)

20××, 12. 12

당행은 귀하를 수익자로 하는 취소불능보증신용장을 아래와 같이 개설합니다.

신용장번호 : STB1212

개설의뢰인 : 미국 캘리포니아주 유니칼주식회사

보증금액 : 미화 4,750,000불 또는 동액상당의 한국원화 이내

목적 : 유니칼주식회사 서울지사("차주")가 서울 Skyline프로젝트 번호 12-12-20을 이행할 수 있는 자재 및 장비구입을 위하여, 귀하가 공여한 대출금 및 동이자에 대한 담보조

본 신용장에 의하여 공여되는 대출금의 이자는 6개월물 리보레이트에 연 0.5%를 초과하지 아니하는 이율을 가산함.

본 신용장은 귀하의 단순영수증 2통 및 차주가 본 신용장에 의거 공여받은 대출원금과 이자를 상환하지 못한다는 귀하의 증명서와 함께 귀 발행 일람출급어음으로 지급됨.

본 신용장은 20××, 12. 12이 만기이고, 그 익일 이후는 무효이다.

본 신용장은 국제상업회의소 2007년 개정발행번호 600 신용장통일규칙을 준수함.

끝맺음말,

서 명

Sample Letter 29

APPLICATION FOR TOTAL TRANSFER OF THE CREDIT

To : Korea Institute Bank
Seoul, Korea

Date : September 11, 20××.
Your Advice No.ADO2985

Gentlemen :

Re : L/C No. TYT-092910
for English Pounds 24,500.50
Favor : Hansung Company, Seoul
Issuing Bank : National Westminster Bank, PLC, London

We hereby irrevocably transfer all of our right under the above mentioned credit to Ankook Manufacturing Co., Busan.

The transferee(hereinafter called "Second Beneficiary") shall have sole rights as beneficiary under the credit; including all rights relating to any amendment, whether increases or extensions or other amendments, and whether now existing or hereafter made. The credit hereafter may be amended, extended or increased, without our consent or notice to us and you will give notice thereof directly to the Second Beneficiary.

The original credit(including amendments to this date, if any) is returned herewith for your endorsement. We request you to notify the Second Beneficiary in such a way you deem advisable for this transfer of credit and of the terms and conditions of the credit as transferred.

We agree to indemnify and hold you harmless against any and all losses, damages and expenses arising from your actions of this transfer.

Yours very truly,

NAME AND SIGNATURE OF SECOND BENEFICIARY	NAME AND SIGNATURE OF FIRST BENEFICIARY

＊ 요약

i) 우리는 여기에 있는 상기 신용장상의 모든 당사의 권리를 안국제조회사 앞으로 취소불능조건으로 양도한다.

ii) 양수인(이하 "제2수익자"라고 칭함)은 이 신용장상의 수익자로서의 모든 권리를 가진다. 이 모든 권리는 금액의 증액 또는 기한의 연장 또는 기타 조건변경이건, 현재 있는 것이나 이후에 발생할 것이건, 여하한 조건변경에 관련되는 것을 포함한다. 이후로는 당사의 동의나 당사에 알리지 않고도 조건변경, 기한연장, 또한 금액증액이 가능하며, 그러한 것에 대하여 귀행은 직접 제2수익자에게 통지할 것.

iii) 원신용장(오늘까지 있었던 모든 조건변경서를 포함)을 귀행의 배서를 위하여 유첨하여 반송함. 귀행이 적당하다고 생각하는 형태로 이 신용장 및 신용장 조건을 양도된 것으로 제2수익자에게 통지할 것을 요청한다.

iv) 본 양도에 따른 귀행의 조치로 인하여 발생되는 여하한 손실, 손해 및 비용에 대하여 배상을 보장하며 귀행에 해를 끼치지 않을 것을 동의한다.

Sample Letter 30

KOREA INSTITUTE BANK
Seoul, Korea

ADVICE OF FULL TRANSFER　　Date : September 14, 20××.
Advice No. AFT-90090213

To : Ankook Manufacturing Co. Busan.

Irrevocable Transferable L/C No. NYT-092190
for GBPounds 24,500.00 dated August 15, 20××.
in favor of Hansung Company, Seoul
for the account of Happy Chester Co.
issued by National Westminster Bank, PLC, London

Gentlemen :

We are pleased to advise you that the above mentioned credit as enclosed herewith has been transferred to you under the date of September 14, 20×× by Hansung Company, Seoul.

All drafts negotiated under this advice are to be accompanied by this letter together with the original letter of credit, and the amount of any such draft must be endorsed on the back hereof by the negotiating bank.

Yours very truly,

＊ 요약 신용장 전액양도 통지서

i) 동봉된 바와 같이 상기 신용장이 20××년 9월 14일자로 한성상사에 의하여 귀사로 양도되었음을 통지함.

ii) 본 통지서에 의하여 매입되는 모든 어음은 원신용장과 함께 본 통지서를 첨부하여야 함. 매입은행은 그러한 어음금액을 신용장 뒷면에 배서할 것.

2. 신용장의 종류

신용장은 수익자가 발행하는 환어음을 인수 · 지급하는데, 운송서류를 담보로 첨부할 것을 조건으로 하지 않는 무담보신용장(Clean L/C)과, 환어음에 운송서류를 첨부할 조건으로 하는 신용장으로서 무역결제에 사용하는 화환신용장(Documentary L/C) 또는 상업화환신용장(Commercial Documentary L/C)이라고 부른다. 따라서 화환신용장을 중심으로 그 통지방법, 효력, 지급방법 등의 관점에서 신용장의 종류를 분류하면 다음과 같다.

(1) ① Revocable L/C(취소가능 신용장) : 개설은행이나 수입업자가 수익자에

게 사전통지없이 신용장을 취소하거나 변경할 수 있는 신용장이다. 'revocable'의 표시가 있거나 'irrevocable'의 명시가 없으면 취소가 능하다. 그러나 매입, 인수, 지급을 위해 은행에 환어음을 제시한 후에는 취소할 수 없다.

② Irrevocable L/C(**취소불능 신용장**) : 신용장이 수익자에게 통지된 후 유효기간 내에 관계당사자 전원의 합의가 없이는 신용장을 취소 · 변경할 수 없는 신용장이다.

(2) ① Confirmed L/C(**확인 신용장**) : 개설은행 이외의 제3의 은행이 개설은행의 요청에 따라 수익자가 발행한 환어음의 지급, 인수 또는 매입을 확약한 신용장으로 가장 안전하다고 볼 수 있다.

② Unconfirmed L/C(**불확인 신용장**) : 개설은행 이외의 제3의 은행에 의한 확약이 없는 신용장이다.

(3) ① General(or Open) L/C(**보통 신용장**) : 어음매입을 특정은행으로 제한하지 않고 아무 은행에서나 매입할 수 있도록 되어 있는 신용장이다.

② Special(or Restricted) L/C(**특정 신용장**) : 수익자가 발행하는 환어음의 매입은행을 특정은행에 한정시키는 신용장을 말한다.

(4) ① Sight L/C(**일람출급 신용장**) : 신용장에 의거 발행되는 환어음이 일람출급인 경우를 말한다.

② Usance L/C(**기한부 신용장**) : 신용장에 의거 발행하는 환어음의 기간(tenure)이 기한부인 경우이다.

(5) ① Transferable L/C(**양도가능 신용장**) : 수익자가 신용장 금액의 전부 또는 일부를 1회에 한하여 국내 · 외의 제3자에게 양도할 수 있는 권한을 부여하는 신용장이다.

② Non-transferable L/C(**양도불능 신용장**) : 위와 같이 제3자에게 양도할 수 없는 신용장을 말하며 수익자만이 해당 신용장에 의거 수출할 수 있다. 신용장에 양도가능(transferable)의 표시가 없으면 양도할 수 없는 것으로 간주한다.

(6) ① Negotiation L/C(**매입 신용장**) : 개설은행이 환어음의 매입을 예상하고 환어음의 발행인, 배서인 및 선의의 소지자에게도 정히 지급할 것을 확약하는 신용장이다.

② Straight L/C(**지급 신용장**) : 신용장에 의한 환어음의 매입여부는 언급

하지 않고 개설은행 또는 그의 지정은행에 환어음을 제시하면 지급하겠다고 확약하는 신용장이다.

(7) ① With Recourse L/C(**상환청구가능 신용장**) : 환어음을 매입한 은행이나 선의의 소지자가 환어음발행인에게 상환청구를 할 수 있는 신용장이다.

② Without Recourse L/C(**상환청구불능 신용장**) : 매입은행이나 선의의 소지자가 환어음 발행인에게 상환청구를 할 수 없는 신용장을 말하며 신용장상에 "without recourse to drawer"와 같이 기재한다.

(8) Revolving L/C(**회전 신용장**) : 일정기간 동안 일정한 금액의 범위 내에서 신용장 금액이 자동적으로 갱신하도록 하는 신용장이다. 동일한 물품의 거래가 빈번할 때 많이 이용된다.

(9) Back to Back L/C(**구상무역 신용장**) : 외국에서 내도한 수출신용장을 담보로 그 신용장의 수익자가 거래은행에서 동액의 수입신용장을 개설할 때 이 신용장을 말한다. 연계무역에 이용되며 동시개설신용장이라고도 한다.

(10) Escrow L/C(**기탁 신용장**) : 환어음의 매입대금이 수익자에게 지급되지 않고 수익자 명의의 Escrow계정에 입금했다가 그 수익자가 원 신용장 개설국가로부터 수입하는 상품의 대금결제에만 사용하도록 규정한 신용장이다.

(11) Local L/C(**내국 신용장**) : 수출업자의 요청으로 수출업자 앞으로 내도한 원 신용장(master L/C)을 견질로 하여 국내의 원료공급자, 하청업자 또는 생산업자를 수익자로 하여 개설한 신용장이다.

(12) Stand-by L/C(**보증 신용장**) : 국내상사의 해외지사의 운영자금, 국제입찰 참가에 수반되는 입찰보증(bid bond), 계약이행보증(performance bond) 등에 필요한 자금을 해외 현지은행에서 받고자 할 때 이들 채무를 보증할 목적으로 국내 외국환은행이 해외의 은행 앞으로 발행하는 무담보 신용장이다.

(13) Baby L/C : 외국에서 원 · 부자재를 수입하여 제조 · 가공 후 상품을 수출하고자 할 때 원래 받는 신용장(Master L/C)에 대하여 원 · 부자재 수입용으로 새로이 개설되는 신용장을 말하며, 국내에서 조달될 때는 Local L/C가 된다.

(14) Cash L/C(**현금 신용장**) : 수입업자의 요청으로 수입업자의 거래은행이 수익자 소재지 자기은행의 본 · 지점이나 Corres Bank 앞으로 일정자금

을 송금해 놓고 그 은행으로 하여금 수익자 앞 신용장을 개설하도록 의뢰하여 개설된 신용장이다. 수입업자는 상품인수 전에 자금이 지출되는 단점이 있다.

(15) Packing L/C(**전대 신용장**) : 수입업자가 개설은행을 통해 수출업자에게 수출대금의 선불을 허용해주는 신용장이다. 네고 시에는 선수금과 이자를 공제한 잔액에 대해서만 환어음을 발행해서 매입은행에 제시한다. Red Clause L/C 라고도 한다.

(16) Thomas L/C : 구상무역의 경우 수출입 당사자 한쪽, 예컨대 A국의 수입업자가 먼저 신용장을 개설하고 B국의 수출업자는 일정기간 내에 수입하겠다는 보증서를 발행해서 B국 수출업자의 매입은행에 제출함으로써 A국의 수입업자가 발행한 수입신용장이 유효하게 되는 신용장을 말한다. Thomas는 중국과의 거래에서 이 방식을 사용했던 일본 회사의 전신약호이다.

(17) Transit L/C : 화폐가 직접 태환되지 않고 서로 상대국의 환거래은행(corres bank)이 없는 국가 간에 무역을 할 경우 양 국가가 거래하고 있는 제3국의 통화로 표시된 신용장이다.

(18) Repayment L/C : 개정된 Buy American 정책에 의해 무역업자가 사용하는 AID 상환에 따른 특수결제방식의 하나이다. AID 수혜국이 기타 AID 수입국 앞으로 수출하는 경우 그 수출대금은 AID 현금으로 상환하지 않고 장차의 대미 수입대금으로 결제하는 조건으로 AID가 신용장 인수은행을 통해 발행하는 무담보 신용장(clean L/C)을 말한다.

(19) Bank L/C(**은행 신용장**) : 수출업자가 발행한 환어음을 개설은행, 확인은행 또는 특정은행이 지급 또는 인수하겠다고 확약하고 있는 신용장이다. 위의 은행 대신 개설의뢰인이 지급 또는 인수를 확약하면 Customer L/C 라고 한다.

(20) Reimbursement L/C : 매입은행에 신용장 개설은행 명의의 계정이 없기 때문에 별도로 개설은행 앞으로 환어음을 발행하여 대금을 추심해야 하는 신용장이다. 또는 매입은행에 신용장 개설은행 명의의 계정에 있어서 이 계정에서 매입자금을 상환받는 경우가 있는데, 이를 Simple L/C라고 한다.

(21) Extended L/C(**연장 신용장**) : 수출업자가 수출상품의 선적 전에 개설은

행 앞으로 무담보 어음을 발행하면 이것을 통지은행이 매입하고 일정기간 내에 당해상품에 대한 모든 운송서류를 매입은행에 제공할 것을 조건으로 하는 신용장이다. 이 신용장은 수출업자에게 자금조달의 편의를 제공하기 위한 것이다.

Useful Sentences(신용장관계)

1. We have instructed the ABC Bank, Seoul to open an irrevocable L/C for U$30,000 in your favor, valid until October 8.
   10월 8일을 유효기일로 한 미화 30,000불에 달하는 취소불능 신용장을 개설할 것을 서울에 있는 ABC은행에 의뢰했습니다.
2. We are pleased to inform you that we have instructed our bankers to open an irrevocable and confirmed letter of credit in your favor amounting to US$10,000 for our order of 10 units of knitting machine No. 9.
   편물기계 제9번 10대에 대한 당사주문을 결제할 미화 10,000불에 달하는 취소불능 확인신용장을 귀사를 수익자로 하여 개설할 것을 당사 거래은행에 의뢰했음을 통지해 드립니다.
3. We trust the advice of credit will soon be in your hands.
   신용장 통지서가 곧 귀사에 도착되리라 믿습니다.
4. It is important that the goods be shipped by August 20, as stipulated in the L/C.
   신용장에 명시된 바와 같이 물품이 8월 20일까지 선적되는 것이 중요합니다.
5. For payment, we have arranged with the ABC Bank, New York for an irrevocable letter of credit in your favor for the sum of US$7,000.
   The credit will be confirmed by the XYZ Bank, Chicago.
   결제에 대해서는 귀사를 수익자로 하여 미화 7,000불의 취소불능 신용장을 개설하도록 ABC은행 뉴욕지점에 의뢰했습니다.
   그 신용장은 XYZ은행 시카코지점에서 확인할 것입니다.

6. We would like to ask you to amend the L/C No. 1234 from the Seoul Bank for your Order No. 17 as follows:
귀 주문 제17호에 대해서 서울은행에서 개설한 신용장번호 제1234호를 아래와 같이 변경하여 주실 것을 요청하는 바입니다.
7. There was an explosion on the m/s New World in which we were to ship your goods, causing her serious damage and her sailing was canceled. This has made it impossible for us to ship your goods within the validity of your L/C which expires on March 10.
귀사 상품을 선적키로 한 신세계호에서 폭발이 났습니다. 따라서 선체가 심각하게 손상됐고 운항이 취소됐습니다. 3월 10일로 만기가 되는 신용장의 유효기일 내에 귀 상품을 선적하기가 불가능해졌습니다.
8. The continuation of the nationwide seamen's strike is paralyzing ocean transportation in Korea.
전국적인 선원들의 파업이 계속되어 한국의 해상운송이 마비상태입니다.
9. According to the L/C we received, the payment is to be made at 30d/s, but we want it to be made at sight as mentioned in your order sheet. Please amend the L/C accordingly.
당사가 수취한 신용장에 의하면 결제조건이 일람 후 30일로 되어 있습니다. 그러나 당사에서는 귀 주문서에 명시한 대로 일람불조건을 원합니다. 신용장을 알맞게 정정하여 주십시오.
10. Because of an unusual shortage of cargo space, we find it impossible to secure space for the shipment of your order No. 123.
이상적인 적화공간부족 때문에 귀 주문 제123호를 선적할 선복을 확보하기가 불가능합니다.
11. Please amend the L/C to FOB basis as our Sales Note No. 125 stipulates, instead of C & F basis as your L/C describes.
귀사 신용장에 운임포함가격으로 명시하는 대신 당사 판매계약서 제125호에서 규정한 대로 신용장을 본선인도조건으로 정정하여 주십시오.
12. This amendment is to be considered as part of the above mentioned credit and must be attached thereto.
본 조건변경서는 상기에 언급한 신용장의 일부분으로 간주됨. 따라서 필히

동 신용장에 부착시켜야 됩니다.

13. This guarantee is payable by the beneficiary's simple receipt and statement countersigned by your bank certifying that Myungbo Trading Co. has failed to execute the contract.
본 지급보증서는 명보무역주식회사가 계약을 이행하지 못했다는 것을 증명하는 내용의 수익자 측 명세서에 귀행이 확인연서하여 수익자의 단순영수증으로 지급됩니다.

14. This credit is available up to USD10,000 each month for six months. Any unused portion of the monthly allotment is forfeited, that is, it is not carried over to the subsequent period.
신용공여는 매월 10,000불까지 6개월간 유효합니다. 월간 할당금액의 미사용잔액은 몰수됩니다. 즉, 다음달에 이월하여 사용할 수 없습니다.

15. Please find out the fate of the credit and handle it promptly.
신용장의 행방을 알려주시고 조속히 처리하여 주십시오.

16. ABC company, Seoul requests an extension of 30 days to the above mentioned credit, as a result of work stoppage in their two plants due to a labor dispute. If you agree, please advise us of the extended shipping and expiry dates.
서울의 ABC상사는 동사 2개 공장의 노동쟁의에 의한 작업중지로 인하여 상기 신용장에 대한 30일간의 기일연장을 요청하고 있습니다. 동의하시면 연장된 선적기일 및 유효기일을 통지하여 주시기 바랍니다.

17. At the time of this writing, we are unable to trace the receipt of your letter of credit.
With the possibility that these were lost in the mail, we would be pleased if you provide us with the authenticated copies.
지금까지도 귀 신용장의 접수를 추적할 수 없습니다.
우송 도중에 분실되었을 가능성을 고려하여 진위가 확인된 사본을 보내주시기 바랍니다.

18. Please inform us via e-Mail as soon as the goods are ready for shipment.
물품의 선적이 준비되면 전자우편으로 당사에 알려주십시오.

19. Your prompt reply by email will be appreciated.
    즉시 이메일로 회신하여 주시면 감사하겠습니다.
20. Please amend(extend) the L/C by fax.
    팩스로 신용장을 정정(연장)하여 주십시오.

Maxim

The early bird catches the worm.

아침 일찍 일어나는 새가 벌레를 잡는다.

Chapter 07

선적통지 및 선적지연통지
Shipping Advice and Notices of Delayed Shipment

수출상은 계약조건에 따라 선적 즉시 또는 선적수배가 끝나는 대로 수입상에게 선적의 주요 내용을 e-mail이나 팩시밀리로 통지하고, 이어서 운송서류(transport documents) 사본 등을 동봉해주거나 팩시밀리로 전송해 준다. 보통 전신으로 먼저 통지한 후 서면으로 확인서를 보낸다.

〈선적통지 서한의 구성요소〉

(1) 주문번호 또는 계약번호 및 날짜
(2) 상품명, 수량, 화인 및 번호
(3) 선박명, 선박출항예정일
(4) 환어음의 취결 및 운송서류 사본의 발송
(5) 기타 전달내용 등

또한 수출상이 계약조건이나 신용장조건 대로 선적이 불가능한 경우 매매계약 위반 및 신용장조건 불일치로 수출대금을 회수할 수 없다. 그러나 선적지연이 불가항력(force majeure)인 경우에는 이를 증명하는 서류(주한 수입국영사 또는 상공회의소 확인)를 지체없이 수입상에게 통지하여야 한다.

Sample Letter 31

Gentlemen :

We confirm our Fax just dispatched, informing you that your Order No. 20 of March 1 for 300 Cassette Tape Recorders RS-5, has been shipped today from Busan by the m/s New World and is due to arrive at your port about May 15.

Enclosed are copies of Invoice No. 105 in duplicate, copies of Bill of Lading No. 25 and Insurance Policy No. TS-1576 as well as Packing List, Certificate of Measurement & Weight.

We have drawn a draft at sight for the invoice amount under the Bank of America Letter of Credit No. 1234 through the Seoul Bank, Busan to whom all documents have been handed.

We hope the goods will reach you safely and we look forward to your further orders.

Yours very truly,

* 요약

카세트테이프 녹음기 RS-5 300에 대한 3월 1일자 귀사 주문 제20호가 금일 신세계호 편으로 부산항을 출항해서 5월 15일 쯤에 귀 항구에 도착할 것이라는 내용을 통지하는 방금 전송한 당사 Fax를 확인합니다.

동봉한 것은 용적 · 중량증명서, 포장명세서, 보험증권 번호 TS-1576 및 선화증권 번호 제25번 및 송장 제105호 사본 2부입니다.

서울은행 부산지점을 통해서 모든 서류가 전해질 것이며 BOA에서 발행한 신용장 제1234호에 근거해서 당사는 송장금액에 대해서 일람불로 환어음을 발행하였습니다. 선적상품이 무사히 도착되기를 희망하며 귀사의 추가주문을 기대합니다.

강의노트

① Commercial Invoice(상업송장)

상거래상 선화증권과 함께 필수적인 선적서류로 사용되며 물품의 거래가 원격지간에 행하여지는 경우 매도인이 매수인 앞으로 해당 물품의 특성과 내용명세를 상세하고 정확하게 작성하여 송부하는 선적화물의 계산서 및 내용명세서로서 송장상의 발행금액과 환어음의 발행금액이 일치하여야 한다.

② **Bill of Lading(선화증권)**

선화증권이란 화주와 선박회사 간의 해상운송 계약에 의하여 선박회사가 발행하는 유가증권이다.

즉, 선주가 자기 선박에 화주로부터 의뢰받은 운송화물을 적재 또는 적재를 위해 그 화물을 영수하였음을 증명하고 동 화물을 일정한 조건하에 수화인 또는 그 지시인에게 인도할 것을 약정한 유가증권이다.

③ **Insurance Policy(보험증권)**

보험증권은 보험계약성립의 증거로서 보험자가 피보험자의 청구에 의하여 교부하는 것으로 계약서는 유가증권은 아니며 단지 증거증권인데, 통상 배서 내지 인도에 의하여 양도된다.

④ **Certificate of Measurement & Weight**

용적 중량증명서로서 송장에 총괄적으로 기재된 중량용적의 내역을 기재한 것이다. 용적(measurement)의 계산단위는 CBM(cubic meter)을 주로 사용하는데, 1 M/T(measurement ton)=40 cubic feet이다.

⑤ **Packing List(포장명세서)**

화물의 포장방법, 개수, 중량, 용량 등을 기재한 서류이다.

일반적으로 상품의 수량은 다음과 같이 개수 혹은 도량형에 의하여 계산된다.

i) 개수－상품수 : 개수(piece), 조(set), 다스(dozen) 등
포장수 : 상자(case), 포(bale), 부대(bag) 등

ii) 도량형－중량 : 톤(ton), 파운드(1b : libra), 킬로그램(kg)
용적 : 입방피트(cft : cubic feet), 용적톤(M/T)
길이 : 야드(yard), 미터(meter)
면적 : 평방피트(SF : square feet)

선적서류의 기본서류는 상업송장, B/L, 보험증권이며 부속서류로는 포장명세서, 원산지증명서(Certificate of Origin), 검사증명서(Inspection Certificate), 영사송장(Consular Invoice) 등이 있다.

⑥ draw a draft '환어음을 발행하다'

환어음을 Bill of Exchange라고도 한다. 환어음의 지급기일(Tenure)을 표시하는데, 일람불어음(Sight Draft)인 경우에는 at 다음에 Sight를 표시하면 되고 기한부어음(Usance Draft)인 경우에는 약정된 기간, 예를 들면 90 days after sight, 90 days sight 혹은 90 days after B/L date 등으로 표시하면 된다.

여기서 환어음(Bill of Exchange)이란 채무자가 채권자 앞으로 발행하는 약속어음과는 달리 채권자가 채무자 앞으로 발행하여 취결되는 것이며, 특히 무역거래에서 사용되는 환어음은 발행지와 지급지가 서로 다른 국가 간에 취결되는 외국환어음이다.

주의할 사항은 신용장상에 송장금액의 90% 등으로 발행케 할 경우 어음발행금액은 Invoice Value의 90% 해당금액이다.
환어음은 은행에 제출 시 2통이 제시된다. 이때에 First Bill of Exchange와 Second Bill of Exchange가 set로 제시되어야 한다.

〈환어음의 주요 당사자〉

i) 발행인(drawer)
어음을 발행하는 자, 즉 수출업자나 채권자

ii) 지급인(drawee)
환어음의 지급을 위탁받은 신용장개설은행

iii) 수취인(payee)
환어음의 지급을 받을 자로서 발행인이 될 수도 있고 발행인이 지정하는 제3자도 될 수 있으나 신용장에 근거를 두고 발행하여 외국환은행에 매입을 의뢰하는 경우의 수취인은 동 서류를 매입한 외국환은행이 된다.

〈환어음의 형태〉

일반적으로 환어음은 다음과 같은 형태를 지닌다.

No. (1)____ Bill of Exchange Seoul (2)____ For (3)____ At (4)____ Sight of this first Bill of Exchange〔(5) Second of the same tenure and date being unpaid〕pay to Korea Institute Bank, Seoul or order (6)____ the sums of (7)____ (8) Value received and charge the same to account of (9) Drawn under (10)____ L/C No.___ dated____ To (11)____ (12)____.

(1) 어음번호 (2) 발행일자 (3) 어음금액(숫자) (4) 어음기일의 종류(tenure of draft) (5) 파훼문구 (6) 지급을 받을 자(payee) (7) 금액(문자) (8) 대가수취문구 (9) 계정결제인(accountee) (10) 신용장개설은행 (11) 어음지급인(drawee) (12) 어음발행인(drawer)

환어음

번호 (1)____ 서울 (2)____

금액 (3) (숫자)____

〔(5) 똑같은 기한 및 일자에 제2환어음에 대하여 지급이 이루어지지 않은 경우〕 등 제1환어음에 대하여 일람출급(또는 기한부) (4)으로 서울 한국협회은행 또는 그 지시인에게 (6) 금액 (7) (문자)를 지급하시오.

(8) 대가수취하였으면 어음금액을 (9)____의 계정으로부터 징구하시오.

동 어음은 (10)____은행의 일자의 신용장번호___에 의거하여 발행되었음

(11)____ 앞 (12) (발행인)____.

위 환어음상에서 for(3) 다음에 숫자로, the sums of (7) 다음에는 문자로 표시한다.

환어음뿐만 아니라 수표, 신용장의 금액을 표시하는데 아래와 같이 숫자(in figures)와 문자(in words)를 병기한다.

숫자와 문자금액이 상이한 경우 문자금액이 우선한다.

US$200.00(Say US Dollars Two Hundred Only)

US$1,234.56(US Dollars One Thousand Two Hundred Thirty-four and Cents Fifty-six Only)

US$11,080.00(Eleven Thousand Eighty U.S.Dollars) 등으로 표기한다.

⑦ Letter of Credit

'신용장' 이란 수익자에 대한 개설은행의 조건부 지급확약이다. 다시 말해서 수입상을 개설의뢰인으로 하고 수출상을 수익자(Beneficiary)로 하여 수입상의 거래은행인 개설은행이 수입상의 요청과 지시에 따라 수출상 또는 그 지시인으로 하여금 신용장에 명기된 조건과 일치하는 운송서류(Transport Documents)를 제시하면 수입업자를 대신하여 지급의 이행 혹은 신용장에 의해 발행된 어음의 지급, 인수를 수출업자 또는 어음 매입은행 및 선의의 소지인(Bona-fide holder)에게 확약하는 증서(Instrument)이다.

* bona fide 선의의(=in good faith), 반대어는 mala fide [méilə fáidi] 악의의, 불성실한

Sample Letter 32

KORÉA TRADING INTERNATIONAL INC.

PHONE : (02)551-3114 11TH FLOOR, TRADE TOWER, DATE : DEC. 9, 20××.
FAX : (02)551-3100 159, SAMSUNG-DONG, KANGNAM-KU. YOUR REF. :
SEOUL, KOREA OUR REF :SPT-4-1132
TRADE CENTER P.O.BOX 23.24

TO : A & J NIAMONITAKIS CO., LTD.
ATTN : MR. JOHN A. NIAMONITAKIS

<“SHIPPING ADVICE”>

Dear Mr. Niamonitakis:

We are very pleased to inform you that we have shipped the Microwave Oven on Dec. 7, 20××.

Please refer to the following details and cover the insurance.

Commodity:	460 Sets of Microwave Oven
Amount:	USD57,040.-
Invoice No.:	F2-20-126
B/L No.:	Bus/PRS-1
On Board Date:	Dec. 7, 20××.
ETA Athens:	Jan. 30, 20××.
Vessel Name:	New World V-922-3

Regarding the Meat Tenderizer, please let us know your L/C schedule. According to your order confirmation, we have already produced the order for early shipment.

We await your prompt reply.

Sincerely yours,

＊ 요약

고려무역(주)이 수입상인 A&J Niamonitakis사에 보내는 선적통지서의 실례.

Sample Letter 33

① Shipper/Exporter 11TH FLOOR, TRADE TOWER, 159, SAMSUNG-DONG, KANGNAM-KU SEOUL, KOREA TRADE CENTER P.O. BOX 23, 24		⑧ No. & date of invoice KGS-SMPL-30 July 14, 20××. ⑨ No. & date of L/C		
② For account & risk of Messrs. M/S. SALEH OMAR BARAYAN EST P.O. BOX 623 JEDDAH 21421 SAUDI ARABIA		⑩ L/C issung bank ⑪ Remarks : * SAMPLES OF NO COMMERCIAL VALUE		
③ Notify party SAME AS ABOVE				
④ Port of loading SEOUL, KOREA	⑤ Final destination JEDDAH, SAUDI ARABIA			
⑥ Carrier SPEED POST	⑦ Sailing on or about July 15, 20××			
⑫ Marks and numbers of Package	⑬ Description of goods	⑭ Quantity/unit	⑮ Unit-Price	⑯ Amount

TOOTH BRUSH	N/M	
MEGAT DX-43	(PAPER PACKING)	1 PCS
MEGAT DX-43	(PLASTIC PACKING)	1 PCS
TIMER	(PAPER PACKING)	1 PCS
TIMER	(PLASTIC PACKING)	1 PCS
ATTENDER TX-51	(PAPER PACKING)	1 PCS
ATTENDER TX-51	(PLASTIC PACKING)	1 PCS
DAVONG	(P.V.C. PACKING)	1 PCS
SUB. TOTAL :		7 PCS

* 요약

고려무역(주)이 발행하여 사우디아라비아의 SALEH OMAR BARAYAN EST사로 보내는 무상견본품에 대한 상업송장이다.

Sample Letter 34

ORDER 1234 SHIPPED M/S NEW KOREA (LEAVING BUSAN SEVENTH) AS DOCUMENTS DRAWN DOLLARS17,000 REQUEST HONOR

＊ 요약 선적통지(전문)

귀하 주문 제1234호 선적서류 대로 7일 부산항의 신한국호에 선적 17,000불 환어음을 발행했음. 지급요망.

강의노트

M.S는 motor · ship의 약어로서 선박의 주기관이 디젤이라는 뜻이다(M.V.=motor vessel).

증기관은 S.S(=steam·ship)

원자력 기관은 N.S(=nuclear·ship)이라 한다.

Sample Letter 35

Gentlemen :

Thank you for your order No. 123 for Electronic Toys, which is now being processed.

Due to unexpected trouble that occurred in the final stage of manufacturing, the execution of your order by the end of June has become impossible.

We assure you that we will do everything we can to expedite shipment, and will cable you immediately when we have arranged shipment.

Yours very truly,

* 요약

현재 생산 중에 있는 전자완구품에 대한 귀 주문 제123호에 감사드립니다.

제조의 최종공정에서 예기치 못한 고장이 나서 귀 주문품에 대한 이행이 6월말까지는 불가능하게 되었습니다.

당사는 선적을 촉진할 수 있도록 최선을 다할 것을 확신하며 선적이 준비되면 즉시 귀사 앞으로 타전하겠습니다.

Useful Sentences(선적통지 및 선적지연통지)

1. Expressions such as 'prompt', 'immediately', 'as soon as possible', and the like should not be used. If they are used, banks will disregard them.(U.C.P. 제3조)
   '신속히', '즉시', '가능한 한 빨리' 및 이와 유사한 표현은 사용되어서는 안 된다. 만일 이들이 사용되었을 경우에는 은행은 이를 무시하여야 한다.
2. We are pleased to inform you that your order No.121 was shipped on April 7 aboard the m/s New Korea that left Busan for New York the next day.
   귀 주문 제121호가 익일 부산항을 출발해서 뉴욕으로 향하는 신한국호 편에 4월 7일자로 선적되었음을 통지해드립니다.
3. Confirming our cable of today, we are pleased to inform you that we have shipped the goods for your order No.121 by the m/s Arirang of the Hanjin line that left Incheon today.
   금일 당사 전문의 확인으로 귀사주문 제121호의 상품을 금일 인천항을 출항한 한진해운의 아리랑호 편으로 선적했음을 통지합니다.
4. The Blue Dragon, the carrier of your goods, set sail from Busan for Yokohama on March 29.
   귀사 상품이 적재된 청룡호가 3월 29일에 요코하마를 향해서 부산을 출항했습니다.
5. As we cabled you today, the m/s New World has left this port carrying the goods for your order No.123.

금일 귀사로 타전한 바와 같이 신세계호가 귀 주문 제123호에 대한 상품을 싣고 이곳의 항구를 출항했습니다.

6. Your consignment of 50 units of video-camera K-93 for your order No. 123 has been dispatched by the m/v New Korea, which is scheduled to arrive in San Francisco about July 10.
   귀 주문 제123호에 대한 비디오카메라 K-93형 50대의 적송품을 신한국호편으로 발송했습니다. 동 선박은 7월 10일 샌프란시스코에 도착할 예정입니다.
7. We are glad to enclose copies of transport documents for this order.
   본 주문에 대한 운송서류의 사본을 동봉합니다.
8. Enclosed are copies of the following documents :
   Invoice 3 copies
   Bill of Lading 2 copies
   Insurance Policy 2 copies
   Packing List 3 copies
   하기서류의 사본을 동봉합니다.
   송장 3부
   선화증권 2부
   보험증권 2부
   포장명세서 3부
9. Enclosed are the relevant documents which we trust you will find in order.
   관련서류를 동봉합니다. 제대로 작성됐으리라 믿습니다.
10. We have today drawn a draft at 30 d/s for the amount of US$10,000 under L/C No. 1234 through the ABC Bank, Seoul.
    당사는 금일 서울에 있는 ABC은행을 통해서 귀사 앞으로 신용장 제1234를 근거로 미화 10,000불의 일람후 30일 출급 환어음을 발행하였습니다.
11. We would appreciate your acceptance of this draft upon presentation.
    동 환어음이 제시되면 귀사에서 인수하여 주시면 감사하겠습니다.
12. Upon completion of your order, we will as usual, draw on you at sight for the full invoice amount.

귀 주문품을 조달하고 종전대로 송장금액에 대해서 일람출급 환어음을 귀사 앞으로 발행하겠습니다.

13. Our terms are also very reasonable. We will draw on you at 30 d/s after your complete order has been shipped.
당사의 지불조건은 대단히 저렴합니다. 귀사 주문품을 모두 선적한 후에 일람후 30일 출급 환어음을 귀사 앞으로 발행하겠습니다.

14. To cover this shipment, we have drawn on you at sight through the ABC Bank here.
이 선적품을 결제하기 위해서 이곳 ABC은행을 통해서 귀사 앞으로 일람출급 환어음을 발행하였습니다.

15. The Documentary Bill of Exchange has been drawn at 30 d/s under L/C No.123 and has been delivered to the Korea First Bank here.
신용장 제123호에 의거하여 귀사 앞으로 일람후 30일 출급 환어음을 발행했으며 이곳 한국제일은행에 제출했습니다.

16. Please give our draft duly honor when it is presented to you by your bankers.
귀사 거래은행이 귀사에게 당사 발행 환어음을 제시하면 정히 결제하여 주십시오.

17. When we have shipped your order, we will cable you to that effect and, at the same time, draw on you at 60 d/s, D/A through the Seoul Bank here.
귀사 주문품을 선적하면 동 취지를 귀사 앞으로 타전하겠으며 동시에 이곳 서울은행을 통해서 귀사 앞으로 일람후 60일 출급 인수인도 조건으로 환어음을 발행하겠습니다.

18. The shipping documents are to be surrendered upon payment of the draft at your end.
선적서류는 귀지에서 (귀사가) 환어음을 지불하면 인도될 것입니다.

19. Though our usual terms are documents against payment, we are prepared in this case to accept documents against acceptance terms.
당사의 통상 결제조건은 지급도이지만 이번 경우에는 인수인도조건을 수락할 용의가 있습니다.

20. We are going to place our order with you subject to shipment during May and the terms of 30 d/s under D/A.
    5월 선적, 일람후 30일 출급 인수인도조건으로 주문할 예정입니다.
21. We trust that the goods will reach you in good order and to your full satisfaction.
    상품이 무사히(양호한 상태로) 도착하고 귀사에 만족을 주리라고 믿습니다.
22. We look forward to the opportunity of filling your order again.
    귀 주문품을 다시 조달할 기회가 있기를 고대합니다.

Maxim

Two heads are better than one.

두 사람의 지혜는 한 사람의 지혜보다 낫다.

Chapter 08

클레임 및 조정

Claims and Adjusments

비즈니스세계에서 가장 정교하고 숙련된 통신이 요구되는 분야이다. 무역거래과정에서 당사자 간에 계약내용의 이행여부와 관련하여 무역분쟁이 일어날 수 있는데, 단순한 Complaint(불만호소)를 넘어서 손해배상과 같은 어떤 구체적 청구를 수반한 경우 이를 Claim이라 한다.

Claim 조정방법으로는 "Compromise is a stabilizer."라는 말처럼 당사자들의 교섭에 의한 화해(Amicable Settlement)나 타협(Compromise)으로 해결하는 것이 가장 좋다.

불행히 타협이 이루어지지 않으면 제3자인 조정인(mediator)에 의한 조정(mediation or conciliation), 중재인(arbitrator)에 의한 중재(arbitration) 또는 소송(litigation) 등으로 발전될 수 있으나, 이 가운데 가장 일반화되어 있는 것은 신속하고 부대비용이 절감되는 경제적인 중재(arbitration)를 통한 방법이다.

이에 따라 우리나라 대한상사중재원(KCAB : Korean Commercial Arbitration Board)은 다음과 같은 표준중재조항(Standard Arbitration Clause)을 계약 내용에 반드시 포함하도록 권하고 있다.

"All disputes, controversies or differences which may arise between the parties, out of or in relation to or in connection with this contract, or for the breach thereof shall be finally settled by arbitration in Seoul, Korea in accordance with The Commercial Arbitration Rules of The Korean Commercial Arbitration Board and under the Laws of Korea. The award rendered by the arbitrator(s) shall be final and binding upon both parties concerned."

(이 계약으로부터, 또는 이 계약과 관련하여, 또는 이 계약의 불이행으로 인하여 당사자 간에 발생하는 모든 분쟁과 논쟁 또는 의견차이는 대한민국 서울에서 '대한상사중재원' 의 '상사중재원칙' 및 대한민국법률에 따라 중재에 의하여 최종적으로 해결한다. 중재인(들)에 의하여 내려지는 판정은 최종적인 것으로 당사자 쌍방에 대하여 구속력을 갖는다.)

〈상사중재의 경제적 기능〉

(1) 자주적 분쟁 해결 가능

영국의 세계적 석학 Schmitthoff는 중재(Arbitration)는 재판보다 낫고, 조정은 중재보다 나으며, 분쟁의 예방은 조정(Conciliation)보다 낫다고 기술하고 있다.

(2) 소송(Litigation)을 능가하는 효율성

① 소송은 3심제이나 중재는 단심제로 분쟁을 신속히 해결해야 한다.

② 중재는 비용이 적게 든다.

③ 중재는 중재인(Arbitrator)을 실정에 맞게 선정할 수 있다.

④ 중재는 비공개리에 진행된다.

⑤ 중재판정(Arbitration Award)은 외국에서도 가능하다.

〈클레임의 3가지 종류〉

(1) Transportation Claim : 운송클레임

(2) Insurance Claim : 보험클레임

(3) Trade Claim : 무역클레임

① 품질불량(Inferior Quality)

② 품질상위(Different Quality)

③ 포장불량(Bad Packing)

④ 파손(Breakage)

⑤ 착화부족(Shortage)

⑥ 선적상위(Different Shipment)

⑦ 선적지연(Delayed Shipment)

⑧ 법규위반선적(Illegal Shipment)

⑨ 계약불이행(Breach of Contract)

⑩ 해약(Cancellation) 등

클레임 조정서한(Adjustment letters)은 서신작성의 기본원칙인 ABCD(Accuracy, Brevity, Clarity, Dignity)를 근간으로 다음 사항들을 숙지하여야 한다.

1. Keep your letter simple and clear. Don't give unnecessary details.
2. If you have made an error, admit it and offer to rectify it.
3. Be prompt in answering complaints and claims. Whenever possible, answer the same day.
4. When you feel the customer is being unreasonable, don't make an outright refusal. Compromise and show willingness to help.
5. Don't permit salesmen to oversell or overstate your product. Honesty and conviction can carry you a long way toward success.
6. Sympathize, advise, and attempt to regain good will.
7. Avoid placing the blame on the customer, make suggestions, and keep the door open to further help or service.

Sample Letter 36

Gentlemen :

Your shipment of our Order No. 20 has arrived today.

Upon unpacking the consignment, however, we found that 50 out of the 300 Cassette Tape Recorders we ordered were different goods. We ordered RS-5 but the 50 out of the 300 units you sent us were RS-4. We don't need RS-4 as we are well stocked in this model.

We would like you to send us 50 units of RS-5 immediately as we are in urgent need of them. As for the 50 units of RS-4 you mistakenly sent us, we will send them back to you for your account.

Your earliest possible shipment of RS-5 would be appreciated.

Yours truly,

* 요약

당사주문 제20호의 선적품이 금일 도착했습니다.

적송품을 열자마자 당사가 주문한 카세트 녹음기 300대 중에서 50대가 물품상위임을 발견하였습니다. 당사는 RS-5를 주문했으나 귀사가 보낸 것은 300대 중 50대가 RS-4입니다.

당사는 이 모델의 재고가 있으며 RS-4는 필요치 않습니다. 당사에서는 긴급히 필요하므로 RS-5 50대를 즉시 송부하여 주십시오.

RS-4 50대는 귀사에서 잘못 보냈으므로 귀사의 비용으로 반송하겠습니다.

RS-5를 조속히 선적해 주시면 감사하겠습니다.

강의노트

① upon unpacking the consignment '적송품을 개장하자마자'

Unpack 물건을 꺼내다(=take out packed(things))

반대어는 pack '포장하다'로 운송 또는 저장(storage)을 위하여 '짐을 꾸리다'이고, package는 '개장(個裝)하다' '일괄하다'로 구별 사용된다.

Upon unpacking this shipment, we found that the goods to be very

inferior in quality to your counter sample and also slightly different in shade.
(선적품을 열자마자, 우리는 품질이 반대견본보다 대단히 열악하고 색조 또한 약간 상이한 것을 발견하였다)

② for your account '귀사의 비용으로'
Please purchase the goods for our account and risk.
(그 물품을 폐사의 계산(비용)과 위험으로 구입해 주십시오)

③ As for '~이 관계되는 한, ~에 관여하는' 항상 문두에서 사용한다(=as far as~are concerned)
As for our means and business integrity, you may refer to our bankers, the Korea First Bank, Seoul.
(폐사의 재정상태와 거래상의 성실성에 관하여는 우리의 거래은행인 한국제일은행에 문의하시기 바랍니다)

Sample Letter 37

Gentlemen :

Your letter of April 15 pointing out our incorrect shipment to you came as a great shock to us.

We at once checked into the matter at our shipping department and found that one of our workers had mistakenly shipped 50 Cassette Tape Recorders RS-4 instead of RS-5.

We will of course replace them with RS-5 by the first available vessel.

As for RS-4, we will bear all expenses you incur in shipping them back to us.

We hope you will please forgive us as we will be careful never to make such a mistake again.

Yours very truly,

＊ 요약

물품상위를 지적한 4월 15일자 귀 서신은 폐사에게 대단한 충격을 주었습니다.
즉시 이 문제를 당사 선적부에 조사해본 결과 한 직원의 실수로 카세트테이프 녹음기 RS-5 대신에 RS-4를 선적했음을 발견했습니다.

당사에서는 물론 첫 번째로 이용가능한 선편으로 RS-5로 대체시키겠습니다.

RS-4에 대해서는 당사에서 반송하는 데 드는 비용을 부담하겠습니다.

그러한 실수가 절대로 생기지 않도록 주의를 하겠으니 귀사에서 용서하여 주시기 바랍니다.

강의노트

① point out '보여주다, 지적하다'
Point out the town on the map. 그 도시를 지도 위에서 지적하여라.

② replace~with '을 ~으로 교체하다' (=substitute)
replacement 대체 the replacement of worn-out parts 낡은 부품의 대체

③ bear '가지다, 보이다, 견디다, 부담하다'
We wish to inform you that his round trip and other expenses will be borne by us.
(그의 왕복 및 기타 비용은 폐사 부담임을 통지합니다)

④ incur '자초하다, 가져오다'
~great expense 막대한 경비가 들게 되다.

Sample Letter 38

Gentlemen :

Your shipment of our order No. 123 for 1,000 units of Electronic Calculators K-77 arrived today. After opening the container, we found that the goods were short by 10 units.

To prove the shortage, we are enclosing a certificate of a Lloyd' s surveyor.

Please examine the matter and send us the goods to meet the shortage as soon as possible.

We trust that this shortage problem will be resolved to avoid similar incidents in the future.

Very truly yours,

* 요약

당사 주문 제123의 선적품인 전자계산기 K-77 1,000대가 금일 도착했습니다. 컨테이너를 열어본 후 물품이 10대가 부족하다는 것을 발견했습니다.

부족을 증명하기 위해 로이즈감정인의 증명서를 동봉합니다.

이 문제를 조사하시고 가능한 빨리 부족분을 보충할 물품을 송부하여 주십시오.

향후 유사한 사건을 피할 수 있도록 이 부족문제가 해결되리라 믿습니다.

강의노트

① Certificate of a Lloyd' s surveyor '로이즈감정증명서'
런던의 로이드협회(the corporation of Lloyd' s certificate)가 각국 주요 항구에 배치하고 있는 로이드감정인이 국제적으로 가장 신용이 있다.

② resolved '결심한(determined); 단호한(decisive)'
resolve '분해하다, 결의하다, 해결하다'

Sample Letter 39

Dear Sirs,

Thank you for your letter of May 1 calling our attention to the apparent shortage of 10 units of Electronic Calculators K-77.

The shortage of 10 units of Electronic Calculators K-77 were caused by unskilled packing on our part. Please accept our profound apologies.

We are confident of being able to send you the substitute by the end of this week.

We shall do everything in our power to see that such an irregularity is not repeated.

Yours truly,

* 요약

전자계산기 K-77 10대의 분명한 부족을 환기시켜 준 5월 1일 귀 서신에 감사드립니다.

그 부족분은 당사 측의 미숙련된 포장 때문에 발생했습니다. 이에 대해 진심으로 사과를 드립니다.

금주말까지 대체품을 송부할 것을 확신합니다.

그러한 변칙적인 일이 재발되지 않도록 주의하는 데 당사에서는 최선을 다하겠습니다.

강의노트

① apparent '또렷한, 명백한, 외관상의'

② calling our attention to '~에 주의를 환기시키다'

We wish to call your attention to the above credit, which we have received from you and delivered to the beneficiary today.

(귀사로부터 받아서 금일 수익자에게 교부한 상기 신용장에 주의를 환기시키고 싶습니다)

③ profound '깊은, 심오한, 오묘한'

명사는 profundity 깊이(=depth)

④ irregularity '불규칙, 변칙, 무질서, 불규칙적인 것'

irregular 불규칙한, 비정상적인

Maxim

Pleasant words are a honeycomb, sweet to the soul and healing to the bones.

친절한 말은 꿀송이와 같아서 마음을 흐뭇하게 하고 건강에도 좋다.

Useful Sentences(클레임 및 조정)

1. We regret to say that three cases of your shipment arrived in damaged condition.

   귀사 선적품 3상자가 파손된 상태에서 도착되었음을 유감으로 생각합니다.

2. Our order for Christmas decorations arrived today, two days after

Christmas.
성탄절 장식품에 대한 당사 주문품이 성탄절이 2일 지난 금일 도착되었습니다.

3. We have received our order No.123 today for 10,000 pairs of socks, but regret to say they are very much inferior in quality to your sample.
당사 주문 제123호인 10,000켤레의 양말을 금일 받았습니다. 그러나 유감스럽게도 귀사 견본품보다 품질이 대단히 불량합니다.
4. We have received today your shipment covering our order No. 47 of February 27. Upon opening the case, we found it contained completely different articles.
2월 27일자 당사 주문 제47호에 대한 귀사 선적품을 금일 받았습니다. 상자를 개장하자마자 그 안에 완전히 상이한 물품이 들어 있는 것을 발견하였습니다.
5. If you examine the enclosed cuttings, you must agree that our complaint is justified.
만일 동봉한 견품을 귀사에서 조사하시면 당사의 불만호소가 정당하다는 것에 동의할 것입니다.
6. Your shipment of different articles has caused us a great inconvenience.
귀사의 상이한 물품선적이 당사에 막대한 불편을 초래했습니다.
7. Enclosed is the surveyor's report on the three damaged cases.
동봉한 것은 파손된 3개의 상자에 대한 감정인의 보고서입니다.
surveyor '감정인' 해사감정인(Marine~), 보험감정인(insurancer, insurance appraiser), 선급 감정인(classification~)
8. We have lost a considerable amount of business on account of your delay in shipment.
당사는 귀사의 선적지연으로 상당한 금액의 거래손실을 입었습니다.
9. Because the goods are inferior in quality, we are returning all 15 cases and ask you to replace them.
물품의 품질이 열악하므로 15상자 전부를 반송하며 그것을 대체하여 줄 것을 요청합니다.

10. We need the correct articles by May 20 at the latest, so please send them to us by air parcel.
당사에서는 정확한 물품을 늦어도 5월 20일까지 필요하므로 그것들을 항공 소포로 보내주십시오.
11. We are obliged to ask you to cover our loss of US$3,000 from the damage of the goods. Please accept this claim and deduct the sum claimed from the amount on your next invoice to us.
물품의 손상으로 당사가 입은 미화 3,000불의 손실을 보상하여 주십시오. 이 클레임을 수락하고 다음번의 당사 송장금액에서 클레임금액을 차감하십시오.
12. Unless the goods arrive by the end of this month, we shall have to cancel our order No. 27.
물품이 금월말까지 도착되지 않으면 당사 주문 제27호를 취소하겠습니다.
13. We are looking forward to your early reply on this matter.
우리는 이 일에 대해서 귀사의 조기회신을 받기를 기대합니다.
14. Please tell us how to dispose of the wrong goods.
상위물품을 처리하는 방법을 알려 주십시오.
15. Please write us and explain why this misunderstanding occurred.
이러한 오해가 발생된 이유를 설명하고 당사로 알려 주십시오.
16. Please provide us with an explanation for the error. We look forward to your reply.
실수에 대한 설명을 당사에 제공하여 주십시오. 귀사의 회신을 기대합니다.
17. We regret to hear that the goods you received are not of the quality you expected.
귀사가 수취한 물품이 기대했던 품질이 아니라는 소식을 듣고 유감으로 생각합니다.
18. We have received your letter of May 10 and regret that the shipment of your order No. 12 arrived much later than contracted.
5월 10일자 귀 서신을 받고 유감스럽게도 귀사 주문에 대한 선적품이 계약일자보다 많이 지연된 것을 알았습니다.
19. Your letter of March 29, telling us that the wrong articles were sent to

you, was received today.
귀사로 상위물품이 보내졌다는 것을 알리는 3월 29일자 귀 서신을 금일 받았습니다.

20. We regret to learn from your letter of February 21 that the goods sent to you arrived in damaged condition.
유감스럽게도 귀사로 보낸 물품이 파손된 상태로 도착되었다는 것을 2월 21일자 귀 서신을 통해서 알게 되었습니다.

21. We have looked into the matter and found that your claims are prefectly justified.
본 건을 조사해 보니 귀사의 클레임제기가 확실히 정당하다는 것을 발견했습니다.

22. We admit that your order has not received our usual careful attention.
귀사 주문에 대해서 당사에서 평소 세심한 주의를 하지 않았다는 것을 인정합니다.

23. We regret that the wrong goods have been shipped due to a mistake by our shipping clerk.
유감스럽게도 당사 선적담당직원의 실수로 상위물품이 선적되었음을 알게 되었습니다.

24. We are prepared to offer you a 20% allowance to compensate you for the defects in the goods shipped.
우리는 선적한 물품의 결함을 보상하기 위하여 20%의 할인을 귀사에게 허용할 용의가 있습니다.

25. We agree to pay one dollar per yard for the quantity you mentioned to compensate you for the loss.
손실을 보상하기 위해서 귀사가 언급한 수량에 대해서 야드당 1불씩 지급하는 데 동의합니다.

26. Enclosed is a check for US$2,000. This remittance is made in settlement of your claim.
동봉한 것은 미화 2,000불의 수표이다. 이 송금은 귀사 클레임의 해결을 위해 이루어진 것입니다.

27. We presume that damage was due to rough handling in transit. We

wish you to negotiate with the shipping company.
파손이 운송도중 난폭한 취급에서 기인된 것이라 추정합니다. 귀사가 선박회사와 교섭할 것을 권합니다.

28. We do not plan to accept responsibility for this claim. You should file your claim for the damage with the insurance company.
동 클레임에 대해서 당사가 책임을 떠맡을 계획이 없습니다. 귀사에서는 보험회사에 손해에 대한 클레임을 제기해야 합니다.

29. We assure you that the goods were in good condition when they left here, and the damage must have occurred during transit.
상품이 이곳을 떠날 때는 양호한 상태였다고 확신합니다. 파손은 운송도중에 발생된 것입니다.

30. We shipped your order before the shipping date specified in your L/C, so the delay was not our responsibility.
당사는 귀 신용장에 명시된 선적기한 전에 귀 주문품을 선적했기 때문에 지연이 당사 책임이 아닙니다.

31. We carefully tested our goods which did not reveal any evidence of inferior quality or workmanship.
물품에 대해서 세심한 검사를 했으나 숙련(솜씨)이나 품질불량의 증거가 나타나지 않았습니다.

32. We are enclosing the report to show that your order has been dispatched from this end as promised.
귀 주문품이 약속대로 이곳에서 발송됐음을 보여주는 보고서를 동봉합니다.

33. We suggest that this claim be settled in accordance with the arbitration rules of the International Chamber of Commerce.
이 클레임은 국제상업회의소 중재규정에 따라서 해결해야 된다는 것을 제안합니다.

34. We hope you please understand our current situation and settle the matter amicably.
귀사에서 당사의 현재사정을 이해하고 그 문제를 우호적으로 해결하기를 바랍니다.

35. We hope the above explanation convinces you that we have abided by

our agreement.

당사는 귀사와의 협정을 준수한다는 상기 설명이 귀사를 납득시키기를 희망합니다.

36. We believe this is a fair adjustment and trust it will be acceptable.

이것이 공정한 조정(해결방법)이라 믿으며 승낙하리라 믿습니다.

37. We have lodged【entered, laid, made, filed】our claim with the insurance company.

당사는 보험회사에 클레임을 제기했습니다.

* claimant : 청구인, claimee : 피청구인

market claim : 가격인하를 구실로 제기하는 클레임

38. In addition, we will hold your company liable for all losses caused by this inexcusable delay.

덧붙여, 이유 없이 지연됨으로 인해 발생되는 모든 손실에 대한 손해배상책임을 귀사에 요구할 것입니다.

Maxim

Better a poor man whose walk is blameless than a rich man whose ways are perverse.

가난하지만 정직하게 사는 자가 거짓된 부자보다 낫다.

Useful Expressions for International Trade English

1. at the request of ~

At the request of Good Friends Co., Ltd, Seoul, we issue this documentary credit No. 1234 in favor of America International Company.

2. ask ~ to ~

We would ask you to forward us another copy immediately, since we did not receive the instrument.

3. disregard, neglect ~

Please disregard our letter dated March 20, 20×× in which we requested you to send us a photocopy of amendment, since we just received it today.

4. self-explanatory, straightforward ~

If you look into your records, all things will be quite straightforward.

5. have(find) difficulty (in) ~ing, find it difficult to V ~

We have difficulty obtaining the agreement from the beneficiary.

We find it difficult to obtain the agreement from the beneficiary.

6. require ~ to ~

L/C required us to add our confirmation.

7. regret ~

We regret to say that we are unable to meet your requirements on this matter.

8. with thanks, with regret, with surprise ~

We are with thanks in receipt of your letter dated July 20, 20×× informing us that the drafts were accepted by the applicant.

9. due to ~, due to the fact that ~

The original credit was sent to beneficiary directly due to clerical error on our part.

We wish to inform you that our customer wants to receive commissions due to him.

10. be crossing with ~

Your amendment dated May 10, 20xx was crossing with our letter dated May 12, 20xx, requesting you to extend the shipping and expiry date at the request of the beneficiary, please disregard our letter above.

We are sure that your letter of March 20, 20×× was crossing with our correspondence dated March 19, 20××.

11. In view of, with a view of, in view that ~

In view that you can properly identify the payee, we see no reason why the check cannot be paid.

12. to the attention of ~

    It will be much appreciated, if you direct your reply to the attention of Mr. K. D. Hong, Assistant Manager.

13. possibility that, possibility of ~

    We can see no possibility that the beneficiary will change his mind later and agree to the cancellation of this credit.

14. Reference is made to ~

    Reference is made to our letter of January 20, 20××.

15. in respect of ~

    Bank charges in respect of transfers are payable by the first beneficiary.

16. We shall appreciate it, if ~ or It will be much appreciated, if ~

    We shall appreciate it, if you send us copy of L/C immediately.

17. cause ~ considerable difficulty (inconvenience) ~

    Your rubber-stamped signature on drafts causes us considerable difficulty in this market.

18. restricted ~

    Negotiation under this credit is restricted to ShinHan Bank Myungdong Br.

19. add ~ to ~

    The advising bank is requested to notify the beneficiary, adding their confirmation to the credit.

20. be borne ~

    All charges outside Korea are to be borne by the beneficiary.

    Please note that confirmation charges are borne by the applicant for the credit.

21. be deemed, be construed ~

    In the absence of such indication the credit shall be deemed to be revocable.

22. in part, in whole ~

    Please acknowledge your agreement to this proposal in whole or in part.

23. with the exception of ~, with the following exceptions ~

    We agree to your proposal with the following exceptions.

24. apologize to ~ for ~

    We must apologize to you for our mistake in this connection.

25. favor ~ with, provide, furnish, extend ~ with

    Please provide us with the authenticated copy of letter of credit, in view that the original credit seems to have gone astray.

26. valued at ~

    We have today dispatched the documents valued at U$500,000.-

27. continue to ~

    Mr. K. D. Hong will continue to be in charge of the International Department as general manager.

28. without delay ~

    Please approach the drawee once again for an immediate payment without further delay.

29. outstanding ~

    A review of our records indicates that the above mentioned items are still outstanding

30. have elapsed ~

    A considerable length of time has elapsed since we had discussed this matter.

31. in case~, in case that ~

    In case that the drawee continues to withhold payment, please inform us immediately by e-mail.

32. A review of our records show that ~, Our records indicate that~, Our

file shows that ~

A review of our file indicates that the items in question remain still outstanding

33. in the event~, in the event that ~

In the event the drawee continues to hold the documents pending, please persuade them into liquidation.

34. further to ~

Further to our letter of June 18, 20×× requesting your prompt acceptance of the above bill, we have to advise you that these items are unpaid until now.

35. upon receipt of ~, upon receiving ~

Upon receiving this letter, please get in touch with the drawee for prompt settlement of this over-due item.

36. as of~, as the date of ~

Please forward us our account statement with you as of December 31, 20xx.

37. instead of ~

It should be read C.I.F Busan port instead of F.O.B Kobe.

38. under advice to us ~

Please remit the proceeds to our account with Citibank N.A. New York under e-mail/fax advice to us.

39. be to ~

Confirmation charges are to be borne by the beneficiary.

40. should have been ~

Documents should have been presented at latest by October 10, 20××.

41. be responsible for ~

The issuing bank will not be responsible for any consequences arising from its failure to follow the procedure set out in the preceding paragraph.

I guarantee that I will be fully responsible for all educational expenses incurred by the applicant, named below, during the course of study at

MSU.

42. so as to enable ~to ~

We wish to request you to extend the expiry date to June 10, 20xx so as to enable the beneficiary to negotiate the drafts.

43. on ~ part, on the part of ~

We notify this letter of credit without any responsibility on our part.

44. upon(on) ~ ing, upon(on) + of

Upon receiving our letter of credit No. 235, please return it to us via airmail.

45. in compliance with~, in accordance with ~

In compliance with your instructions, we forwarded one set of non-negotiable documents to Baewha Trading Co., Ltd. Seoul.

46. Please accept our apologizes for ~

Please accept our apologies for our clerical error in this matter.

47. impose on~ to ~

We wish to impose on you to accept the amendment dated July 20, 20xx.

48. avoid duplication~, avoiding duplication ~

We would like to ask you to pay the drafts, avoiding duplication.

49. In reply to ~

In reply to our letter, please mention our reference No. 1234.

50. consider ~ as null and void

Please consider our request of credit standing regarding ABC trading as null and void.

51. protect through ~, protection was made through~

We issued draft for U$30,000.- for protection of which was made through The Chase Manhattan Bank, New York.

52. at ~ disposal, at the disposal of ~

Please utilize this line of credit at your disposal.

We are holding the documents at your disposal.

53. cannot trace receipt of ~

We cannot trace receipt of your letter of March 18, 20××.

54. the cover ~

Please note the cover was made through Seattle First National Bank, Seattle.

55. It has come to our attention that ~

It has come to attention that the above items have been outstanding for a considerable length of time.

56. express our sincere appreciation (thanks) for ~

We wish to express many thanks for the excellent service you provided to us for many years.

57. mature on ~, mature in ~

We are enclosing draft No. 1234 which matures on March 20, 20××.

58. On behalf of ~

On behalf of our company, we wish to congratulate you on your opening ceremony.

59. in ~ name, in the name of ~

We wish to open a current account with you in the name of our Busan branch.

60. be prepared to ~

We are prepared to add our confirmation to the attached credit, if you pay us confirmation Charges at the rate of 7 1/8% per 3 months.

61. terminate ~

Please terminate our notice deposit for U$200,000.- on March 20, 20×× and remit the amount to our a/c with Irving Trust Co., New York.

62. be interested in ~ ing

We are interested in maintaining a closer relationship with you.

63. with value of ~, with value dated ~

As instructed by you, we debited your A/C with CMB New York with value of July 20, 20××.

64. amount to ~, amounting to ~

We are enclosing beneficiary's drafts amounting to U$500,000.-

65. Reference is made to ~

Reference is made to your letter of March 20, 20××.

66. under ~

Under these circumstances, we regret that we cannot comply with your requirements.

67. locate ~

We cannot locate the drawee, please furnish us with further particulars.

68. It is needless to say that ~, It goes without saying that ~

It goes without saying that the amendment of February 20, 20×× must be adhere to in its entirety.

Maxim

Slow and steady wins the race.

천천히 그리고 꾸준히 달리는 자가 경주에서 이긴다.

Part **IV**

기타 관계통신문

제1장 기타 관계통신문

제2장 FAX Communication and e-Mail

Global Business English

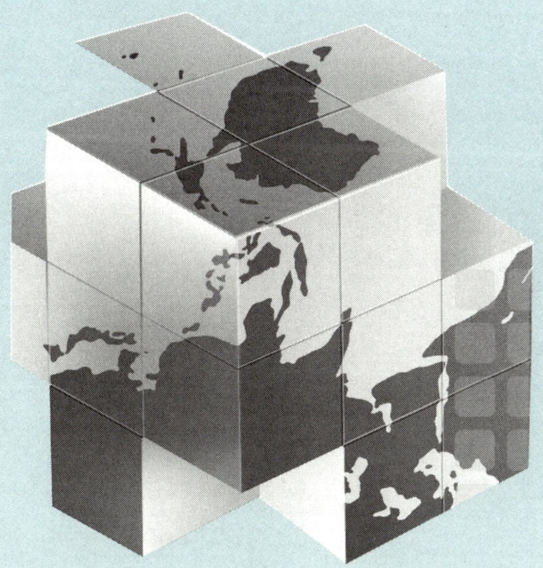

Global Business English

Chapter 01

기타 관계통신문

기타 관계통신문에서는 일반대중이나 여러 거래처에 같은 내용을 인쇄하여 Inside Address만 개별타자하여 발송하는 Circular Letter의 주요 사례를 중점적으로 다루고 있다.

Circular Letter는 회사의 신설, 지사설치, 주소변경, 주요 인사이동 등을 통지하는 일반통지(General Announcement), 방문 및 면담, 전근통지와 후임자 소개 및 거래처 소개를 내용으로 하는 Courtesy Letter, 판매안내장(Sales Circular) 및 영업안내장(Trade Circular) 등이 있다.

다양한 Circular의 작성을 위해서는 본서의 사례를 기본으로 하여 상황에 따라서 가감 변형하여 활용하는 것이 보다 효과적일 것이다.

1. 고용계약서(Employment Contract)

EMPLOYMENT CONTRACT

This contract of employment is made between Seoul Trading Co., Ltd. (hereinafter called the "Employer"), and Carol Ann York (hereinafter called the "Employee") :

Job Description and Terms of Employment : The Employee, on a part-time(4 working hours a day from Monday through Friday) non-regular staff member basis, undertakes to fulfill the following responsibilities for the Chairman and President :

	-Secretarial Work -English correspondence and speech -Writing and typing -Revision of English-related documents
Contract Term :	This contract is effective for one year, commencing August 10, 20××.
Remuneration :	The Employer undertakes to pay the Employee ₩1,000,000 per month, after taxation, payable monthly in local currency.
Miscellaneous :	The Employer reserves the right to terminate this contract without the Employee's consent if the latter neglects her duties or otherwise acts in a manner that seriously impairs the reputation of the employer. It is further agreed that if the Employee is forced to return to the United States, this contract shall be null and void.

On this tenth day of August 20××, the Employer and the Employee agree to the above mentioned as witnessed by their signatures affixed below.

"Employer"　　　　　　Carol Ann York "Employee"

＊ 요약

(주)서울무역과 Carol Ann York 사이에 체결한 고용계약서이다.

강의노트

① remuneration 보수 · 보상 · 봉급(wages, salary)
remunerate : ~에 보답하다, 보수를 주다(pay, reward)

② impair 손상시키다, 상처입히다

③ affix 첨부하다, (서명 따위를) 써넣다, (도장을) 찍다(=impress)

2. 이력서(Resume)

Personal DATA	
Name in Full	Jae-Hyun Chun
Place/Date of Birth	Seoul, Korea/March 29, 20××
Marital Status	Married
Present Domicile	Pirundaero 1 Gil 34, Jongno-Gu, Seoul Phone Number : 732-1234(home)
EDUCATION	
Feb. 1979	Seoul Senior High School
Mar. 1980 ~ Feb. 1984	Department of Business Administration, College of Business Administration, Seoul National University
Mar. 1984 ~ Feb. 1986	Department of Business Administration, Graduate School, Seoul National University, MBA Degree Major course studied : Managerial Accounting
WORK EXPERIENCE	
Oct. 1985~Sept. 1988	The Bank of Daehan, Seoul Branch
Sept. 1988	Daesung Bank, Business Division Ⅱ as Assistant Manager
Apr. 1993	Training & Education Dept. Banking Training Center
SERVICE AND LICENCES	
May 1984~July 1985	Served for 14 months in Korea Army
Sept. 1985	Acquired an International Trade Specialist Licence (or Certificate)
Nov. 1988	Acquired a Quality Control Specialist Licence (or Certificate.)

I hereby declare that the above mentioned statements are true and correct in all details.

＊ 요약

영문 이력서의 실례이다.

영문 이력서를 작성할 때 위와 같이 요약식으로 하면 "Resume", 서술식으로 전개하면 "Personal History" 그리고 Resume와 Personal History를 절충한 형태를 "Curriculum Vitae"라 한다.

3. 연수생 파견(Despatch of Trainee)

Dear Sirs,

We wish to send one of our staff members to your company as a trainee in the middle of July this year and would like to know if you can accept him as a trainee for six months. Please consider the following information about our candidate:

1) Name and position :
   Mr. Yong Deok Kim, Assistant Manager
2) Period of training :
   For six months starting in the middle of July, this year.
3) Subject of training
   International Trade and L/C Automation System.

Enclosed is a copy of his personal history.

We wish to inform you that his round-trip ticket and other expenses will be at our expense.

If you agree, please forward us a formal invitation letter issued by the Korean Consulate to obtain his passport and visa.

We sincerely hope that you seriously consider the above proposal and we wish to extend our best regards.

Sincerely yours,

＊ 요약

해외 거래업체에 6개월 동안 국제무역 및 신용장 전산화에 대한 연수를 위하여 김영덕 대리의 파견을 제의하는 서한

4. 소개장(Letter of Introduction)

Dear Sirs,

We take pleasure in introducing to you, Mr. J. H. Kim, President of Seoul Trading Co., Ltd., Seoul, a valued client of our bank.

Mr. Kim expects to leave shortly on a business trip abroad, which will include a visit to Seattle, and should he have occasion to call upon you during his stay in your city, we would appreciate you extending to him your usual fine courtesy and assistance in order to further the objectives of his trip.

Sincerely yours,

＊ 요약

거래처 대표이사인 J.H. Kim이 Seattle 방문 시 협조를 요청하는 서한

5. Cocktail Reception에 초청

IT GIVES ME GREAT PLEASURE TO CORDIALLY INVITE YOU TO A COCKTAIL RECEPTION TO BE HOSTED BY MR. ANDRIES WOUDHUYSEN, EXECUTIVE DIRECTOR IN CHARGE OF L AND W TRADING CO., LTD. ASIA-PACIFIC.

DATE : FRIDAY, JULY 7, 20××.
TIME : 6 : 30 P.M.
LOCATION : HYATT REGENCY SEOUL
LOTUS ROOM, SECOND FLOOR

MR. WOUDHUYSEN WILL BE ACCOMPANIED BY OTHER SENIOR EXECUTIVES OF L AND W TRADING CO., LTD. WHO ARE RESIDING IN ASIA, INCLUDING MR. ROBERT FALLON, MANAGING DIRECTOR IN CHARGE OF CORPORATE FINANCE,

MR. SCOTT BAUER, VICE PRESIDENT IN CHARGE OF INSTITUTIONAL FIXED INCOME SALES, AND MR. GEORGE SCHOTT, VICE PRESIDENT IN CHARGE OF COMMODITY TRADING AND SALES.

WE WOULD GREATLY APPRECIATE IT IF YOU COULD REPLY BY FAX TO MISS TSUSHIMA IN OUR TOKYO OFFICE AT 81-3-591-2717 AND INDICATE IF YOU WILL BE ABLE TO ATTEND THE RECEPTION.

WE SINCERELY HOPE TO SEE YOU ON THE 7TH OF JULY.

VERY TRULY YOURS,

＊ 요약

L. AND W 무역회사의 아시아 · 태평양 지역담당 전무인 Mr. Andries Woudhusen이 주최하는 Cocktail Reception에 초청장을 Fax로 보낸 실례이다.

6. 직책 및 부서명 영문 표기

- 대표이사 : Chairman of the Board of Directors & President
- 전무이사 : Managing Director & Deputy President
- 상무이사 : Managing Director & Executive Vice President
- 상임감사 : Standing Auditor
- 이　　사 : Managing Director & Vice President
- 부　　장 : General Manager
- 차　　장 : Deputy General Manager
- 과　　장 : Manager
- 대　　리 : Assistant Manager
- 일반상품부 : General Merchandise Department

  섬유제품과 : Textile Goods Section

기계전자과 : Machinery & Electronic Section
잡화상품과 : Sundry Goods Section
생활용품과 : Sports & Leisure Goods Section

- 인력개발부 : Human Resources Department
- 총 무 부 : General Affairs Department
- 심 사 부 : Credit Control Department
- 경 리 부 : Accounting Department
- 수 출 부 : Export Department
- 수 입 부 : Import Department
- 자 금 부 : Finance Department

7. 방문 및 면담요청

DEAR SIRS,

I SHALL BE VISTING NEW YORK AT THE END OF THIS MONTH AND, IF CONVENIENT TO YOU, WOULD LIKE TO VISIT YOUR OFFICE ON 1ST SEPTEMBER, 20×× AT 3:00PM TO DISCUSS MUTUAL BUSINESS OPPORTUNITIES.

YOUR EARLY REPLY, AS TO WHETHER THE TIME SUGGESTED IS SUITABLE OR NOT, WOULD BE APPRECIATED.

I AM LOOKING FORWARD TO SEEING YOU AGAIN.

8. 게시문

게시문은 간결하면서도 쉽게 알아볼 수 있도록 숙어적인 것이 좋다. 다음은 흔히 사용되는 게시문들이다.

- 고장 : Out Of Order
- 수리 : Under Repair
- 출입금지 : Off Limits, No Entrance
- 무용자 출입금지 : No Admittance Except On Business
- 금연 : No Smoking
- 침을 뱉지 말 것 : No Spitting
- 소음금지 : No Nuisance
- 담배버리는 곳 : Cigarette Butts
- 휴지통 : Trash, Waste Basket
- 비상용 출구 : Emergency Exit
- 출구 : Exit, Way Out
- 입구 : Entrance, Way In
- 측면입구 : Side Entrance
- 음료수 : Fit For Drinking, Portable Water
- 예약필 : Reserved
- 1월 1일부터 유효 : Effective Jan. 1
- 통행금지 : No Thoroughfare
- 편도통행 : One Side Only
- 배회하지 말 것 : No Loitering
- 주차금지 : No Parking
- 일방통행 : One Way Only
- 페인트 조심 : Wet Paint, Fresh Paint
- 근무시간 : Business Hours, Office Hours
- 우(좌)측 통행 : Keep to the Right(Left)
- 사용금지 : Not In Use
- 접수부 : Information Desk
- 입장무료 : Admission Free
- 금일휴업 : Closed Today
- 손대지 마시오 : Hands Off
- 접근 금지 : Keep Off
- 잔디밭에 들어가지 마시오 : Keep Off the Grass
- 비매품 : Not For Sale
- 매물 : For Sale
- 판매필 : Sold
- 금일품절 : All Sold Out Today

- 소지품 조심 : Beware Of Pickpockets
- 공사중 : Under Construction
- 속도제한 : Speed Limit
- 위험 : Danger, Dangerous
- 적화장 : Loading
- 하역장 : Unloading
- 불조심 : Beware Of Fire

9. 송별연회(Farewell Reception) 불참을 통보함

Ambassador Richard Walker
United States Embassy
Seoul

Dear Ambassador Walker :

I am very sorry that I will be unable to attend your farewell reception scheduled for October 4, 20××, as I will be out of town on business.

I would like to thank you for all the kindness and wonderful hospitality which you extended to me during your stay in Korea. Even though there will be a great distance between us, I want to continue the amicable friendship we have developed over the years.

I do hope we have an opportunity to meet in the near future, but until then, I wish both you and Mrs. Walker all the best in your future endeavors.

Sincerely,

10. 자유중국정부의 방문 초청에 감사함

Ambassador Tsou Chien
Embassy of the Republic of China
Seoul, Korea
Dear Ambassador Tsou Chien :

It is with great honor and heartfelt thanks that I accept your government's invitation to visit your country during the period of October 29 through November 2, 20××. This visit will allow me to observe first-hand the remarkable development your country has achieved through your devoted and endless efforts.

Korea and the Republic of China have become very close friends during the past few years and you may rest assured that I will personally do all that I can to help strengthen the bond between our two countries.

Again, my deepest gratitude for your very kind invitation.

Sincerely,

11. 전근을 통지하고 후임자를 소개함(I)

Gentlemen :

I take pleasure in introducing Mr. H. G. William, who will assume the overall responsibilities for ABC Group in Korea. Mr. William was previously associated with our group's operations in Hong Kong.

I will be leaving Korea towards the end of October, 20×× to assume the overall responsibilities of ABC Group in India.

I take this opportunity to express my sincere gratitude to you for the kind patronage, guidance and cooperation extended to me during my 2-year stay in Korea. I am confident that my associate Mr. William will continue to receive the same privileges from you and our relationship, both personal and organizational, will grow closer in the future.

Yours sincerely,

12. 전근을 통지하고 후임자를 소개함(Ⅱ)

Dear Sirs,

I wish to inform you that I have recently been assigned to the Import Department as a General Manager. I expect to take up my new responsibilities there by the end of February.

May I take this opportunity to thank you most sincerely for the cooperation and assistance accorded to me during my time spent in the Export Department. It has been my privilege to work here and become personally acquainted with you and your colleagues.

I am confident we will have the opportunity to continue our friendship in the future, and please do not hesitate to contact me whenever I may be of assistance to you.

Mr. J. H. Koh, who was formerly General Manager of Korea First Finance Ltd., our wholly-owned subsidiary in Hong Kong, has been named to succeed me. I trust you will extend to him the same support you have shown to me in the past.

Sincerely yours,

13. 영업점 이전을 통지함

Shifting of Office Premises

Dear Sir(s),

We have the pleasure to announce that effective July 15, 20××, we shall be operating our business in our new office premises located at:

Seoul Plaza Building 8th Floor
150, 2-ka, Taepyung-Ro, Chung-Gu, Seoul

It is our sincere desire that in shifting our branch to much more spacious, modern and beautiful premises we shall be able to provide you with more personalized and efficient services, catering to all your requirements.

While we welcome your august visit to our new office premises, we sincerely regret any initial inconvenience you may encounter due to the changing of our branch location.

Please note that our post office box number, telephone and fax numbers will remain unchanged.

14. 해외지사 개설 통지

Dear Sirs,

We take pleasure in announcing the opening of our Frankfurt branch, upgraded from a representative office effective March 22, 20×× at the following address :

Dae Han Trading Co., Ltd.
Frankfurt Branch
Mainzer Landstrasse 27-31(HDI Haus)
6000 Frankfurt/Main 1
Germany
General Manager : Mr. Young-Jae, Park
Fax No. : 02-3990-775
Telephone No. : 0611-271079

This branch is adequately staffed and equipped to engage in a full range of international operations.

We cordiallly invite you to our Frankfurt branch. Attached are specimen signatures of the officers who have been authorized to sign on behalf of this branch.

We sincerely hope that you will continue the assistance and cooperation as you have given to our other offices.

Sincerely yours,

15. 신간 Economic Review를 송부함

Gentlemen :

ECONOMIC REVIEW

We are pleased to enclose with this letter a copy of the first issue of the Company's Economic Review which we trust you will find informative and useful.

The Review will look regularly at economic conditions from a Korean point of view and will also feature articles of special interest.

The company's economists will provide most of the material that appears in this publication, but we shall also be calling upon specialists in other fields to contribute articles of topical interest.

We trust that the information contained therein will prove useful in your dealings with the Korean Market.

Yours sincerely,

16. 신용장분실통지

CAUTION NOTICE

Gentlemen :

We regret to inform you that the letter of credit has been lost.

The details of the credit are described as follows :

Irrevocable letter of credit No.IPU038210

Issued date : October 10, 20××

Amount : Deutsche Marks 425,000

Issuing Bank : Lloyds Bank PLC, Berlin, Germany

Beneficiary : Hansung Company, Seoul, Korea

Commodity : 425 pcs. of Men's Blazer

Regarding the above, we duly request that any process of banking thereunder must consequently be stopped and bankers are hereby cautioned against taking possible action on it. Also, it is requested that if presented, the credit must be taken into custody and forwarded immediately to us.

Incidently, at the request of the beneficiary, our bank may reproduce it in a negotiable form on the strength of its copy. When doing so, the reproduced credit will bear the following markings thereon.

"This advice superseded the original instrument dated October 19, 20×× issued by Lloyds Bank PLC, Berlin which was reported lost."

Please acknowledge receipt of this Caution Notice by signing and returning to us the attached form, and we will consider that this Notice has been kept in your bank with your keen attention and nothing has been dealt with by your bank for the original instrument unless your acknowledgement or any information of your handling thereto is in our hand within seven days from the date of this circular.

Faithfully yours,

＊ 요약

ⅰ) 신용장 분실을 알리게 됨을 유감으로 생각합니다. 동 신용장의 명세는 아래와 같습니다.

취소불능신용장 번호 : IPU038210

발행일 : 20××년 10월 10일

금 액 : 독일 마르크화 425,000

발행은행 : 독일 베를린 소재 로이즈은행(주)

수익자 : 한국 서울 소재 한성기업

상품명 : 남성 상의 425장

ⅱ) 따라서, 상기 신용장에 관하여는, 여하한 은행업무의 절차진행을 중지할 것을 정히 요청하며, 또한, 은행은 동 신용장에 대하여 어떠한 조치를 취하지 않도록 주의를 환기함. 만약 신용장이 제시되면, 보관(수중에 넣음)하시어 즉시 당행에 송부바랍니다.

ⅲ) 또한, 수익자의 요구에 따라, 동 신용장 사본을 근거하여 양도가능한 형식으로 신용장을 당행이 재생산할 수도 있음. 그렇게 하는 경우에는 재생 신용장에는 다음과 같은 표시를 할 것임.

"본 통지서는 20××년 10월 10일자 베르린 소재 로이즈은행(주)이 발행한 분실 통보된 신용장을 대체함."

iv) 유첨양식에 서명하시고 본 주의공고의 접수확인통보를 당행에 송부바람. 확인통보나 기타 동 신용장 취급에 관한 통보가 본 회람장 발송일로부터 7일 이내에 당행에 도착되지 아니하면, 당행은 귀행이 본 주의공고를 상당한 주의를 가지고 접수보관하고 있으며, 원신용장에 대하여 아무런 취급도 하지 않는 것으로 간주합니다.

강의노트

① caution notice '주의 통지'
② PLC : 공개주식회사(영국=public limited company)
③ on the strength of : ~을 근거로 하여(=on the base of)
④ the original instrument : 원신용장

17. Global Trade Interaction사의 구인광고

JOB OPPORTUNITY
SECRETARY FOR SALES DEPT.

GLOBAL, one of the largest multinational trading corporations in the world, is looking for a qualified secretary.

Qualification

1. University degree, preferably majored in English.
2. Good communication skills in English.
3. Positive/Motivated attitude.
4. Excellent PC Skills(Lotus, Harvard, Excel & Window)
5. Minimum 1-2 years experience as a secretary.

Applicants should send a resume with a recent photo and telephone number no later than August 15, 20×× to the H. R. Dept., C. P. O. Box 1234, Seoul.

GLOBAL TRADE INTERACTION, KOREA

18. 자기소개서

성장과정

While I was in elementary school, I heard a "pungmul", which is a traditional Korean percussion instrument and quickly joined a club, practicing and performing the pungmul. Before and after school, we practiced passionately at least three or four hours a day. The hard work finally paid off when our club won the prestigious Gyeonggi Province Governor's Trophy and then a prize at a National Pungmul Tournament. I usually played the "ggwaenggwari", which is a small gong. I took part performing "sangse" by leading the club on the stage. It was a unique and valuable experience that helped me to develop leadership skills and promote community spirit.

자기소개

Majoring in International Trade at Baewha Women's University was my highest desire and an ambitious dream for me was to become a professional worker in the business field utilizing practical skills, global vision, and an open mind. Last year, during summer vacation in China, I gained practical business skills through hands-on experience while participating at a business experience program for university students. I organized a team in order to sell several items to ordinary people on the street of China. It was invaluable learning what kind of items customers in China were looking for, and particularly, detailed design and proper price levels of selling products preferred on the market.

능력 및 장점

One certain thing that I can say about myself is that I always take a positive view of my life. Not only because of how my warming parents raised me with so much love, but because of the way I live. I try to see the bright side of whatever I face every day.

since last winter of 20xx, I have worked at the Korean bakery franchise, Tous Les Jours. It was my first part-time job and there were so many things to learn from the get-go. As I mentioned before, I am very cheerful. My attitude never changed at work. I did my best in welcoming and guiding customers. A few weeks later, it turned out that several costumers became regular patrons of the bakery thanks to my sunny character. Therefore, I can assure you that my initial approach, kind manner, and open mind will be a big asset for ABC Trading Co.

지원동기 및 입사 후 포부

I am well aware that ABC Trading Co. requires an applicant to have a cheerful character, very skilled in computing, writing, and speaking in English. To meet these qualifications, I have studied English conversation every day with a native speaker and with friends who have studied abroad. Currently, I hold a QA certificate and I am highly skilled in Excel, ACCESS, and PowerPoint. I can promise you that with my mantra "Be the best at whatever you do", I will bring much passion and commitment to work. I will put forth my best effort to help promote ABC Trading Co. to attain large profits.

19. 이스라엘 방문 협조에 감사함

May 30, 20××
His Excellency Ambassador Amnon Ben-Yohanan
Embassy of Israel
3 Nibancho, Chiyoda-Gu
Tokyo, Japan

Your Excellency Ambassador Amnon Ben-Yohanan :

It is with deep regret that I must apologize for not being able to visit you this past week after my trip to Israel. Unfortunately, I went directly to Seoul from Hong Kong, without stopping in Japan.

My visit to Israel was extremely informative and useful. The hospitality was beyond reproach and the people with whom I met were very helpful.

I will be in Japan around the 8th of June and would like to meet with you to discuss the outcome of my trip, if your schedule will allow for a brief visit.

During my trip, I met with Mr. William Lowell, the counsellor for economic affairs and I was very impressed with his expertise. We had many useful discussions and I would be very pleased to go over these details with you if, in fact, we are able to meet next month.

Again, my deep regrets for not being able to stop in Tokyo and visit with you, and my most heartfelt thanks for all your assistance in making my visit to Israel a success.

Sincerely,

20. 싱가포르 사무소 주소변경통지

To Our Correspondent :

Re : Change of Address of our Singapore Representative Office

In accordance with the Singapore Government's new numbering system for high rise buildings, effective from March 1, 20××, our Singapore Representative Office's address will be changed to :

65 Chulia Street 30-01
OCBC Centre
Singapore 0104

Their location, telephone and fax number will remain unchanged.

We cordially invite you to contact our Singapore Representative Office whenever we may be of service to you there.

Yours faithfully,

21. 추천장 I (해외유학)

Dear Professor Browne :

I am writing this letter to recommend Suzi Lee as a promising scholar deserving of acceptance into your graduate school of Economics.

In the limited time I have known her, Suzi has shown herself to be both bright and industrious, one who is energetic and endlessly fascinated by her study of Economics. While our Economics department produces well-educated graduates, it is my belief that she has had as much to do with her intellectual development as her professors. She has taken full advantage of all the resources the university has had to offer her. I often see her in the library doing research and consulting one of her professors. I have become better acquainted with her in her senior year; since she has taken two of my upper-level courses in Macro Economics, I have seen an already good student become even better. I consider her among the top two or three Economic students I have taught in my ten years of teaching at the university, and I think that she has genuine potential to contribute to the academic world.

It is my firm belief that her academic success will not be defined by her own abilities, but by the opportunities presented her. She is a budding economist and it is my hope that you accept Suzi Lee into your graduate program.

Sincerely,

____

Myung Gyu Koh, Ph.D.
Professor of Economics
Baewha Women's University

22. 추천장 Ⅱ(취업)

Dear Mr. or Madam :

I am writing this letter to recommend Minsu Kim to your company.

A very capable graduate of Korea University, he has demonstrated exemplary leadership skills, proven himself as a team player, and become an accomplished scholar.

I have known him for three years and watched him develop into one of the most well-rounded students I have seen in my ten years at the university. He has performed very well in the classroom and his transcript speaks for itself. Not only has he been a good student, but his papers also show real academic potential. After teaching him in four courses over a period of three years, I have seen noticeable development in both his writing and critical thinking skills. Minsu has also played on the university baseball team and has gone from being a third to a first string player. Both inside the classroom and on the playing field, he has shown persistence, adaptability and self-improvement.

Minsu has served as an outstanding leader for both his class and his school. Traditionally, the class representative acts as mediator between the departmental students and faculties. He has consistently shown a strong sense of responsibility in performing his duties as class representative. He has empowered the office of class representatives by convincing the university administration to upgrade the status of the office of class representatives from having only very localized responsibilities to gaining a seat in the student government. As a result, the structure of the student goverment changed dynamically because the majority of power, typically held by supporters of the student body president, was weakened. The student government has never been the same.

Minsu is an outstanding/exceptional student who has excelled academically, and he is certain to be a valuable asset to his future employer. He is responsible and assertive. He is a team player and a leader. He is both ready to work and prepared to adapt himself to his changing surroundings. It is my hope that you give Minsu Kim the opportunity to prove himself at your company as he has here at Korea University.

Very truly yours,

Kildong Hong, Ph.D.
Professor of Business Administration
Korea University

23. Michigan State University 입학허가통지

MICHIGAN STATE
UNIVERSITY

Dear Jaehyun,

We are pleased to report you have been recommended for admission to Michigan State University. However, before we can send the I-20 and letter of admission, appropriate financial proof and English language proficiency information must be submitted. Following is a list of documents or information that must be received by this office. If you have already forwarded the information or documentation requested, please disregard this notice. A Personal Identification Number(PID) is printed below your address. Please include this number when corresponding with us. PLEASE NOTE: Official translation must be furnished when records/transcripts are not in English.

ACTIVITIES - You must account for all periods of time indicated. For each time period, list the activity; for example, education, travel, homemaker, employment, unemployment, etc. Include the month, year, city and state for each activity. PLEASE BE SPECIFIC, your application WILL NOT BE COMPLETED until activites are received. Please use back of letter to list activities.

February 20×× to July 20××

Thank you,

Office of Admissions and Scholarships

24. 구직서신 Ⅰ(Effective Job Application Letter Ⅰ)

458-125, Donam-Dong,
Seongbuk-Gu, Seoul 136-060

July 10, 20××

Ms. Maria Williams
Human Resources Director
Collins & Aikman Corporation
127-19, Sogong-Dong
Chung-Gu, Seoul 100-070

Dear Ms. Williams :

I am applying for the position of Trade Manager which was advertised in June 28 issue of the the Korea Buyer's Guide. I have enclosed my resume, and I would like to schedule an interview. I will call you early next week.

I look forward to speaking with you soon.
Sincerely yours,
Kil-Soon Hong

Enclosure

25. 구직서신 Ⅱ(Effective Job Application Letter Ⅱ)

Soo Jung Lee
342, Shinlim-Dong, Kwanak-Gu
Seoul, Korea

August 15, 20××

Personnel Manager
Samsung Company
CPO Box 1343
Seoul, Korea

Dear Sir:

In response to your advertisement in the Korea Times, I am applying for the position of Trade Manager.

I believe I have the necessary qualifications, and I would like to be considered for this position. An examination of my personal history statement will show that I am well trained and have vast experience in international trade. In addition, my involvement in extracurricular activities has provided me with the skills required to work well with other people.

My proven academic performance in international trade will serve your company well. I would very much like the opportunity towork in your company and put my knowledge and training into practice.
Thank you for your time and consideration. Please call me at your earliest convenience to discuss the possibility of an interview.

Sincerely yours,
Soo Jung Lee

26. 상황별 속담연구

1. A bird in the hand is worth two in the bush.
   앞으로 더 많이 얻을 수 있으리란 기대감 때문에 현재 가지고 있는 것을 버리지 말라.
2. A friend in need is a friend indeed.
   어려울 때 친구가 진정한 친구이다.
3. A little learning is a dangerous thing.
   선무당이 사람 잡는다.
4. A picture is worth a thousand words.
   백문이 불여일견이다.
5. A leopard cannot change his spots.
   타고난 천성은 고칠 수 없다.
6. A problem shared is a problem halved.
   고민을 함께하면 문제는 반으로 줄어든다.
7. A stitch in time saves nine.
   때를 놓치지 않고 신속하게 행동해야 생길 수 있는 문제를 예방할 수 있다.
8. Actions speak louder than words.
   말보다는 행동이 중요하다.
9. After death, call the doctor.
   소 잃고 외양간 고치기
10. All that glitters is not gold.
    사람이나 사물을 겉모양만 보고 판단해서는 안 된다.
11. As you sow, so shall you reap.
    콩 심은 데 콩 나고 팥 심은 데 팥 난다.
12. Beauty is in the eye of the beholder.
    아름다움은 보는 이의 눈에 달려 있다.
13. Better late than never.
    늦어도 안 하는 것보다는 낫다.
14. Blood is thicker than water.

피는 물보다 진하다.

15. By other's faults wise men correct their own.
    타산지석
16. Do unto others as you would have them do unto you.
    남에게 받고 싶은 대로 남에게 해주어라.
17. Don't count your chickens before they are hatched.
    떡 줄 사람은 꿈도 안 꾸는데 김칫국부터 마신다.
18. Don't cry before you are hurt.
    일이 일어나기도 전에 미리 걱정하지 말라.
19. Don't put all your eggs in one basket.
    한 가지 일에 모든 것을 걸지 마라.
20. Easier said than done.
    말하기는 쉬워도 실천하기는 어렵다.
21. Every dog has his day.
    쥐구멍에도 볕들 날이 있다.
22. Every man knows his own business best.
    자기의 일은 자신이 가장 잘 안다.
23. Everybody's business is nobody's business.
    모두의 일은 어느 누구의 일도 아니다.
24. Hunger is the best sauce.
    시장이 최고의 반찬이다.
25. Ignorance is bliss.
    모르는 게 약이다.
26. It never rains but it pours.
    불행한 일은 겹치기 마련이다.
27. It's the nature of water to run downhill.
    물은 아래로 흐르는 것이 순리이다.
28. Like father, like son.
    부전자전
29. Look before you leap.
    신중하게 행동하라.

30. Many drops make a shower.
    작은 물방울이 소낙비를 이룬다.
    =Water will wear away stone.
31. More haste, less speed.
    급할수록 천천히
32. No news is good news.
    무소식이 희소식이다.
33. No pain, no gain.
    고통 없이는 얻는 것도 없다.
34. One cannot have one's cake and eat it too.
    양쪽 다 좋게 할 수는 없다.
35. One man's music is another man's noise.
    한 사람에게는 음악인 것이 다른 사람에게는 소음일 수 있다.
36. One swallow doesn't make a summer.
    한 가지 징조를 보고 너무 성급히 결론을 내리지 말라.
37. Out of sight, out of mind.
    눈에서 멀어지면, 마음도 멀어진다.
38. Practice makes perfect.
    연습이 완벽하게 만들어 준다.
39. Rome was not built in a day.
    로마는 하루 아침에 이루어지지 않았다.
40. Slow and steady wins the race.
    천천히 그리고 꾸준히 달리는 자가 경주에 이긴다.
41. Still waters run deep.
    생각이 깊은 사람은 조용하다.
42. Strike while the iron is hot.
    쇠가 뜨거울 때 쳐라.
    =Make hay while the sun shines.
    기회를 놓치지 마라.
43. The grass is always greener on the other side.
    남의 떡이 더 커 보인다.

Useful Sentences(기타 관계통신문)

1. I would like to apply for the position of Translator/Interpreter at your company, as advertised in yesterday's "Korea Herald".
어제 코리아헤럴드에 광고된 귀사 번역 및 통역요원직에 응시하고자 합니다.
2. If you feel that my qualifications meet your requirements, please feel free to contact me in regards to an interview. I enclose a stamped, addressed envelope for your reply.
본인의 자격이 귀사의 요구조건과 일치한다고 생각되면 면접에 임하겠습니다. 우표를 붙인 회신용 봉투를 동봉합니다.
3. I regret to inform you that the vacancy has been filled.
공석이 충원됐음을 귀하에게 알리게 되어 유감으로 생각합니다.
4. In an effort to always provide the best possible service for all our customers, we have reorganized our export department into the following two departments.
당사 고객에게 최상의 서비스를 제공하기 위해서 당사에서는 수출부를 하기 2개 부서로 개편하였습니다.
5. We take pleasure in informing you that the following personnel changes have been made in our general merchandise department effective from February 3, 20××.
20××년 2월 3일자로 당사 일반 상품부에 대한 인사이동을 아래와 같이 단행하였음을 통지하여 드립니다.
6. We are pleased to enclose a copy of our revised price list which we trust you will find informative and useful.
당사는 귀사가 유익하게 사용할 개정가격표 1부를 동봉합니다.
7. We are pleased to announce that we have installed two new copy machines in addition to the copiers now in operation. The new copiers are available from today, March 1, 20××.
당사에서는 현재 사용중인 복사기 외에 신규 복사기 2대를 설치했음을 알립니다. 신규복사기는 20××년 3월 1일, 금일부터 이용가능합니다.

8. I would like to convey to you my sincere congratulations on your new appointment as president of ABC Trading Company.
   귀하가 ABC 무역회사의 사장으로 임명된 것을 진심으로 축하합니다.
9. The main products we are handling are textile, sundry goods and sweaters.
   당사의 주요 취급품은 스웨터, 잡화, 섬유류입니다.
10. We are pleased to inform you that the following two firms have agreed to merge under the new name of New World Trading Co. Ltd.
   하기 두 회사가 신세계 무역회사라는 새로운 회사명으로 합병하는 데 동의하였음을 알려드립니다.

Maxim

The purposes of a man's heart are deep waters, but a man of understanding draws them out.

사람 마음속의 계획은 깊은 물과 같지만 통찰력을 가진 사람은 그것을 길어낸다.

Chapter 02

FAX Communication and e-Mail

제1절 FAX Communication

FAX란 일반전화 회선을 이용하여 모사전송기(Facsimile Machine)를 통해 국내 및 국제 간에 송 · 수신하는 전보를 말한다.

FAX는 Facsimile의 약칭으로서 불어 Facere(make, do)와 Similis(similar, like)의 합성어로 "make similar", "an exact copy or reproduction"의 뜻의 명사뿐만 아니라 동사(to fax someone)로도 사용된다.

FAX는 현대 통신혁명의 총아로서 이용이 날로 증가되어 이제는 마치 전화만큼이나 유용한 통신수단이다.

FAX는 Telex와 달리 문자, 숫자, 기호, 부호는 말할 것도 없고 설계, 도안, 사진, 도표, 수출입 면장이나 그 밖의 어떠한 형태의 문서까지 원형 그대로 일반전화 회선을 이용하여 거리에 관계없이 팩시밀리가 설치된 곳이면 신속한 전송이 가능하다.

1. FAX의 작성요령

FAX의 작성요령은 Letter의 경우와 다를 바 없으며, 구성 및 배열에 있어서도 근본적으로 동일하다.

다만, 격식을 중시하는 공공기관이나 일부 회사의 경우 Letter를 FAX 송부하기 위하여 Cover Letter를 의미하는 "Lead Sheet"를 별도로 덧붙이는 경우도 있으나, 대부분의 경우 Letter의 형식을 일부 변형하여 FAX 발송서식을 자체적으로 디자인하여 동 서식을 "Lead Sheet" 없이 직접 사용하기도 한다.

Guidelines

- All faxes should have a cover sheet.
- Focus on the four principles "FCCC."
- F=Fast C=Correct C=Clear C=Concise

2. FAX Message의 구성요소

(1) FAX의 기본요소(Basic Parts)

FAX COMMUNICATION
Korea Good Friends Co., Ltd. ①

12, Pirun-Dong, Jongno-Gu, Tel: 02-3990-775 * * * * ③
Seoul, Korea ② Fax: 02-3990-737 * * * * ④

Date : ____________ ⑤

To :______________ ⑥ Attn. : ______________ ⑦

Fax No.

From : __________ ⑧

No. of pages including this one : __________ ⑨

Message : ⑩

① 송신인 회사명
② 송신인 주소
③ 송신인 전화번호
④ 송신인 팩시밀리 번호
⑤ 송신년월일
⑥ 수신처 팩시밀리 번호

⑦ 수신인명과 그 회사명
⑧ 송신인명
⑨ 송신매수
예 Pages : This only (total 1 page)
Pages : This + 2 (total 3 pages)
Pages : Cover + 4 (total 5 pages)
Pages : 5 (total 5 pages)
⑩ 메시지

(2) FAX의 선택요소(Optional Parts)

1. Subject →
2. Confidential
   Yes ( ) No ( )
3. CC Notation →
4. Enclosures :
   Yes ( ) No ( )
5. Need Response
   Yes (Within __ Days) No( )
6. Reference
7. Checked by

1. 제목 2. 비밀사항 여부 3. 사본배부처 4. 동봉물
5. 회신의 필요 여부 6. 참조 7. 승인자명

3. FAX 송신표의 형태

(1) PR 형태의 송신표

Facsimile Cover Sheet

Please deliver the following pages to :

Name :____________________________

Firm :____________________________

Fax :____________________________

This information was sent by :

Name :

Date :

The number of pages transmitted(including this page):

____

Thank you.

If this transmission is unclear, please call or fax :

Tel : 02-3990-775

Fax: 02-3990-737

(2) 절약 형태의 송신표

Korea Trading Co., Ltd.
Seoul, Korea
Tel : 02-576-8022
Fax : 02-553-1234

FACSIMILE COMMUNICATION

To :	From :
Company/Firm :	Reference : [1]
Department/Location :	
Fax Number :	Date :

Number of pages (including this page) :

Message :

1) 관련[참고]사항(Our fax No. 786/Your letter of Feb.3 등)

(3) 효율 형태의 송신표

FAX COMMUNICATION
Korea Trading Co., Ltd

Tel. (02) 568-7788
123, Samsung-Dong, Kangnam-Gu   Fax. (02) 568-7860
Seoul, Korea
Date : ______/______/______
To : ________________   Copy :[1]________________
Fax No.
Attn :
From :
Enclosures : ☐ Yes ☐ No[2]
No. of pages including this one :
Message :

1) 관계자명(CC와 동일)
2) 메시지 이외의 문서 · 도면 유무

4. Fax 작성 시 주의사항

FAX 통신문의 문체는 보통 서신문을 그대로 사용하는 것이 원칙이다. 비즈니스 문서에서 약어를 사용할 경우 수신자가 쉽게 판독할 수 있는 공식약어나 축어를 활용하는 것이 중요하다.

약어표 (Abbreviation Table)

■ 일반공식약어

OJT : On the Job Training
NG : No Good
ZIP : Zone Improvement Program
POB : Post Office Box
SHEX : Sundays and Holidays are Excepted
E & OE : Errors and Omissions are Excepted
SWIFT : Society for Worldwide Interbank Financial Telecommunication
SPQR : Small Profit and Quick Returns
N.B. : Note Well(Latin어 Nota Bene)
LST : Local Standard Time
ETA : Estimated Time of Arrival
ETD : Estimated Time of Departure
RSVP : Please Reply(Repondez S'il Vous Plait)
C/O : Care of, Certificate of Origin
VIP : Very Important Person
DM : Direct Mail
IOU : I Owe You
T/D : Time Deposit
KBS : Korea Broadcasting System
IBRD : International Bank for Reconstruction and Development
GNP : Gross National Product
BOK : Bank of Korea
IMF : International Monetary Fund
WTO : World Trade Organization
CPA : Certified Public Accountant
AVP : Assistant Vice President
PN : Promissory Note
LIBOR : London Interbank Offered Rate
FCFS : First Come, First Served
OECD :Organization for Economic Cooperation and Development
B/O : By the Order of/Buyer's Option

P/O : Payment Order
FYI : For Your Information
BIS : Bank for International Settlement

■ 단위(Units)

Gr : Gram(그램)
kg : kilogram(킬로그램)
St : Set(조)
m : meter(미터)
m^2 : square meter(제곱미터)
m^3 : cubic meter(평방미터)
l : liter(리터)
Kl : Kilo-Liter(킬로미터)
Gt : Gross Tonnage for Vessel(총톤수)
Dt : Displacement Tonnage(배수톤수)
Mt : Metric Ton(메트릭톤)
Kw : Kilo-Watt(킬로왓트)
Dz : Dozen(타)
Gs : Gross(그로스)
Pr : Pair(쌍, 켤레, 족)
kg(Ms) : Kilogram(Including Containers)〔킬로그램(금속함유량)〕
kg(Ic) : Kilogram(Including Containers)〔킬로그램(용기포함)〕
kg(St) Kilogram(Set)〔킬로그램(조)〕
Gr(Ic) : Gram(Including Container)〔킬로그램(용기포함)〕
Sh : Sheet(매, 장)
Cc : Cubic Centimeter(입방센티미터)
kg(DW) : Kilogram(By Dry Weight)킬로그램(건조중량)
CR : Carat(캐럿)
MW : Mega Watt(메가왓트)
u piece/item(개, 본, 매, 두, 필, 대, 량, 기, 척, 착)
TU Thousand Unit(천본, 천매)

■ 숫자 사용원칙

※ If the amount is under one million

–use figures

–1,650

–$160,000

※ If the amount is over one million

–use a combination of figures and words

–$16 million

–6.5 billion

Number Review

1,000,000	1 million
10,000,000	10 million
100,000,000	100 million
1,000,000,000	1 billion
10,000,000,000	10 billion
100,000,000,000	100 billion
1,000,000,000,000	1 trillion

■ FAX Etiquette

- Never read faxes meant for others. It is the same as opening their mail. Don't use the fax machine to send very long documents unless you've discussed it with the recipient. Call the recipient before you send a fax, especially if the recipient doesn't know you. Always include a cover page. Avoid sending unsolicited resumes by fax when job hunting.

제 2 절 e-Mail

'e-Mail' 은 Electronic mail의 약어로서 컴퓨터를 이용하여 Message를 주고 받는 국제 간 P/C 통신이다. e-Mail은 가장 최근에 도입된 통신수단의 하나로 비용이 상대적으로 저렴하며, 수신문서의 보관 및 검색이 용이할 뿐 아니라, 고유의 Password를 사용하여 비밀유지가 가능하다는 점 등 여러 가지 장점을 보유하고 있다.

현재 우리나라에 도입되어 있는 가장 대표적인 e-Mail 방식이 바로 SWIFT System인 바, SWIFT란 'Society for Worldwide Interbank Financial Telecommunication' 의 약자로 일부 사회주의 국가 및 미개국을 제외하고 전 세계 대부분의 국가은행에서 적용되고 있으며, 국제 간 송금거래, 국제대출거래, 추심거래와 신용장거래 등을 포함한 은행 간의 국제거래를 신속 정확하게 처리하여 주고 있다.

SWIFT는 전산조직을 이용한 EDI(Electronic Data Interchange)체계로 통신전문의 표준화, 발 · 수신의 자동화를 통하여 통신비용을 절감시키고 은행업무의 생산성을 높이는 데 기여하고 있을 뿐만 아니라 보안성 유지까지도 겸비하고 있다.

또한 SWIFT 활용의 범위를 확대하는 차원에서 범국가적인 사업인 KT Network 구축사업이 추진되고 있는 바, 이의 기반이 되고 있는 EDIFACT도 e-Mail의 산업 간, 국제 간 통합이용의 한 범주에 속한다.

EDIFACT란 Electronic Data Interchange for Administration, Commerce and Transport의 약어로 행정, 상업 및 운송분야의 표준화된 기업 간 거래서식 또는 기업, 은행, 행정기관의 공공서식을 상호 간에 합의한 통신표준에 따라 컴퓨터와 컴퓨터 간에 교환하는 전자교환시스템을 뜻하며, 이에 포함되는 공공서식이라 함은 E/L, L/L 등의 무역 서류, B/L 등 운송관계 서류, 면장 등 세관관계 서류 및 보험관계 서류를 말한다.

1. What is e-Mail?

- e-Mail : A facility to allow you to electronically correspond with one person, or a mailing list comprised of many people. e-Mail accounts must be established for both the sender and receiver for e-mail to work.
- e-Mail, short for electronic mail, is a system in which a computer user can exchange messages with other computer users using a communications network. To use e-Mail you must have access to a computer that is linked to the outside world via a modem, phone line, or fiber optic cable(ethernet).

2. Some e-Mail Ground Rules to Live by

- As in all written communications, it is essential to use proper grammar, punctuation, spelling, and sentence structure.
- Try to avoid flamming.
- Be unambiguous.
- Write clearly and carefully.
- Avoid cluttering your messages with excessive emphasis.

Humor Parade

Conversation overheard in a college sorority house :

Visitor : "I've got a friend I' d like you girls to meet…."

Freshman : "Is he cute?"

Sophomore : "Can he dance?"

Junior : "Does he drink?"

Senior : "Where is he?"

어느 대학 여학생기숙사에서 엿들은 대화 한 토막 :

방문객 : 여학생 여러분에게 소개하고 싶은 친구가 있는데…

1학년 : 그 사람 잘 생겼어요?

2학년 : 그 사람 춤출 줄 알아요?

3학년 : 그 사람 술 마셔요?

4학년 : 그 사람 어디 있어요?

△ sorority house : 여학생 기숙사, △ freshman : 1학년, △ sophomore : 2학년, △ junior : 3학년, △ senior : 4학년

Appendix
부 록

I
1. 대한상공회의소 시행 무역영어 국가검정시험 세부내용
2. 국제무역사시험 시행요강
3. 대한상공회의소 국가공인자격 검정시험 기출문제
   - 무역영어 제1회 1·2급 기출문제

II INCOTERMS 2010의 개관

III Western Business Idioms

IV Enrich Your Word Power

V 무역용어 약어표

[부록 I]

1. 대한상공회의소 시행 무역영어 국가검정시험 세부내용

■ 무역영어 국가검정시험 시행안내

<table>
<tr><th>등급</th><th colspan="2">시행과목</th><th>배점</th><th>제한
시간</th><th>문항수</th><th>수준</th><th>합격기준</th></tr>
<tr><td rowspan="3">1급</td><td>1과목</td><td>영문해석</td><td>100</td><td rowspan="3">90분</td><td rowspan="3">과목별
객관식
25문항</td><td rowspan="3">4년제 대학 경상계열 졸업자와 대기업의 무역실무 관리책임자로서 갖추어야 할 무역실무 전반에 관한 지식</td><td rowspan="9">매과목 100점 만점에 전과목 평균 60점 이상 (단, 1급은 과목당 40점 미만인 경우 불합격)</td></tr>
<tr><td>2과목</td><td>영작문</td><td>100</td></tr>
<tr><td>3과목</td><td>무역실무</td><td>100</td></tr>
<tr><td rowspan="3">2급</td><td>1과목</td><td>영문해석</td><td>100</td><td rowspan="3">90분</td><td rowspan="3">과목별
객관식
25문항</td><td rowspan="3">전문대학 및 4년제 대학교 경상계열 재학생과 기업의 무역실무자로서 갖추어야 할 지식</td></tr>
<tr><td>2과목</td><td>영작문</td><td>100</td></tr>
<tr><td>3과목</td><td>무역실무</td><td>100</td></tr>
<tr><td rowspan="3">3급</td><td>1과목</td><td>영문해석</td><td>100</td><td rowspan="3">90분</td><td rowspan="3">과목별
객관식
25문항</td><td rowspan="3">실업계열 고등학교 재학생 및 졸업자로서 기본적으로 갖추어야 할 지식</td></tr>
<tr><td>2과목</td><td>영작문</td><td>100</td></tr>
<tr><td>3과목</td><td>무역실무</td><td>100</td></tr>
</table>

■ 무역영어 검정시험 출제기준

1·2급	3급
1. 무역실무 전반에 걸친 무역통신문	1. 무역통신문의 구성 및 형식
2. 해외시장조사, 신용조사방법, 수출입 개요 등	2. 거래관계의 개설(신용조회 및 보고, 거래제의)
3. 무역관계법(실무에 적용되는 것에 한함)	3. 거래관계의 성립(청약, 주문, 계약)
4. 무역계약	4. 신용장(발행신청, 통지 및 수정)
5. 대금결제	5. 선적과 운송서류(선적보험, 운송서류, 보험)
6. 운송, 용선계약, 적화보험	6. 기본 무역영어
7. 무역클레임과 상사중재	7. 상용회화
8. EDI에 의한 수출입 통관	

※ 1·2급의 문제출제는 상기 범위 내에서 난이도로 조정하여 출제

2. 국제무역사시험 시행요강

■ 시험과목

① 제1교시 : 90분

시험과목	세부교과목	문항수
무역규범(40)	대외무역법 · 통상통관/환급, FTA 및 전자무역	객관식 80문항 (4지선다형)
무역결제(40)	대금결제 및 외환실무	

② 제2교시 : 90분

시험과목	세부교과목	문항수
무역계약(40)	무역계약 및 운송	객관식 80문항 (4지선다형)
무역영어(40)	무역영어 및 무역관련규칙	

■ 합격기준(Passing criteria)

전체 평균 60점 이상(단, 40점 미만 득점과목이 있을 경우 불합격)

■ 응시대상(Applying requirement)

무역업체 임직원, 대학생, 일반희망자 등(학력 및 경력 제한 없음)

■ 원서교부 및 접수(Acceptance)

무역아카데미 홈페이지를 통한 인터넷 접수

3. 대한상공회의소 국가공인자격 검정시험 기출문제

• 무역영어검정시험 기출문제(1회) : 1 · 2급

무역영어 제1회 1급 기출문제

※ 다음 문제를 읽고 가장 알맞은 것을 고르시오.

〈제1과목〉 영문해석

[문 1~2] Read the following letter and answer the question.

DREAMROAD MASTER INC.
4400 South Hose Avenue, Milwaukee 15321

Date: September 25, 20××
Our Contract No. 323
Your order No. 5386

DREAMROAD MASTER INC. as Seller hereby confirms having this day sold to you as Buyer the following goods on terms and conditions below:

Description	Qty	Unit Price	Amount	Total Amount
SLH-76BH SLH-77BH	12-PCS 05-PCS	@USD 890.00	USD 10680 USD 4900	USD 15580

DELIVERY TERM : C.I.F. Incheon
SHIPMENT : End of November
PORTS OF SHIPMENT : Seattle
PAYMENT : Drafts to be drawn at 30 days after sight under an irrevocable letter of credit

Please refer to General Terms and Conditions on the reverse side hereof which are also integral parts of the contract.
Accepted and confirmed by Kims Trading Co. Ltd.

DREAMROAD MASTER INC.

1. Which of the following is CORRECT according to the letter above?
   ① Kims Trading Co. Ltd. will pay the bill at the end of November.
   ② Dreamroad Master Inc. will deliver the goods on FOB base.
   ③ The seller's goods will be ported at Incheon.
   ④ The total sum is USD 15580.

2. What is the main purpose of the letter above?
   ① Sales Contract
   ② Memorandum of Understanding
   ③ Purchase Order
   ④ Agreement on General Terms

3. What is the main purpose of the letter below?

> Thank you for your order, No. F-8601, which we received yesterday. Unfortunately, we cannot offer the 30% trade discount you requested. 20% is our maximum discount, even on large orders, as our prices are extremely competitive. Therefore, in this instance, I regret that we will have to turn down your order.

① Decline of order ② Request for discount
③ Request for large order ④ Reply to complaint

4. The following is a letter from an exporter to an importer. Which of the following is true?

> We want to thank you for your order of May 24 for our digital camera, Model K-10. However, we regret to inform you that we are unable to fulfill your order for the time being.
>
> Currently, we have no stock available for the items requested and cannot say with certainty as to when we are able to make a delivery
>
> However, we can offer to you our new model K-11, which is far superior to Model K-10 in quality and performance. The price of Model K-11 is only slightly higher at USD135.50. At present it is the best-selling model in our domestic market.
>
> If you feel that the new model is a little expensive, we would like to recommend our model K-9, which is similar to Model K-10 in features, performance, and overall quality, but at a much lower price of USD105.00.
>
> We await any further requests you may have.

① The importer has ordered digital cameras, Model K–10, and the exporter will be able to make a delivery after a short while.

② The price of Model K–11 is higher than Model K–10 by USD135.00, and that of Model K–10 is lower than Model K–9 by USD105.00.

③ The exporter recommends the two models of digital camera; one is more expensive than what the importer wants to buy and the other one may be less expensive.

④ Both Model K–9 and K–11 are the best selling models in the domestic market because of their quality and performance.

5. Which of the following fits LEAST in the letter below?

> We deeply regret to learn from your letter on July 10 that you are not satisfied with the goods which we shipped on June 15 for your order No. 123.
>
> (A) We are very sorry to hear that you are experiencing a problem with our dress materials. Please understand that this is a very unusual case for us, so we are very concerned about any inconvenience we may have caused you.
>
> (B) Upon receipt of your letter, we contacted the manufacturers to check into the matter and asked our shipping department to trace this matter throughly.
>
> (C) As the matter is under investigation now, we are not yet able to make our position clear. As soon as the cause of the problem is determined, we will contact you again and discuss how this problem can be solved. Of course, we are ready to take responsibility if we are found to be at fault.
>
> (D) We feel urged to search for an alternative solution even though we both may suffer some loss. Therefore, we will take your goods at a reasonable discount if you would prefer to do so. In the meantime, we would like to ask you to send us by

> airmail a few samples of the goods, at our expense, for our inspector to examine.

① (A) ② (B)
③ (C) ④ (D)

6. Which of the following puts the paragraphs in the box below in the correct order?

> (A) We like the quality of your products and also the manner in which you handled our inquiry and would very much welcome the opportunity to do business with you. We would be pleased to place an order with you if you could reduce the price by 10% to USD19.95 per piece. We will place our first order with you as soon as we receive a reply granting the discount.
>
> (B) Although we feel your products have some advantage with respect to quality, the prices you quote simply leave us with no margin. We are sure that we will not be able to successfully market your products at such a high price because the primary demand here is for products in the mid-price range.
>
> (C) We would like to thank you for your offer of the 15th of June for women's jackets.
>
> (D) We consider your offer to be quite acceptable to us in general. However, we regret to inform you that the prices you quoted are far higher than we expected.

① (C) – (D) – (B) – (A) ② (A) – (B) – (C) – (D)
③ (B) – (C) – (A) – (D) ④ (D) – (C) – (B) – (A)

7. Which of the following can be inferred from the letter below?

> Thank you for your letter of 4 May in which you offered us a whole agency for products in Indonesia. First, let me say that we can handle an agency of the type you describe, and we agree that the demand for good quality textile is increasing here. However, before we proceed with your offer any further, we need the following information.

① The sender may have additional buyers in Indonesia after the agency contract is made.
② The two parties are interested in franchising.
③ The receiver wants to get some more information about the agency in Indonesia.
④ The sender is willing to sign the agency contract provided that some terms and conditions are cleared.

8. Which of the following is correct according to the letter?

> We refer to your offer for USD2million CIF 2,000 (two thousand) XG 3001 computers in your Catalogue No. 2011. We are interested in goods at this moment.
> Would you please send us a few samples for our further consideration? We may then put a purchase order in due course.

① Buyer wants to see seller's catalogue.
② Buyer is not satisfied with the price terms.
③ Seller wants the buyer to arrange the vessel for ocean shipment.
④ Seller shall insure at his expense the goods when the deal is done.

9. Which of the following is correct regarding the documents presented as follows?

A credit is issued for USD100,000 covering a shipment of mobile phones not allowing partial shipments. Prior to the presentation of documents, an amendment is received reducing the amount of the credit to USD50,000. The beneficiary, however, presents documents in the amount of USD100,000 without notice of refusal to the advising bank.

① The beneficiary appears to accept the amendment as he failed to notice refusal of amendment.
② The beneficiary has not accepted the amendment.
③ The beneficiary would not receive payment from the issuing bank.
④ The beneficiary should notice its refusal to the applicant.

10. Which of the following is correct about the buyer's claim, according to CISG?

Seller delivered an offer to Buyer on 1 July, which read:
"I will hold this offer open until 30 September" To this offer, Buyer delivered the following to the Seller on 15 July: "I do not accept your offer because the price is too high," but on 10 August the Buyer delivered the following to Seller: "I hereby accept your prior offer of 1 July." Seller immediately responded that he could not treat this "acceptance" because of earlier rejection. Buyer reminded Seller that the offer was valid until 30 September.

① Buyer is not in a position to insist upon his second acceptance.
② Seller shall agree to the buyer's second acceptance.
③ Seller shall amend his offer.
④ Buyer can withdraw his first acceptance.

11. Which of the following are the correct titles for (A), (B), (C), and (D)?

(A) If a credit indicates that a documents is to be issued by a named person or entity, this condition is satisfied. It may appear to be issued by a named person or entity using its letterhead, or, if there is no letterhead, the document appears to have been completed and/or signed by, or on behalf of, the named person or entity.
(B) Detailed mathematical calculations in documents will not be checked by banks. Banks are only obliged to check total values against the credit and other required documents.
(C) Under international standard banking practice, it is expected that documents issued by the beneficiary will be in the language of the credit. When a credit states that documents in two or more languages are acceptable, a nominated bank may, in its advice of the credit, limit the number of acceptable languages as a condition of its engagement in the credit or confirmation.
(D) Documents presented under a credit must not appear to be inconsistent with each other.

① (A) Inconsistency in the documents
(B) Language
(C) Issuer of documents
(D) Mathematical calculations
② (A) Inconsistency in the documents
(B) Issuer of documents
(C) Mathematical calculations
(D) Language
③ (A) Mathematical calculations
(B) Inconsistency in the documents
(C) Language

(D) Issuer of documents

④ (A) Issuer of documents

(B) Mathematical calculations

(C) Language

(D) Inconsistency in the documents

12. A credit requires presentation of an Insurance Certificate. Which of the following insurance documents would be acceptable for a CIF shipment where the invoice value is USD125,000?

> A. Insurance certificate for USD137,500
> B. Insurance policy for USD140,000
> C. Insurance declaration under open cover for USD137,500
> D. Insurance certificate for USD125,000

① A ② A+B

③ A+B+C ④ A+B+C+D

13. According to the flow of the letter below, where is the MOST appropriate place for the sentence below?

> Please issue a new policy on the same terms with the current policy for the same amount of USD75,000.
>
> ---
>
> (A) We enclose a complicated form declaring a further consignment, valued USD2,325. (B) This will be the last full declaration under the above policy as the undeclared balance now stands at only USD825, which will not be sufficient to cover our new consignment in December. (C) When we make the next shipment, we shall declare it against the present policy for USD825 and against the new policy for the amount by which the value of the shipment exceeds this amount. (D)

① (A) ② (B)
③ (C) ④ (D)

14. Please put the following sentences in order.

(A) The offer we made is virtually a rock–bottom one sacrificing our own margin, so we are convinced that you will be able to carry out a most profitable business at this time.
(B) We have received your letter of May 23, confirming your acceptance on the phone for Silk Scarfs.
(C) Shipment will be effected during July, of course. We have enclosed our Sales Note No. 58 and also copies of cables exchanged between us.
(D) Immediately upon receipt of your letter of credit for the above, we will make every arrangement necessary to clear the goods by the first available vessel to New Orleans.

We thank you again for this initial order and wish to assure you that your order will receive our best attention.

① B–A–D–C ② A–B–D–C
③ C–D–A–B ④ D–A–C–B

15. Which of the following does NOT fit with the others in the letter below?

(A) As we have done business with your company for the past 18 months on the basis of payment on invoice, we would now like to request that you grant us open credit terms with monthly settlement.
(B) For more information concerning our company's promptness in paying invoices, we refer you to the following credit

references:

Nathan Kane Export Company, 867 Oxford Street, Nashville, TN

Samsom, Inc. 91 North 34 Ave., Palo Villas, CA

If you require additional information, we will be glad to supply it.

(C) For that reason, I would like to request your permission to propose your name for membership at the Centreville Polo Club at the next bimonthly meeting scheduled for Monday, October 4.

(D) You may check our credit rating with Mr. Howard Williams, Branch Manager of the Bank of America, 532 Orchard Street, IN.

① (A) ② (B)

③ (C) ④ (D)

16. Please put the following sentences in order.

(A) However, the delivery consisted of men' s coats instead of the women' s coats I asked for.

(B) As I have firm orders for the design I asked for, I would be grateful if you could send the correct consignment to me.

(C) I received a consignment of winter coats, Cat. No. 2206, to the above order yesterday.

(D) Also, please collect the wrongly delivered goods as soon as possible. Thank you in advance.

① B–A–C–D ② B–D–A–C

③ C–A–B–D ④ C–B–D–A

17. Which of the following is true according to the letter below?

> We received with thanks your letter of credit No. AT-8938 covering your order No. 2467 for multimedia speakers.
> However, we found it stipulated that transshipment is prohibited. Since no direct vessel to Sydney is available from here, transshipment at Kobe is unavoidable.
> We therefore request that transshipment be allowed and that an amendment notice for the letter of credit replacing the clause, "transshipment is prohibited" with the clause, "transshipment is allowed" be sent to us.
> Please note that the amendment notice should reach us by the end of this month at the latest in order for the shipment to be made on time.
> Your prompt attention to this matter will be much appreciated.

① According to the above letter, the importer has ordered a variety of computer accessories.

② The receiver of the above mail will find out that transshipment is allowed as transshipment is necessary at any port city en route to the final destination, Sydney.

③ The sender of the above mail is requesting that transshipment be allowed and that the letter of credit be amended so that the delivery will be able to proceed.

④ The amendment notice needs to be completed within one month and to be delivered to the importer soon after the amendment. Then the shipment will be on time.

18. The passage below is a reply to a letter. Which of the following is MOST likely to be found in the previous letter?

> Thank you for your inquiry regarding your consignment to Seoul. All our charges including freight, airway bill fee, insurance and our own commission are shown on the attached schedule.
> To enable us to prepare your airway bill we shall need the information requested in the enclosed form. Three copies of a certified commercial invoice and a certificate of origin will also be necessary.
> Your consignment should be in our hands by 10 am on the morning of departure. Please telephone me when you are ready to deliver the consignment to our officer at the airport so that we can prepare to receive and deal with it promptly. Alternatively, we can also make arrangements to collect the goods.

① We have been informed that the consignment of electronic shavers has arrived to our customer in Seoul without any damage. Thank you for treating our goods carefully.

② Shortly, we shall have a consignment of electric shavers, weighing about 50 kg, for a customer in Tokyo. We wish to send this by ship from LA.

③ The consignment will be handled on arrival by United Air Services who will make all the arrangements for delivery. The bill of lading, invoice, and our account for commission and charges are enclosed.

④ Please send us details of the cost and any formalities to be observed. The invoice value of the consignment is USD15,000 and we require insurance to cover this amount plus the costs of sending the consignment.

[문 19~20] Read the following model contract and answer the questions.

9.1 Upon the Effective Date and subject to the payment by the Franchisee of the Initial Fee, the Franchisor shall deliver to the Franchisee the start-up package, i.e., all relevant know-how, including written technical information financial data, the Manual and any other specifications specifically relating to the System and the Proprietary Rights and their utilization thereof which is available to the Franchiser as of the Effective Date.
Insofar as such know-how shall be delivered in a material form or recorded in a material form, such materials shall be provided to the Franchisee on loan only.

9.2 Any know-how not furnished under Article
9.1, such as general knowledge and experience, shall be conveyed by the Franchiser in the manner provided for in Articles 9.4, 9.8. and 15.1.

9.3 The Franchisee shall not have the right to file patent, copyright, design and/or trademark applications and/or to acquire any other intellectual property rights concerning such know-how, the Proprietary Rights and/or the System in any country of the world without the prior written consent of the Franchiser.

19. What is the main purpose of the model contract?

① To clarify the specifications of the know-how.

② To clarify the obligations of the Franchisee about the know-how.

③ To clarify the rights that the Franchisee shall acquire about the know-how.

④ To clarify the obligations of the Franchiser and the Franchisee about the know-how.

20. Which of the following is NOT true according to the above contract?

① The Franchiser shall provide the start-up package to the Franchisee who has paid the Initial Fee.

② The start-up package means all relevant know-how, including written technical information, financial data, the Manual and other specifications.

③ Insofar as the know-how shall be delivered in a material form, such materials shall be offered to the Franchisee with ownership rights.

④ Any know-how not under Article 9.1, such as general knowledge and experience, shall be conveyed by the Franchiser in the manner written in other Articles.

21. The passage in the box is a reply to a letter. Which of the following is correct about the previous letter?

> We are sending you a representative selection of our most popular lines. Your suggestion to make monthly payments is quite satisfactory, and we will allow you
> a commission at 10% calculated on gross profits.
> The goods are being shipped by Voyage II, leaving Indonesia for Korea on 10 April. We will send the bill of lading and other shipping documents as soon as we receive them.

① previous letter was to propose to send a trial delivery of the cutlery for sale on consignment terms.

② The previous letter was to confirm the trading conditions that both parties have agreed upon.

③ The previous letter was to negotiate the conditions about payments and sales commission.

④ The previous letter was to request information on the delivery schedule and the sending of some documents.

[문 22~23] Read the following letter and answer the questions.

> Thank you for your fax of 6 April informing us that the goods supplied to you were damaged. Since you may think that we should be responsible for the damage, we must clarify our position as follows:
>
> First, the goods were inspected throughly by us before packing and loaded onto the ship in perfect condition. The clean-on-board Bill of Lading shows that everything was in order at the time the goods were loaded onto the ship.
> Second, the packaging was in full compliance with the standards of packing for international ocean transportation and the specifications of the packaging were agreed upon by you in the contract.
> Third, since this transaction is based on FOB, we are free from liabilities for the shipment upon loading onto your designated vessel.
> It is likely that the damage of the goods was caused by rough handling during the voyage or when they were unloaded at your port. We would suggest that you file a claim with the insurance company or shipping company.
> If you need any assistance, we will be more than willing to cooperate with you in expediting the process of your claim.
>
> Yours sincerely,

22. Which of the following BEST describes the exporter's position?

① The exporter does not want to be involved in the problem at all since he does not have any responsibility for the problem.

② The exporter does not want to involve himself in the matter at all since he is sure that the responsibility is upon the shipping company.

③ The exporter intends to assist the importer in resolving the problem although the exporter is convinced that the cause of the damage is not upon him.

④ The exporter intends to assist the importer in resolving the problem since he feels responsible for the damage.

23. Which of the following is NOT true according to the passage above?

① The letter above is a response to the fax that the importer sent to the exporter about the damage of the shipment.

② The goods were examined completely before packing and were moved to the ship without any damage.

③ The bill of lading indicates that all of the goods were shipped onto the designated vessel.

④ The packaging complied with strict domestic standards, and the specifications of the packaging were based on the contract.

24. Which of the following can be taken as the date of shipment?

A presentation is made under a credit that prohibits partial shipment. Bill of Lading presented represents: bills of lading dated 10 July, 11 July, and 12 July covering the full shipment of goods on the same vessel and voyage.

① 10 July ② 11 July

③ 12 July ④ any of those 3 days

25. The following are excerpts from a model of a TECHNICAL LICENSE AGREEMENT. Which of the following is true?

> 1. Licensor hereby grants to Licensee, upon the terms and conditions hereinafter specified, an exclusive and non-assignable license to use the Licensed Trademarks during such time as this Agreement subsists in such manner as not to deceive the public, on and in connection with the Licensed Products. Licensor will not grant a License to use the Licensed Trademarks in the Contract Territory to any other third party in Korea during the term of this Agreement.
> 2. Licensee shall be entitled to use Licensed Trademarks on Licensee's letterhead, invoices and all advertising and promotional materials in such form and in such manner as shall be approved at the first consulting in writing with the Licensor.
> 3. Each Licensed Trademark shall be used only after it has been duly registered with the Patent Office, and after this Agreement has also been duly registered with the Patent Office.
> 4. This License to use the Licensed Trademark is provided on a royalty free basis and Licensee shall have the right to use combined trademark on the Licensed products.

① During the Agreement term, Licensor can grant a License to any other third party in Korea.

② Licensee shall have the right to use Licensed Trademarks on Licensee's materials as agreed upon in writing with the Licensor, provided that the trademark is registered.

③ Right after the agreement with the Licensor, Licensee shall use each Licensed Trademark.

④ Licensee shall have the right to use combined trademark on Licensed products with royalties paid.

〈제2과목〉 영작문

26. Which of the following is most appropriate to appear right after the passage in the box?

> On 30 April I ordered 100 barbecue grills to be delivered at the end of May. Persistent bad weather has seriously affected sales so I find that my present stock will probably satisfy demand in the present season. I am therefore writing to ask you to cancel part of my order and to deliver only 50 of these grills instead of the 100 ordered.

① We are sorry you find it necessary to make this request.
② I hope you will understand why we must hold you to your order.
③ We are naturally disappointed that there should be any need for this request
④ I am sorry to make this request so late, but hope that you will be able to agree.

27. Which of the following is the best place for the sentence below to be placed?

> As instructed, we have drawn upon you for the net amount of USD 5000 at sight through the Korea Exchange Bank.
>
> March 10, 20××
>
> (A) We have the pleasure to enclose the invoice and B/L for 400 cases of SUNNYSIDE Goods Shipped by S.S. "ChungAhHo", in execution of your order of 25th February.
>
> (B) We trust the goods will reach you in due course and give you entire satisfaction.
>
> (C) We would ask you to give our draft your kind protection as usual. We trust this purchase will bring you a good profit, and

result in further orders. (D)

① (A) ② (B)

③ (C) ④ (D)

28. Which of the following is INCORRECTLY modified from the underlined parts in the box below?

You will see from the attached accounts that turnover in the past nine months of trading has been disappointing. There are a couple of reasons for this:

1. **Advertising**: Our agreed advertising budget of10,000 is not enough to promote your products, even though we use only newspapers and magazines.
(A) It would be useful to double this budget with a view to extending advertising into neighbouring countries, where there are good opportunities to become established.
(B) You will see from the attachment concerning the market research I have done through questionaries to retailers, that there is a positive response in Jordan, Kuwait, and the Emirates.

2. **Competition**:
a. As I am sure you are aware, your main competition is from manufacturers in the Far East, who undercut your prices by at least 40%.
(C) While they do not sell the same quality products, a number of large companies are becoming established here and are likely to start targeting the upper end of the market with better quality goods. I am monitoring the situation and will

let you know of any developments.

b. (D) Some competitors copy designs, so it is important for us to get your new designs as quickly as possible and put them on the market first.

① (A) Doubling this budget would be useful, given a view to extending advertising into neighbouring countries in which there are good opportunities to become established.

② (B) You will see from the attachment about the market research conducted through questionaries to retailers, which there is a positive response in Jordan, Kuwait, and the Emirates.

③ (C) Although they do not sell the same quality products, quite a few large companies are becoming established here and seem to start targeting the upper end of the market with better quality goods.

④ (D) Since some competitors copy designs, it is pivotal for us to get your new designs promptly and put them on the market first.

29. Which of the following is MOST likely to appear right BEFORE the passage in the box?

In response to your inquiry, we are pleased to send you an estimate as follows:

Item: Digital Camera System
Model: DCS-9
Quantity: 1
Price: US$2,000 CIF Brisbane

Please note that the above price is not a firm offer. The various functions of this model are explained in detail in the enclosed brochure. We are currently receiving a lot of orders from all over the world, and we hope you will place some orders. We look forward to hearing from you as soon as possible.

① Thank you very much for stopping by our booth at the IFI Exhibition in Hong Kong last month.
② Thank you for your letter of July 17, in which you expressed your willingness to open an account with us.
③ Please send me, if available, export guides for Australia and New Zealand. I would appreciate your placing me on the mailing list to receive them upon publication.
④ Thank you for your letter of September 12 expressing your interest in our digital camera system DCS-9.

30. Which of the following is MOST appropriately rewritten to have the same meaning?

① We should be grateful for your view about the firm's general standing and your opinion on whether they are likely to be reliable for credit up to two million dollars. Any information provided will of course be treated in strict confidence.
→ We ask your assessment on the company's status and your view regarding their capability to deal with a two million dollar credit. We will keep any information confidential.
② We understand their requirements with us may amount to approximately two million dollars a quarter, and should be glad to know whether you feel they will be able to meet commitments of this size. Any other information you can provide would be very welcome.
→ They may require us approximately two million dollars a quarter and should know they can meet such commitments. Any other information would be grateful.
③ Please let us have a report on the reputation and financial standing

of the company and in particular your advice on whether it would be advisable to grant credit for this first order. Your advice on the maximum amount for which it would be safe to grant credit on a quarterly account would also be appreciated.

→ We want to know whether the company is in a good reputation and is financially stable and whether it is wise to grant credit for the first order. We also wonder about the appropriate amount of granting on a yearly account.

④ We have been doing business with this company for over 7 years on quarterly-account terms. Although they have not usually taken advantage of cash discounts they have always paid their account promptly on the set dates. The credit we have allowed this company has at times been well over two million dollars.

→ Our business on a quarterly basis has been over 7 years. The company pays us with cash without any delay, and we grant over two million dollars in credit to the company.

31. Which of the following is most UNLIKELY to appear right before the passage below?

Since we have a very limited amount of time to ship the goods in May, we must urge our manufacturers to expedite an early delivery of the goods. However, we cannot proceed without receiving your L/C. It will be impossible for us to secure the goods on time if we do not receive the L/C by May 25. Therefore we need you to open your L/C immediately. When we receive it we will make the arrangements for your order as quickly as possible.

① We would like to bring to your attention the fact that we have not received the letter of credit covering your order.

② Although you placed an order with us for a printing machine with the special instruction of prompt shipment, your letter of credit has not yet reached us.

③ We would like to ask you to extend the validity and shipping dates of the credit N0. 300 to May 25 and confirm the changes to us by fax.

④ The letter of credit to cover our contract is not in our hands, although the shipment is to be made by the end of this month.

32. Which of the following best completes the dialogue below?

> Kim: What's the FOB price of the newest MP3 Player, the Palm-20G?
> Johnson: (A)__________ It will also be able to store 20 gigabytes worth of files.
> Kim: How about the previous model, the Palm-10G?
> Johnson: The Palm-10G costs $290.
> Kim: Really? Could you explain why the price gap between the two is so huge?
> Johnson: (B)__________
> Kim: I see. Can you offer a quantity discount if I order 10,000 units of the Palm-20G?
> Johnson: (C)__________

① (A) It's $390. It will come in black, white, and blue.
(B) The Palm-10G only stores 10 gigabytes with very few other functions.
(C) Yes, then you will get 10 dollars off per unit.

② (A) Yes, then you will get 10 dollars off per unit.
(B) The Palm-10G only stores 10 gigabytes with very few other functions.

(C) It' s $390. It will come in black White, and blue.

③ (A) Yes, then you will get 10 dollars off per unit.
(B) The Palm–10G only stores 10 gigabytes with many other functions.
(C) It' s $390. It will come in black, white, and blue.

④ (A) It' s $390. It will come in black, white, and blue.
(B) The Palm–10G only stores 10 gigabytes with many other functions.
(C) Yes, then you will get 10 dollars off per unit.

33. Which of the following best fits the blank in the box?

> This is to certify I, the undersigned, Sujin Han, President and Representative Director of Germs Cosmetics Co., Ltd. with its principal office at C.P.O. Box No. 772–1, Jongro–gu, Seoul, Korea, hereby authorize Mr. JunSung Park, Director of Germs Cosmetics Co., Ltd., whose signature is shown hereunder, as a true and lawful attorney of the company.
>
> Mr. JunSung Park is empowered to carry out all necessary procedures on my behalf concerning the attainment of approval from the Government of Poland and the signing of all required documents related to the establishment of Joint Venture Company of Cosmetics in Poland.
>
> __________
>
> Date : May 12, 20××
> Authorized Signature
>
> | | |
> |---|---|
> | Sujin Han | JunSung Park |
> | President and | Director |
> | Representative Director | |
> | Germs Cosmetics Co., Ltd. | Germs Cosmetics Co., Ltd. |

① This Power of Attorney shall be effective for a period of seven (7) days after my signature shown hereunder.
② This Letter of Guarantee will expire on July 1, 20××, and it will become of no effect whatsoever returned to us or not.
③ This letter shall be available by your sight draft on us accompanied by your signed statement certifying that Germs Cosmetics Co., Ltd. has been awarded to the tender.
④ This Letter of Credit shall be subject to the Uniform Customs and Practice for Documentary Credits.

34. Which of the following best fits the blank in the letter below?

> In reply to your fax message dated April 23, 20××, we have already submitted all related documents to the issuing bank, and have requested to open the L/C in your favor by today.
>
> The L/C will reach you within a couple of days through the BankOne Seoul branch.
>
> Please note that all terms and conditions of the L/C such as price, shipping date, packing method are exactly same as the "Sales and Purchase Contract No.6712" signed on February 28, 20×× between us.
>
> ______________

① Meanwhile, please let us know the shipping information as soon as shipment has been made.
② Otherwise, we may revise the price on the Contract due to the price increase of the raw materials.
③ We hope you will pay attention to this matter, and we look forward to receiving your prompt reply.

④ Regarding your order, we regret to inform you that we have not been informed of any Letter of Credit opening information from you.

35. Please fill in the blanks using the given information.

To : Daniels Co., Ltd. P/O No. : XYZ-101250

Date : Jan. 12, 20××

Gentlemen,

We are pleased to issue our purchase order for the following commodities in accordance with the terms and conditions given below.

Description	Quantity	Unit Price	Total Amount
Printer	(A) _____	USD 50.00	USD200,000
			USD 200,000,- FOB Korea seaport

- Delivery : By January 30, 20××
- Terms of payment : (B) _________
- Country of origin : Republic of Korea
- Shipping port : Incheon seaport, Korea
- Unloading port : Charleston, SC, U.S.A.
- Packing : (C) _________
- Inspection : Maker's inspection to be final
- Insurance : To be covered by us

Your prompt order confirmation would be very much appreciated.

① (A) 4,000
(B) Standard import packing
(C) By an irrevocable letter of credit payable at sight

② (A) 3,500
(B) By a stand–by letter of credit
(C) Standard export packing

③ (A) 5,000
(B) By a levy of 5% special additional duty
(C) By non–transferable Credit

④ (A) 4,000
(B) By an irrevocable letter of credit payable at sight
(C) Standard export packing

36. Which of the following is MOST likely to appear right BEFORE the passage in the box?

> We are a large chain of retailers and are looking for a manufacturer who can supply us with a wide range of jackets for the teenage–girls and ladies market.
>
> As we usually place very large orders, we would expect a quantity discount in addition to a 30% trade discount off net list prices, and our terms of payment are normally 30–day bill of exchange, documents against acceptance.
>
> If these conditions interest you and you can meet orders of over 500 garments at one time, please send us your current catalogue and price–list. We hope to hear from you soon.

① We are pleased to accept the kind invitation of yours to the party at 5:00pm on Saturday, May15th at the Mayfield Hotel.

② We were impressed by the selection of jackets that were displayed on your stand at the 'Womenswear Exhibition' that was held in Milano last month.

③ Thank you for your letter of February 26 inquiring about Jacket. We are pleased to hereby submit an offer to you as follows.

④ Please be assured that if there is any way that International Air Cargo can assist you with your exporting problems, we would be delighted to hear from you.

37. Which of the following is MOST likely to appear right AFTER the passage in the box?

We greatly regret to inform you that a temporary derangement of machines in our maker's factory has rendered us unable to ship the goods of your Order No.2398 by June 15 as arranged. We have just sent you a cable as follows, asking for your understanding for an extension of L/C for 10 days. ORDER 30 MACHINERY DERANGEMENT UNABLE SHIPMENT AS CONTRACTED EXTEND L/C SHIPPING DATE AND EXPIRY DATE TEN DAYS RESPECTIVELY Every effort, of course, is being made to quicken the shipment, and we trust that we can effect our shipment by the next direct steamer.

① We have given them credit facilities for at least ten years and have always found that they have paid on due dates without any problems. I might also add that our credit is in excess of the one mentioned in your letter.

② Please accept our profound apologies for this inconvenience. We assure you that we will take every precaution against such an incident from arising again in the future.

③ Your order for 700 units of electronic calculators is acknowledged with thanks. We stated that estimated delivery would be two weeks from receipt of order.

④ For your reference, two copies of our shipping documents are being enclosed in this letter. We trust all documents are in good order and will meet your requirement.

38. Which of the following LEAST fits the blank in the letter below?

> We are pleased to learn from your letter of March 2 that you would like to act as our agent in Korea.
>
> We are quite interested in your proposition since we have been looking for a way to expand into the Korean market for quite a long time.
>
> We truly hope that this will give us the opportunity to do so. We would like to discuss the possibility of establishing exclusive agency ties with your company.
>
> Our marketing manager in charge of overseas markets plans to visit East Asia, including China, Japan, and Korea, in May. He will be able to visit your company and discuss this proposition in detail. ____________.
>
> We believe that this will be the beginning of a mutually beneficial relationship.

① In the meantime, we are particularly interested in your products, and would like to have more detailed information on your entire business range.

② In the meantime, we are sending you a catalog describing our entire line of products as well as a copy of our company profile.

③ We welcome your specific inquiries for any of our lines and assure you that we will make every effort to meet your requirements.

④ We will be very pleased if you could inform us of the details of the products you are especially interested in.

39. Which of the following is INCORRECTLY modified from the underlined parts in the box below?

> 7.2 Quality Standards: Licensee shall strictly observe Licensor's quality standards, for any Product manufactured and use in the manufacture and assembly of the Products equipment, tooling, materials and components that conform to such standards.
>
> (A) Licensee shall furthermore establish and maintain such test and inspection procedures as are necessary to ensure the fulfillment of its obligations under this sub-section. (B) If any Product fails to meet the above-mentioned standards, Licensor shall assist Licensee in identifying the deficiencies and furnish recommendations to Licensee for correcting them. (C) Where assistance is required in the Territory, Licensee shall pay the cost of the dispatch of technical personnel by Licensor. (D) Licensee shall not market or use any Products that fail to meet the above-mentioned quality standards without Licensor's prior consent.

① (A) Licensee shall furthermore establish and maintain such test and inspection procedures necessary to fulfill its obligations under this sub-section.

② (B) In case any Product doesn't meet the above-mentioned standards, Licensor shall help Licensee identify the problems and offer recommendations to Licensee in order to correct them.

③ (C) Unless assistance is required in the Territory, Licensor shall dispatch technical personnel at the expense of Licensee.

④ (D) Licensee shall market or use any Products only after Licensor gives consent.

[문 40~41] Read the following passage and answer the questions.

NOW, THEREFORE, in consideration of mutual conditions and covenants hereinafter, the parties agree as follows;

Article 1. Description of Goods

Refrigerator

Article 2. Quantity

200 sets

Article 3. (A) __________

"DongHwa" presented its preferred price USD500,000.- to "Mitzhara", and "Mitzhara" shall present its price idea to "DongHwa" by June 11, 20×× in order for the parties to enter into a "Supply and Purchase Agreement."

Article 4. (B) __________

The parties shall enter into a "Supply and Purchase Agreement" within 30days after settlement on the price.

Article 5. Other Conditions

Other conditions shall be discussed in due course, and the details will be clearly expressed in the "Supply and Purchase Agreement" to be made.

Article 6. (C) __________

This LOI shall become effective upon signing and effective only for a period before signing the "Supply and Purchase Agreement" is made between the parties.

40. Please fill in the blanks of the above letter of intent.

① (A) Agreement (B) Duration (C) Importer
② (A) Product (B) Agreement (C) Price
③ (A) Price (B) Agreement (C) Duration
④ (A) Exporter (B) Duration (C) Payment

41. Which of the following is MOST likely to appear right AFTER the passage?

① IN WITHESS WHEREOF, the parties hereto have caused this LOI to be executed by their respective duly authorized representatives as of the day and year first above written.
② The exemption provided by this article is effective for the period during which the impediment exists.
③ Please cover us for the amount of USD 2,000 at 3% on W.A. including breakage as per your quotation just received on all goods in transit to our warehouse.
④ LOI, the following terms have the following meanings: "Dollars" means the lawful currency of the United States of America.

42. Which of the following BEST fits the blank in the box below?

We are holder of Policy No. 876 issued by your London office on 3,000 bags of Coffee per s.s. Apollo Ho valued at USD 3,000. During the voyage the vessel encountered heavy seas and consequently 500 bags was damaged by sea-water. ________ Kindly adjust the claim and forward us the check in settlement at your earliest convenience.

① Some garments were apparently missing and quite a few others were seriously stained and thus cannot be sold as new articles.
② Because of the large number of complaints filed by the customers, our client has returned nearly entire order.
③ We agree to your selling the remainder of the goods at 15% below the list price.
④ We enclose the Lloyd's Surveyors' certificate of damage and also the policy, which covers all risks.

43. The passage below is an Article excerpt from the ICC Model Contract for the Turnkey Supply of an Industrial Plant. Which of the following is the BEST summary for the excerpt below?

> 28.1 **Taxes and other charges payable in the Country.**
> All taxes, duties or other charges which may be incurred by the Supplier in the Country in relation with this Contract and its performance shall be paid and borne by the Purchaser. In case of taxes, duties or other charges which, according to local laws or regulations, are to be paid by the Supplier, and the Purchaser will reimburse the amounts paid by the Supplier, within thirty (30) days following payment by the Supplier.
> 28.2 **Taxes and other charges payable outside the Country.**
> All taxes and duties or other charges incurred by the Supplier outside the Country in relation with this Contract and its performance will be borne by the Supplier.
> * Note: Country means the country where the Plant is to be installed.

① All taxes, duties or other charges incurred by the Supplier in the Country and outside of the Country will be the Supplier's responsibility within one month following payment by the Supplier.

② All taxes, duties or other charges incurred by the Supplier in the Country will be compensated by the Purchaser, and the similar charges paid by the Supplier outside the Country will be the Supplier's responsibility.

③ All taxes, duties or other charges incurred by the Supplier in the Country will be paid by the Purchaser within one month following payment by the Supplier.

④ All taxes, duties or other charges incurred by the Supplier in the Country will be paid by the Supplier, and the similar charges paid by the Supplier outside the Country will be the Purchaser's responsibility.

44. Which of the following is appropriately rewritten to have the same meaning?

① We have informed your agents, Eddis Jones, who will make arrangements for the consignment to be sent on to you as soon as they receive the shipping documents for clearance. → It has been informed that your agents, Eddis Jones, will deliver the consignment, upon receiving the shipping documents.

② We apologize for the delay. You will know from previous experience with us that we make every effort to stick to schedules. This incident was an unfortunate exception. → We are not responsible for the delay. However, considering our relationship, we try our best to meet the shipping schedules. This incident was unfortunately exceptional.

③ The cargo should be marked on two sides with a shipping mark which includes the destination port. This should correspond with the mark on your shipping documents. → A shipping mark including the destination should be placed on two sides of the cargo. The mark should match with the one on your shipping documents.

④ She is the Manhattan, and is currently docked in Boston. She is a bulk carrier with a cargo capacity of seven thousands pounds. She has a maximum speed of 24 knots, so would certainly be capable of ten trips in the period you mentioned. → The Manhattan is in Boston. The vessel has a cargo capacity of seven thousands with a highest speed of 24 knots, so that it will make ten trips during the mentioned period.

45. Which of the following is MOST likely to appear right after the passage in the box?

We will send you the goods ordered on June 1 by M/S "East Sea" sailing today from Busan. We are enclosing an invoice and B/L for same. We have taken every care in packing and handing the goods, so that they will reach you in good order. In order to assist you in opening and checking the goods, they were divided into three parts, each part having an individual number, so that you will find on each case a number corresponding to that which is on the invoice.

① We trust that they will give you entire satisfaction, and hope that we shall have many opportunities in the future to demonstrate our ability to fill orders promptly and carefully.

② We are much obliged for the arrangements you promised us by phone this morning to reserve ship's space for two tons on the M/S "East Sea" which is due to sail from Busan.

③ The goods are five cases of our Cotton Products destined for Los Angeles where they will be warehoused by our shipping agents.

④ Concerning the loss during transportation, we have put all the necessary particulars into your insurance claim forms to cover the loss.

46. Complete the letter using the sentences in the box below.

> (1) You will find a copy of the consignment note and invoice enclosed, and we will hold the boxes for your inspection.
> (2) Therefore we assume that damage occurred while the consignment was in your care.
> (3) It consisted of 10 boxes of CDs, three of which were badly damaged.
> (4) However, the nature of the damage to the goods suggests that the consignment was roughly handled.
>
> Consignment Note 27332
> The above consignment was delivered to our premises at the above address on 3 October.
> (A)______ We have contacted our suppliers, and they informed us that when the goods were deposited at your depot they were in perfect condition. (B)_______ The boxes were marked FRAGILE. (C)______ We estimate the loss on invoice value to be $2000 and as the goods were sent 'carrier's risk' we are claiming compensation for that amount. (D)_______

① 1-3-2-4　② 3-2-4-1
③ 3-1-4-2　④ 4-1-2-3

47. Which of the following should be replaced for the coherence of the letter below?

> (A) The surveyor's report is enclosed with statement from the shipping agent. When the United Oceanline arrived at Busan on May 10, it was noticed that one side of case number 15 containing radio receivers was split. Therefore the case was opened and the contents were examined by a local insurance surveyor in the

presence of the shipping company' s agents.
(B) The case was invoiced as containing 30 Hacker 'Mayflower' radio receivers, 9 of which were badly damaged. As you hold the insurance policy, I should be grateful if you would take up this matter with the insurers. (C) Nine replacement receivers will be required.
Please arrange to supply these as soon as possible and charge them to our account. Thank you in advance for your trouble on our behalf. (D) If there are any queries, please do not hesitate to call me.

① (A) ② (B)
③ (C) ④ (D)

[문 48~49] Read the following memo and answer thequestions.

Shipper/Exporter PK CHEMICAL CORP. LOTTE GWANAK TOWER BLDG., 639-57, SHINDAEBANG-DONG, DONGJAK-GU, SEOUL, 154-581 KOREA [TEL NO.]02-840-0164	No.& date of invoice No.& date of L/C or Contract
(A) ________ SHANGHAI WAIGAOQIAO FREE TRADE ZONE LANSHENG DAEWOO INTERNATIONAL TRADING CO., LTD. 30F, LANSHENG BUILDING, NO.8 HUAL HAI	L/C issuing bank

<table>
<tr><td colspan="4">ROAD(M) SHANGHAI 200021
CHINA</td><td colspan="2"></td></tr>
<tr><td colspan="4">(B) ________
SHANGHAI WAIGAOQIAO FREE
TRADE ZONE LANSHENG
DAEWOO INTERNATIONAL
TRADING CO., LTD.
FAX:021-63190177</td><td colspan="2" rowspan="3">Remarks
EACH PACKAGE
OF:
QUANTITY :
1.1MT
WEIGHT :
1.1MT(NET),
1.10314MT(GROSS)

PACKING
CONDITIONS :
EXPORT
STANDARD
PACKING</td></tr>
<tr><td colspan="2">Port of Loading
ULSAN, KOREA</td><td colspan="2">Final
Destination
ZHANGJIAGAN
G, CHINA</td></tr>
<tr><td colspan="2">(C) ________
MV. SEA STAR</td><td colspan="2">Sailing on or
about
JUN. 04, 2010</td></tr>
<tr><td>Marks and
numbers of
PKGS
N/M</td><td>Description
of goods</td><td>No.
of
bags</td><td>Net-
Weight</td><td>Grosswei
ght</td><td>Measure
ment</td></tr>
<tr><td></td><td colspan="5">910 BAG 1,001,000 KGS
1,003,867 KGS 1,251,250 CBM</td></tr>
<tr><td colspan="6">COMMODITY:
PURIFIED TEREPHTHALIC
ACID(PTA)
QUANTITY:1001MTS

________</td></tr>
</table>

48. Which of the following BEST fits the blanks in the box?

① (A) Consignee
(B) Notify Party
(C) For Transshipment to

② (A) For Account&Risk of Messrs.
(B) Port of Discharge
(C) Freight Prepaid

③ (A) Notify Party
(B) For Account&Risk of Messrs
(C) Clean on Board

④ (A) For Account&Risk of Messrs.
(B) Notify Party
(C) Vessel& Voyage No.

49. What type of document is the memo above?

① Packing List
② Bill of Lading
③ Commercial Invoice
④ Certificate of Origin

50. Which of the following is correct in terms of grammatical structure and meaning?

> We are sorry to learn from your letter of May 10 of the difficulties you are having with the radios supplied to your order number 8562.
>
> ___
>
> (A) All our radios are manufactured identical in design and performance and we cannot understand why some of them should have given trouble your customers.
>
> (B) It is normal practice for each radio to individually examine

through our Inspection Department before being exported. However, from what you say, it seems that a number of radios escaped the usual examination. We sympathize with your problem but regret that we cannot accept your suggestion to take back all the unsold stock.

(C) Indeed there should be no need for this since it is likely that the number of faulty radios can be very large.

(D) We will gladly replace any radios found to be unsatisfactory, and are prepared to give you a special discount of 5% to compensate you.

We trust you will accept this as being a fair and reasonable solution of this matter. Please contact us if you have any further questions.

① (A)　② (B)
③ (C)　④ (D)

〈제3과목〉 무역실무

51. 항공운임요율에 관한 설명으로 옳은 것을 모두 고른 것은?

ㄱ. Class Rate는 모든 품목에 적용되는 할인 및 할증요율 이다.
ㄴ. Normal Rate는 화물 1건당 45kg 미만의 화물운송에 적용되는 요율이다.
ㄷ. 중량단계별 할인요율은 중량이 낮아짐에 따라 요율을 낮게 적용하는 요율이다.
ㄹ. 특별품목할인요율(SCR)은 항공운송을 이용할 가능성이 높은 품목에 대하여 낮은 요율을 적용하는 요율이다.

① ㄱ, ㄴ　　② ㄱ, ㄷ
③ ㄴ, ㄷ　　④ ㄴ, ㄹ

52. 우리나라 중재법상 중재판정을 취소할 수 있는 사유나 요건에 해당되지 않는 것은?
① 중재판정이 중재합의의 대상이 아닌 분쟁을 다룬 경우
② 중재판정의 취소를 구하는 당사자가 중재인의 선정 또는 중재절차에 관하여 적절한 통지를 받지 못한 경우
③ 중재판정의 정정, 해석 또는 추가 판정의 정본을 받은 날부터 3개월 이내에 제기하여야 한다.
④ 중재판정에 관한 승인 또는 집행판결이 확정된 후에 중재판정 취소의 소를 제기할 수 있다.

53. 다음은 FPA조건으로 보험계약을 체결하는 경우 운송물의 종류에 따라 일반적으로 특약이 필요하다고 생각되는 부가 위험을 열거한 것이다. 가장 관련이 적은 것은?
① 갑판적재화물 – washing overboard: WOB
② 도자기제품 – contamination
③ 석탄 – spontaneous combustion
④ 신문용지 – rain and/or fresh water damage: RFW

54. 신용장통일규칙(UCP600)에서 선하증권의 서명요건(signature)에 관한 설명 중 맞지 않는 것은?
① 운송인, 선장(함장) 또는 이들 대리인의 서명과 함께 운송인의 명의가 있어야 한다.
② 선장의 대리인이 서명하는 경우 대리인이란 자격, 운송인과 선장의 명의가 있어야 한다.
③ 운송인의 대리인이 서명하는 경우 대리인이란 자격과 운송인의 명의가 있어야 한다.
④ 선장이 서명하는 경우 선장이란 자격과 운송인의 명의 외에 선장의 명의는 없어도 된다.

55. '전자무역촉진에 관한 법률'에서 정한 전자무역기반사업자의 업무에 해당하지 않는 것은?

① 전자무역거래의 대행 사업

② 전자무역 기반시설과 외국의 전자무역망 간의 연계업무

③ 전자무역문서의 중계사업

④ 전자무역기반시설을 활용한 전자무역서비스 관련 사업

56. 다음은 Incoterms 2010의 DAT 규칙과 DAP 규칙에 관한 설명이다. 이 중 올바른 것은?

① DAT 규칙-물품이 도착운송수단에 실린 채 매수인의 처분 하에 둘 때 인도발생
DAP 규칙-물품이 도착운송수단으로부터 양하된 상태에서 매수인의 처분 하에 둘 때 인도발생

② DAT 규칙-수출국에 의하여 강제되는 선적전검사비용은 매도인부담
DAP 규칙-수출국에 의하여 강제되는 선적전검사비용은 매수인부담

③ DAT 규칙-매도인은 매수인에 대하여 운송계약을 체결할 의무가 있으나, 보험계약을 체결할 의무는 없다.
DAP 규칙-매도인은 매수인에 대하여 운송계약과 보험계약을 체결할 의무가 있다.

④ DAT 규칙-당사자들이 터미널에서 다른 장소까지 물품을 운송하는데 수반하는 위험과 비용을 매도인이 부담하도록 의도하는 때에는 DDP 규칙을 사용할 수 있다.
DAP 규칙-당사자 간에 매도인이 물품을 수입통관하고 수입관세를 부담하며 수입통관절차를 수행하도록 원하는 때에는 DDP 규칙을 사용할 수 있다.

57. 신용장통일규칙(UCP 600)의 해석에 관한 내용으로서 맞지 않는 것은?

① "first class", "well known" 등이 서류발행인에 붙어 있으면 수익자를 제외한 누구든지 발행을 허용한다.

② 은행 지점이 다른 국가에 있으면 이를 다른 은행으로 보고 동일 국가에 있으면 같은 은행으로 본다.

③ "from", "within" 등이 환어음 만기일에 사용된 경우에는 이는 해당일자를 포함하여 계산한다.

④ "from", "to", "till" 등이 선적기일에 사용된 경우에는 이는 해당일자를 포함하여 계산한다.

58. 매수인의 계약불이행 시 매도인에게 손해가 발생되는 경우, 매도인은 손해배상청구를 통하여 보상받을 수 있다. 국제 물품매매계약에 관한 UN협약(CISG) 상 아래 열거한 내용 중에 매도인의 구제조치에 포함할 수 없는 것은?

① 매도인은 물품을 전매한 경우에 발생되는 각종 경비 및 가격차이 등으로 인한 손해배상을 청구할 수 있다.

② 매도인이 판매시점을 놓치게 된 경우 가격하락이 발생하면 그 손실만큼 손해배상을 청구할 수 있다.

③ 매도인이 생산을 개시한 경우라면 해당하는 손실을 청구할 수 있다.

④ 매도인은 차기 계약분의 대금에서 감액을 요청할 수 있다.

59. 참기름(HS 2306.90.1000)을 인도(India)로부터 수입하려고 한다. 다음 중 우선적으로 적용하는 관세율은?

① 한 · 인도 FTA 협정세율 55.1%

② 기본세율 5%

③ 농림축산물양허관세 5%(수입추천서 발급시)

④ 한 · 아세안 FTA 협정세율 0%

60. 무역대금결제방식에 대한 다음 설명 중 옳지 않은 것은?

① 송금결제방식 중 실무적으로 가장 많이 사용되는 방식은 'wire transfer' 라고도 불리는 전신송금방식이다.

② 외국환은행이 외국에 있는 타 은행과 환거래의 서비스를 상호 교환하여 이행하기로 하는 약정을 'correspondent agreement' 라 한다.

③ 송금결제방식을 합의하는 경우에는 계약서의 'terms of payment' 란에 'T/T in advance....' 등과 같이 기재하며 송금받을 은행명과 계좌번호를 함께 기재하기도 한다.

④ 신용장결제방식의 경우에는 환어음의 지급인란에 수입 자가 아닌 개설은

행 또는 기타 은행을 기재하는 경우가 대부분이며, 이는 추심결제방식에서도 그러하다.

61. 무역클레임의 설명 중 가장 부적절한 것은?

① 수출자가 일방적으로 계약내용을 불이행하여 해당화물의 선적을 거부하는 경우에 수입자는 계약이행을 요구할 수 있다. 이 경우에 수입자는 해당하는 손해에 대한 손해배상청구를 할 수 없다.

② 수입자가 시중에서 입수한 유명제품의 상표를 도용하여 제품을 주문하고 대량으로 수입하여 판매를 하였다. 제3자인 상표권자는 클레임을 제기할 수 있다.

③ 국제매매계약을 체결한 후에 갑작스럽게 국제시세가 하락하여 수입자 측이 가격 인하를 요구하면서, 물품 인수를 거절하고 있는 악덕클레임을 마켓클레임(market claim)이라고 할 수 있다.

④ 클레임(claim)과 불평(complaint)을 구별하기는 힘들지만 꼭 구별한다면 클레임이 객관적인 측면을 지닌 청구권이라면 불평은 주관적인 색채가 짙다.

62. 전자무역 관련 국내 법률에 대한 설명으로 가장 옳은 것은?

① '전자무역촉진에 관한 법률' 은 공인전자문서보관소, 전자무역기반사업자, 전자무역문서, 전자무역전문서비스업자 등에 관해 규정하고 있다.

② '전자거래기본법' 은 전자선하증권의 발행, 양도(배서) 및 권리이전 등 전자선하증권의 운용에 대한 법적근거를 규정하고 있다.

③ '정보화촉진기본법' 은 공인인증기관, 공인인증증서, 인증업무의 안정성 및 신뢰성 확보 등에 관해 규정하고 있다.

④ 전자적 형태의 무체물의 정의 및 수출입 확인에 관한 규정은 '대외무역법(시행령)' 에서 규정하고 있다.

63. 국제물품매매계약에 관한 UN협약(CISG)에서는 피청약자가 승낙을 의도하고 있는 경우에는 청약상의 조건을 실질적으로 변경하지 아니하는 조건의 추가, 제한 또는 변경이 있더라도 승낙으로 인정하고 있다. 다음 중 CISG에서 특정하고 있는 실질적인 조건의 변경의 사유에 해당되지 않는 것을 고르시오.

① 물품의 품질 및 수량조건
② 화인조건
③ 물품의 인도장소 및 인도시기
④ 분쟁해결에 대한 추가적 대금의 지급방법

64. 개정된 관세법상 환경오염방지물품 등에 대한 감면세와 관련된 적용대상으로서 틀린 것은?
① 오염물질(소음 및 진동 포함)의 배출 방지 또는 처리를 위하여 사용하는 기계기구시설장비
② 폐기물 처리(재활용을 포함)를 위하여 사용하는 기계기구
③ 기계전자기술 또는 정보처리기술을 응용한 공장 자동화 기계기구설비 및 그 핵심부분품
④ 방위산업에 소요되는 시설기계류 및 기초설비품, 방위산업제품을 제조 · 가공 · 수리 또는 정비하기 위한 부분품 및 원재료

65. 해상보험에서 공동해손에 관한 다음 설명 중 옳은 것은?
① 공동해손이 성립하기 위해서는 공동해손행위가 우연히 이루어 져야 한다.
② 공동해손의 정산은 헤이그-비스비 규칙에 따라 이루어 진다.
③ 공동해손희생손해는 공동해손 정산이 완료된 후 보험자로부터 보상받을 수 있다.
④ 공동해손비용손해는 공동해손 정산이 완료된 후 피보험자가 부담하는 부분을 보상한다.

66. Incoterms 2010의 사용방법에 관한 다음의 설명 중 잘못된 것은?
① 당해계약에 인코텀즈 2010 규칙을 적용하고자 하는 경우에는 그러한 취지를 계약에서 명확히 해 두어야 한다.
② 선택된 인코텀즈 규칙은 당해물품과 그 운송방법, 운송계약이나 보험계약의 체결에 관한 의무를 매도인과 매수인 중에서 누가 부담하도록 의도하는지에 적합하여야 한다.
③ 선택된 인코텀즈 규칙은 계약당사자들이 당해 장소나 항구를 가급적 정확하게 명시하여야 한다.

④ 인코텀즈 규칙은 운송계약이나 보험계약 체결의 당사자, 물품의 인도시기와 장소 및 이에 따른 비용부담자 등을 규정하고 있기 때문에 인코텀즈 규칙은 그 자체로 매매계약을 완벽하게 해 주는 기능을 하고 있다.

67. 다음 중 해외투자시 M&A 계약의 장점이 아닌 것은?
① 막대한 인수자금이 필요할 수 있다.
② 사업착수까지 시간을 단축할 수 있다.
③ 선진기술의 도입이 가능할 수 있다
④ 기존판매망과 고객기반을 인수 할 수 있다.

68. Incoterms 2010의 DAP 규칙에서 매도인의 의무에 관한 다음의 설명 중 올바른 설명만을 묶은 것은?

A. 물품이 지정목적지에서 도착운송수단으로부터 양하된 상태로 매수인의 처분 하에 놓이는 때에 매도인이 인도하는 것을 의미한다.
B. 매도인은 자신의 비용으로 물품을 지정목적지까지 또는 그 지정목적지에 합의된 지점이 있는 때에는 그 지점까지 운송하는 계약을 체결하고 또한 매수인에 대하여 보험계약을 체결하여야 한다.
C. 특정한 지점이 합의되지 않거나 관례에 의하여 결정되지 않는 경우에, 매도인은 지정목적지 내에서 자신의 목적에 가장 적합한 지점을 선택할 수 있다.
D. 매도인은 매수인에게 매수인이 물품의 인도를 수령할 수 있도록 하는 데 통상적으로 필요한 조치를 취할 수 있도록 하기 위하여 필요한 통지를 하여야 한다.

① A, D　　② B, C
③ C, D　　④ A, B

69. 신용장통일규칙(UCP 600)의 적용범위에 관한 설명으로 맞지 않는 것은?
① UCP 600은 임의규범이고 모든 신용장에 강제로 적용되는 것은 아니다.
② UCP 600은 SWIFT 신용장이 발행된 경우 이에 자동으로 적용된다.

③ UCP 600 신용장의 경우 ICC 규칙인 ISBP도 이에 자동으로 적용된다.
④ UCP 600 신용장의 경우 ICC 규칙인 eUCP도 이에 자동으로 적용된다.

70. 지식재산권 관련 국제협약과 보호대상물이 잘못 짝지어진 것은?
① 문학적, 예술적 저작물 보호에 관한 베른협약(1971) –저작물
② 저작인접권 보호에 관한 로마협약(1961) – 산업재산권
③ 산업재산권 보호에 관한 파리협약(1967) – 특허권
④ 집적회로(IC) 배치설계권 보호에 관한 워싱턴조약(1989) – IC 배치설계권

71. 상표 라이센스계약에 관한 설명으로서 옳지 않은 것은?
① 상표 라이센스계약이란 상표에 대하여 사용을 허락하는 계약이다.
② 상표 라이센스의 대상은 상표에 체화된 신용(goodwill)을 말한다.
③ 상표 라이센스가 사용료를 수반하는 경우나 특허, 노하우 등과 결합되었을 경우에 우리나라는 공정거래위원회의 심사를 받아야 한다.
④ 우리나라는 상표를 보호하는 방법으로서 등록주의가 아닌 사용주의를 채택하고 있다.

72. 남북한교역물품에 대한 원산지 확인에 관한 내용으로서 옳은 것은?
① 남한의 원산지증명서 발급기관은 세관에만 한한다.
② 북한의 원산지증명서 발급기관은 조선민족경제협력연합회이다.
③ 반입된 물품의 원산지가 북한인 경우에는 Made in NOK(North of Korea)로 표시한다.
④ 개성공단에서 반입된 물품의 전체 직접재료비 중국내공급분이 40% 이상인 경우는 국내산으로 본다.

73. 국제물품매매계약에 관한 UN협약(CISG)상 매도인의 물품인도의무에 관한 설명으로 옳지 않은 것은?
① 매도인은 인도기일이 계약에 의하여 지정되어 있는 경우에는 그 기일에 물품을 인도하여야 한다.
② 매도인은 인도시기가 계약에 의하여 지정되어 있지 않은 경우에는 계약

체결 후 즉시 물품을 인도하여야 한다.

③ 매도인은 인도기간이 계약에 의하여 지정되어 있는 경우에는 그 기간 내의 어느 시기에 물품을 인도하여야 한다.

④ 매도인이 물품의 운송을 주선하여야 하는 경우에, 매도인은 상황에 맞는 적절한 운송수단 및 그 운송에서의 통상의 조건으로 운송계약을 체결하여야 한다.

74. 국제운송에 관한 로테르담규칙(2009)의 주요 내용에 대한 설명 중 잘못된 것은?

① 전자운송기록에 관한 규정을 신설하였다.

② 운송인뿐만 아니라 송하인의 권리와 의무에 관한 규정을 신설하였다.

③ 적용대상 운송증권을 해상화물운송장 및 전자선하증권으로 확대하고 있다.

④ 항해과실 면책과 면책리스트를 폐지하였다.

75. 국제자원개발계약에서 자원국이 계약상 능동적인 지위에서 투자자의 기술을 도입하여 생산과 경영에 공동으로 참여하는 계약의 형태는?

① 생산분담계약(production sharing contract)

② 생산특허계약(production license contract)

③ 이권계약(concession agreement)

④ 모험계약(risk contract)

무역영어 제1회 2급 기출문제

※ 다음 문제를 읽고 가장 알맞은 것을 골라 답안카드의 답란(①, ②, ③, ④)에 표기하시오.

〈제1과목〉 영문해석

[문 1~2] Refer to the following e-mails.

Dear Mr. Leslian,

I am Jeremy Kim from the purchasing department at Herb Garden. I found your aroma products at the trade fair in Madrid last year.

But at that time, we were importing all the aroma related products from the company which went out of business last month.

We are currently looking for new suppliers. We will choose a company which offers us the best price and quality.

We would appreciate it if you send us sample products and a price list. And please let us know what discount we can get on large orders.

Sincerely,

Jeremy Kim

Dear Mr. Kim,

I am glad to hear that our aroma products are of interest to you. If you are looking for a reliable supplier with resonable prices, you have come to the right place. Aroma World was established in 1930 and has since been the leading company.

Our products are high in quality and prices are reasonable.

Attached you will find the price list and we are sending you samples of our products by FedEx. If you have any other questions, don't hesitate to contact me.

Sincerely,

Keith Leslian

1. Why did Jeremy Kim contact Mr. Leslian?
   ① To order products
   ② To take an order
   ③ To get information about the products and prices
   ④ To hold a conference

2. Which of the following is NOT true about Aroma World?
   ① It was established approximately 80 years ago.
   ② It participated in a trade fair.
   ③ It is dispatching some sample products.
   ④ It worked with Herb Garden before.

3. Put the following sentences in order.

I am replying to your inquiry of February 17 in which you asked about World Tire of McGuire Bros. of Portland, Oregon.

1) We have given them credit facilities for at least seven years and have always found that they have paid on due dates without any problems.
2) I contacted them yesterday and they confirmed that they wanted us to act as their referees, and I am pleased to be able to do so.
3) You can have every confidence in offering this company the facilities they ask for.
4) The company has an excellent reputation in North America for both service and the way they conduct their business with their associates in the trade.

① 4 – 1 – 2 – 3 ② 3 – 2 – 1 – 4
③ 4 – 2 – 3 – 1 ④ 2 – 4 – 1 – 3

4. 다음을 읽고 옳은 것을 고르시오.

Dear Mr. Tanner,

The above order has been shipped clean aboard the Southern Cross, due in Wellington on 12 June.

The shipping documents have been passed to the Eastland Bank, London, and will be forwarded to the New Zealand Bank, Wellington, who will advise you.

As agreed, we have drawn on the Eastland Bank at sixty days after

> sight for USD 6,200.00, and we will get a discount from them.
>
> Neil Sohn
> Senior Shipping Clerk
> Delta Computers Ltd.

① Mr. Tanner will get USD6,200.00
② Mr. Tanner will get more than USD46,200.00
③ Mr. Sohn will get USD46,200.00
④ Mr. Sohn will get less than USD46,200.00

5. How long is Mr. Chung staying at the hotel?

> M : Hi, I made a reservation under the name Minhoon Chung.
> W : Welcome to Los Angeles, Mr. Chung. Yes, I see you have a single room for two nights. Would you like a room near the pool?
> M : That won't be necessary. I am here for business and I have a lot of work to do while I am staying here. I would rather stay in a quiet room with a great view.

① one day ② two days
③ three days ④ four days

[문 6~7] Read the following letter and answer the questions.

> We would like to draw your attention to our order of May 30 for the Wafer ISTA-2A. The order is now two weeks overdue for delivery.
>
> Please let us know the current situation of the order and the expected date of delivery.

We are receiving numerous complaints from our customers due to the delay and this will certainly cause us serious problems.

We definitely need the goods by the end of July. Otherwise the order will (　　).

6. What is the purpose of the letter above?
① advising shipment
② urging prompt shipment
③ lodging a claim
④ extending the shipment period

7. Which of the following is most appropriate to fill in the blank ?
① cancel
② delay
③ be delayed
④ be cancelled

8. In the email below, what will Mr. Brown get along with this email?

Dear Mr. Brown,

The goods were shipped on 17 April 20×× – on the America, due in Liverpool on 27 April.
We have informed your agents, Eddis Jones, who will make arrangements for the goods to be sent to you as soon as they receive the shipping documents for clearance.
We are sure that you will be impressed by the machines, and we enclose a catalogue of our new models for your further consideration – see especially pp.103–110.

We look forward to hearing from you again soon.

Yours truly

① an invoice
② an order sheet
③ machines
④ a catalogue

[문 9~10] 다음을 읽고 물음에 답하시오.

Dear Mr. Merton,

(A) Please find attached an order (R1432) of glasses from our principals, KM Corporation.

(B) I am an owner of an import company specializing in cosmetic goods. I think it would be a good business opportunity to introduce your products to my country for both of us.

(C) They have agreed to pay by letter of credit, which we discussed on the phone last week, and they would like delivery before the end of this month

(D) If the colors they have chosen are not in stock, they will accept an alternative provided the designs are those stipulated on the order.

Please send any further correspondence relating to shipment or payment direct to KM Corporation and __________.

Many thanks
Linda Lowe

9. Choose the one does NOT fit in the letter.

① (A)
② (B)
③ (C)
④ (D)

10. 위 이메일의 마지막 문장을 채우기에 가장 적합하지 않은 것을 고르시오.

① let us have a copy of the commercial invoice when it is made up.

② send us a copy of the commercial invoice when it is done.

③ we'd like to have a copy of the commercial invoice when it is made up.

④ tell us how you make the commercial invoice when you finish making one.

11. 다음 문장과 가장 유사한 뜻을 가진 문장을 고르시오.

We can't possibly fill this huge order: it's more than our total output for at least one month.

① Unfortunately, we do not have the capacity to supply an order as large as this.

② We can't let you have 15% off because we price our products as cheaply as possible.

③ We have stopped manufacturing this product as there is no longer sufficient demand.

④ There is a way we can deliver in such a short time.

12. Put the following sentences in the correct order.

A) At the same time please let us have the term of trade in detail. B) We are interested in your recently introduced XA-3 sports sedan. C) If price is competitive, you can be assured of our large orders in the near future. D) We would like to have your quotation for this product together with a catalog and brochure for it.

① D−B−A−C ② B−C−A−D
③ B−D−A−C ④ D−A−B−C

13. Which of the following would NOT be included in the reply to the email below?

> Dear Mr. Swift,
>
> I saw the brochure you sent to me last week and I must say that I was quite impressed with the wide variety of ceramics.
> We have heard about your company many times, but we didn't know that you have the widest selections in ceramics and have such a long history.
> I would like to visit Korea to see the products and have a meeting with you. I am busy until March, so I'd like to visit you in the first week of April if it's okay with you.
>
> Sincerely,
> Abraham

① We are glad that you have a good impression of our products. We guarantee you the best products and quick shipping.
② I will be away to go on a business trip to Canada in the first week of April. So, I'd like to ask you to visit us in the second or third week of April.
③ They have asked us to instruct you to indicate "fragile" on the shipping mark.
④ If you see our products in person, you will be surprised at the distinctive decorative elements.

14. Which of the following was NOT mentioned in the letter?

> Dear Mr. Choi
>
> Our bank has advised us that the proceeds of our letter of credit against your invoice No, G1197/S, have now been credited to your account.
> Although we have paid for some time on this basis, it does not really suit our accounting system, and as we feel you know us well enough by now, we would like
> to make future payments on quarterly statements by international banker's draft.
> If you require a reference, please contact either Mr. Pierson or Mr. Gerlach of Patterson& Co., Louis Drive, Dawson, Ontario, who will be happy to vouch for us.
> Please confirm that these new terms are acceptable to you.
>
> Richard Mason

① Richard Mason wants to change the payment method.
② Richard Mason placed orders with Mr. Choi's company.
③ Richard Mason and Mr. Choi agreed to change the payment method after they develop trust.
④ Mr. Gerlach works at Patterson& Co.

[문 15~16] 다음을 읽고 답하시오.

> Your bank has been given as a reference by the NPN Co., Ltd., in their business proposal.
> We would be grateful if you furnish us with information to make some evaluation regarding their credit worthiness. We are particularly interested in their line of business, financial responsibility, mode of business, and reputation in your community.
> We will keep your information in strict confidential.

15. Which of the following is LEAST likely to be included in a reply to the letter above?

① We shall be glad to reciprocate the courtesy on any similar occasion.

② The company enjoys an excellent reputation in the business community here.

③ The company was established in 1996 as a cosmetics manufacturer.

④ The company has maintained account with us since 2009.

16. Which of the following best represents the sort of the letter above?

① Bank statement ② Trade inquiry

③ Trade reference ④ Bank reference

17. Put the following sentences in the correct order.

> (A) We hope you will excuse us for the delay and ask for your patience.
> (B) As a result, we regret that these temporal difficulties prevent us from meeting your draft at maturity.
> (C) We would be grateful if you can grant us a delay of one month.
> (D) We have been faced with unexpected financial difficulties by the influence of world financial crisis

① (A)-(C)-(B)-(D) ② (B)-(D)-(A)-(C)
③ (C)-(A)-(D)-(B) ④ (D)-(B)-(C)-(A)

[문 18~19] Read the following and answer the questions.

> Thank you very much for your inquiry regarding A-620 Digital Camera. We would like to submit our offer subject to our final confirmation as follows:
>
> Goods : A-620 Digital Camera
> Quantity : 10,000 sets
> Price : USD300/unit CIF London
> Shipment : Within 1 month after receipt of L/C
> Packing : Export standard packing
> Payment : Irrevocable negotiation L/C at 60 d/s
> We await your prompt reply with great anticipation.

18. What is the purpose of the letter above?
① Order
② Firm Offer
③ Quotation
④ Sales Note

19. Which of the following is NOT correct according to the letter above?
① A Bill of Exchange is not necessary.
② The price includes freight to London.
③ It is on a deferred payment basis.
④ The seller may ship number of 10,000 sets.

[문 20~21] Read the following and answer the questions.

> Upon checking the goods, we discovered a shortage of 10 units. There was not any sign from which we can judge that they were tampered with in transit as the boxes packed were received in good condition.
> Although we think that the shortage is due to a mistake in packing, we would like to have your explanation.
> If you have an evidence that you shipped the goods correctly, please send it to us soon, because we need your evidence in order to process our claim to the shipping company.

20. What is the purpose of the letter above?

① inquiry for inspection
② shipping inquiry
③ surveyor' s inspection
④ compromising

21. If the seller present the evidence that he shipped the goods correctly, what the buyer is supposed to do?

① lodge a claim to the seller
② try to compromise with the shipper
③ lodge a claim to the shipping company
④ try to compromise with the shipping company

22. Which of the following could be the best title for the letter below?

> I enclose leaflets explaining our three fully comprehensive industrial policies which offer the sort of convert you required. Policy S314 would probably suit you best as it offers the widest protection at 45% with full indemnification. I would stress that

this is a competitive one. If you are pleased with the terms, please complete the enclosed proposal form and return it to us with your payment for premium of USD 7,000.00.

① Request for a comprehensive insurance
② Full range of comprehensive insurance policies
③ An issuing of a cover note for a comprehensive insurance
④ Quotation for a comprehensive insurance

23. Which of the following is LEAST likely to be included in the reply to the letter below?

We are a large steel company and wish to export goods of steel tubing, approximate weight of 16 tons and lengths varying from 2 to 6 meters. The goods are destined for Hamburg.
Could you pick them up at our works in Sheffield and deliver them to Hamburg by the end of April? If you can handle these goods by the given date, please send us the details of your sailing and freight charges. We can promise you regular shipments if you quote a competitive rate.

① You will see that the first available vessel we have will be the MV Orient, which will accept cargo from February 20 to 28 when she sails. She is due in Hamburg on March 23.
② You will see from our list of tariffs that charges are calculated by cubic meter or cubic kilogram and that we offer substantial rebates for regular shipments.
③ We inform you that we have shipped 16 tons of steel tubing by MV orient which left Sheffield today.

④ The most suitable containers of your consignment would be a half-height container which is 20' x8' x4' or, in meters, 6.1x2.4x1.3. This can carry a payload of 18,300kg.

24. 다음 회화의 순서가 가장 적절한 것은?

(1) W : Hi Mr. Bristol, This is Emily at Hain corporation.
M : Hi Emily, I was about to call you because of my trip to Korea.
(2) W : Then, you are staying here for the weekend.
Do you have any plan for the weekend?
M : I want to go sightseeing. I signed up a weekend Seoul Tour for foreigners.
(3) W : I heard that you will visit us. So, I thought I should call you to check your schedule and arrange meetings.
M : It's very kind of you. It's so easy to work with you.
(4) W : You should have told us that you wanted to go sightseeing. I could be your tour guide myself.
M : I knew you would do that but I think I didn't want to bother you.
(5) W : Thank you. Anyway, when are you coming and how long are you going to stay here?
M : I will arrive at Seoul next Friday morning and I'm thinking of five days four nights trip.

① (5)-(3)-(4)-(1)-(2)
② (2)-(3)-(1)-(4)-(5)
③ (1)-(2)-(4)-(5)-(3)
④ (1)-(3)-(5)-(2)-(4)

25. Choose the one does NOT fit in the letter.

> 1. Since we have a very limited amount of time to ship the goods during June we must urge our producers to expedite an early delivery of the goods.
> 2. As a result, we are experiencing a temporary inability to meet your payment request.
> 3. However, we cannot proceed without receiving your L/C.
> 4. It will be impossible for us to secure the goods in time if we do not receive the L/C by June 20.

① 1 ② 2
③ 3 ④ 4

〈제2과목〉 영작문

26. Below is to seek a bank reference. Fill in with right words

> We would appreciate your sending us information ( ) the company's credit standing. We would especially like to know how long the company has had ( ) with you and whether or not any of their debts are ( ).

① for – loan – paid ② on – borrowing – paid
③ about – loan – outstanding ④ regarding– account– past due

27. Fill in the blank.

> I'd like to thank you first for placing an additional order. However, we are running out of ( ).

> When we asked our supplier, they said that it will take approximately 2 weeks. So, we would like to ask you to extend the time of delivery by a week.

① all of raw material
② some raw materials
③ some the raw materials
④ any of raw materials

28. Fill in the blanks.

① avoid – make – Authorities – observed

> To (　　) difficulties with the Customs (　　) here, please (　　) sure that our Shipping Instructions be carefully (　　).

② avoid – Authorities – make – observed
③ make – Authorities – observed – avoid
④ avoid – observed – Authorities – make

29. Fill in the blanks.

> Your order No. 5 will be completed (　　) March 20 and shipped (　　) the "Easters Quees" scheduled (　　) leave Pusan on March 30. would you please open a letter of credit well in time (　　) the shipment.

① around – on – to – for
② on – in – to – of
③ by – on – to – on
④ on – on – on – on

30. Which would be used to have a similar meaning?

> In 20××, we sold 10,083 mobile phones to India, which was about the target.
> →Last year we could ( ) the target by selling ( ) 10,000 mobile phones in India

① meet – a little more than
② achieve – just below
③ get – little more to
④ obtain – just about

31. 다음 문장의 괄호 안에 들어갈 적합한 단어나 구를 고르시오.

> We are prepared to give you a 10% allowance ( ) in the goods.

① to compensate the defects
② to complain the quality
③ to repay the amount
④ to claim for loss

32. Choose most suitable one for bracket

> Commercial risk arises from factors like the non-acceptance of goods by buyer. In order to prevent such a commercial risk, a bank is involved ( ) seller by way of issuing letter of credit.

① in favour of ② on behalf of
③ for account of ④ on account of

33. 다음 문장을 가장 적절하게 바꾼 것을 고르시오.

We are very sorry. We didn't send you an email upon issuing the LC. → We are very sorry for (   ).

① not sending you an email upon issuing the LC.
② sending not you an email upon issuing the LC.
③ didn't send you an email upon issuing the LC.
④ didn't send an email to you upon issuing the LC.

34. Choose the most appropriate words to complete the sentence.

Should the number of (   ) be exceeded the charterer must pay (   ) ; should the work be completed in less than number of days allowed, they receive (   ).

① lay days – demurrage – dispatch money
② running days – dispatch money – demurrage
③ lay days – dispatch money – demurrage
④ shipping days – demurrage – dispatch money

35. 다음 괄호 안에 순서대로 들어갈 가장 적절한 단어를 고르시오.

We can (   ) you the rate of freight for green tea sets (   ) USD 50.00 per one cubic meter. We are sure nobody can quote (   ) this low rate.

① quota – in – at ② quota – in – on
③ quote – at – at ④ quote – at – on

36. 다음 문장의 빈 칸에 가장 알맞은 단어들로 연결된 것은?

> • Large national budget deficits do not cause large trade ______.
> • Company Gamma buys free-travel coupons from people who are awarded the _____ by Zetta Airlines for flying frequently on Zetta Airlines.

① improvement – tickets
② budget – receipts
③ deficits – coupons
④ currency – fare

37. 다음 문장의 빈 칸에 가장 알맞은 단어들로 연결된 것은?

> We hereby agree with the drawers, _____ and bona fide holders of drafts that the same shall be duly honored on presentation to the ______.

① endorsers – drawee ② banks – letter of credit
③ payees – discrepancies ④ beneficiaries – purchase

38. 빈칸에 알맞은 단어를 고르시오.

> We would be very pleased if you could give us some information about their financial standing and the way they have met their liabilities. We are especially
> interested to know whether you think that a (   ) of up to US$2,000,000 D/P can be granted safely.

① draft ② invoice
③ debit ④ credit

39. 다음 문장들의 빈칸에 알맞은 단어로 연결된 것은?

> • Please accept our apologies for the last minute problems caused ____ our oversight.
> • We are seeking a long-term strategic alliance with an internationally _____ company like yours.

① to – recognize ② of – recognizing
③ on – to recognize ④ by – recognized

40. 다음 문장으로 빈 칸을 채울 때 알맞은 순서로 배열된 것을 고르시오.

> We asked you to pack goods individually with stuffing. However, ___________.
> (1) as a result, most of them were broken.
> (2) they were not individually packed and were without stuffing.
> (3) we noticed that you didn' t even attach the fragile stickers.

① (1)-(3)-(2) ② (1)-(2)-(3)
③ (3)-(1)-(2) ④ (2)-(3)-(1)

41. 문맥상 빈칸에 들어가기에 어색한 것을 고르시오.

> We are sorry to inform you that shipping is being delayed due to unfavorable weather conditions. Korea is under the influence of a typhoon and ________.

① it will be stormy until this weekend.
② we will not be able to ship the goods until the weather gets better.
③ workers are leaving the country
④ We will ship the goods when the typhoon is gone.

[문 42~43] read the following and answer.

Plastic Toys under B/L number No 201105 We have today received the subject goods damaged. In the mean time, we were informed from our supplier the goods were shipped in order. Therefore we assume that the damage occurred during transit while the boxes (a) FRAGILE and KEEP AWAY FROM HEAT. We estimate USD10,000 worth loss and we are asking compensation from you as the goods were sent '(b)' s risk. We attache the S/R for your attention, and we are holding the boxes for your inspection.

42. Which is most suitable for bracket (a)

① shown ② marked
③ printed ④ known

43. Who is most suitable for bracket (b)

① carrier ② shipper
③ insurer ④ buyer

44. Choose the one which contains no errors.

① We owe your name to the website at www.gobizkorea.com as reliable importers of industrial electronic products such as motors, transmitters and stabilizers, which we are eager to furnish to our clients.

② They posses total assets worth of USD10 million with factory facilities having a total floor area of 100,000 cubic meters.

③ With over 50 sales branches through EU market, we provide an overseas service that is specially tailoring to meet the requirements of textile industry backed up by vast stocks holding at our distribution centre.

④ Our merchandise covers rucksack, cosmetic bag, PDA case and etc. The above products are made of the finest materials and the highest craftsman and not second to none in design and durability.

45. 논리상 다음 괄호 안에 가장 적절하지 않은 문장을 고르시오.

Your account balance of USD10,000 for the invoice dated Jun 5 was due on July 30 but it has not been paid yet. But we are giving you 2 month more credit exceptionally in view of your financial difficulties at this moment. (　　)

① Please remit the money no later than October 30.

② If you do not pay immediately, we will forward this claim to a collection agency.

③ We look forward to receiving your payment in due course.

④ We look forward to continuing our valuable relationship with you.

46. 다음 중 문법상 틀린 곳이 있는 문장을 고르시오.

① One of our clients recommended your company to us as a reliable shipping company.

② We give customer satisfaction the first priority, so quick and safe delivery is very important to us.

③ We would like to do business with you if your freight charge is reasonable.

④ If you send to us your freight rate, we would be appreciated.

47. Which the most appropriate as the Opening Sentence in the inquiry?

① We have today issued a transferable L/C in your favor through EDI system, which will be soon notified by your bank.

② We learn from the homepage of "http://www.ec21.com/belcon" that you are exporters of Men Half Sleeve Printed Shirts in Singapore.

③ Although the prices of your Men Half Sleeve Printed Shirts are competitive, we are anxious to know their quality.

④ We clicked the homepage of "http://www.ec21.com/belcon", and learn that you are importers of the best Men Half Sleeve Printed Shirts.

48. Choose the most appropriate words to complete the sentences on credit inquiry.

> ... The company you mentioned is a private company running as a family concern by three brothers and was founded fifteen years ago. It (   ) a good reputation.
> As far as our information goes it is punctually (   ) its commitments and a credit in the sum you mentioned seems to be safe. This information is strictly (   ) and given without any responsibility (   ).

① plays – satisfying – coincident – on your part
② plays – meeting – confidential – on our part
③ enjoys – satisfying – coincident – on your part
④ enjoys – meeting – confidential – on our part

[문 49~50] 다음은 무역서신의 일부이다. 읽고 물음에 답하시오.

> We were pleased to receive your enquiry of our range of sweaters. We can confirm that there would be certainly no trouble in supplying you from our wide selection of garments. We can offer you a discount which would be 5% (   ) normal prices of more than 20,000

pieces. We always deal in cash. However, we are prepared to review this once we have established a firm relationship with you.

49. 문맥상 괄호 안에 가장 적절한 것은?

① off ② from

③ for ④ in

50. 위 서신으로 내용으로 옳지 않은 것은?

① 위 서신의 작성자는 의류공급업체이다.

② 위 서신의 작성자는 현금방식에 의한 결제를 선호한다.

③ 위 서신의 작성자는 특정한 의류의 공급에 차질이 있을 것에 대하여 미리 양해를 구하고 있다.

④ 위 서신의 작성자는 장차 외상거래의 가능성을 부인하지 않는다.

〈제3과목〉 무역실무

51. 무역거래시 계약서 작성의 유의사항으로 틀린 것은?

① 무역계약은 양도나 증여계약이 아니므로 계약 당사자는 상대방에 대한 의무를 규정하여야 한다.

② 계약서에 명시적으로 합의하지 않았거나 거래관습도 없는 경우를 위하여 준거법을 지정하여야 한다.

③ 계약자유의 원칙에 따라 당사자가 합의한 계약은 일국의 강행법규에 제한을 받지 않는다.

④ 준거법상의 내용이 명시조항이나 거래관습과 충돌하면 명시조항, 거래관습이 우선한다.

52. 다음 중 국제채권추심을 진행하는데 도움을 주는 공공기관으로서 적합한 곳은?

① 중소기업진흥공단 ② 대한무역투자진흥공사

③ 한국무역보험공사 ④ 신용보증기금

53. 해상적하보험계약과 관련된 다음 설명 중 옳지 않은 것은?
① 적하보험에 있어서 보험금액은 보통 송장가액의 110%가 된다.
② A/R조건에서는 TPND위험을 담보한다.
③ 보험가액과 보험금액은 동일한 개념이다.
④ WA조건에서는 RFWD를 담보하지 않는다.

54. 국제매매계약에서 예상치 못한 사태가 발생하여 계약상 의무를 일시적으로 이행할 수 없게 되는 경우, 그 사태의 지속 기간에 대해서만 양당사자의 귀책사유에 속하지 않도록 인정하는 개념은?
① Force Majeure ② Impossibility of performance
③ Impracticability ④ Frustration

55. 신용장거래에서 선하증권(B/L)의 요건에 관한 설명으로서 옳은 것은?
① 양륙항이 지리적인 구역으로 요구된 경우 B/L의 양륙항도 특정의 지리적인 구역으로 기재할 수 있다.
② 기명식 B/L이 요구된 경우 지시식 B/L은 안 되며, 지시식 B/L이 요구된 경우 기명식 B/L은 안 된다.
③ 해상선적 B/L이 요구된 경우 B/L 제목에 "Marine", "Ocean", "Port-to-port" 등의 표기가 있어야 한다.
④ 복수 B/L이 요구된 경우 원본의 발행 통수와 관계없이 1통의 원본과 나머지를 사본으로 제시할 수 있다.

56. 다음은 국제비즈니스계약서 조항의 일부이다. 괄호 안에 알맞은 것은?

The Principal hereby appoints the ( ) to be its exclusive ( ) and the ( ) hereby accepts the appointment in the territory for period of five years subject to the terms and conditions set forth herein. Nothing contained in this Agreement shall be deemed or construed constituting the ( ) as a legal representative of the

> Principal for any purpose whatsoever, or ...

① Licensee ② Seller
③ Agent ④ Constructor

57. 신용장에서 단순히 "Invoice"라고 요구한 경우, 다음 중 수리되지 않는 것은?
① Consular Invoice ② Pro-forma Invoice
③ Customs Invoice ④ Final Invoice

58. Incoterms 2010의 FCA 규칙에서 매도인의 의무에 관한 설명 중 잘못된 것은?
① 매도인은 자신의 위험과 비용으로 물품이 인도된 사실을 매수인에게 통지하여야 한다.
② 원칙적으로 매도인은 매수인에 대하여 운송계약과 보험계약을 체결할 의무가 없다.
③ 지정장소가 매도인의 영업구내인 경우에는 물품이 매수인이 제공한 운송수단에 적재된 때 인도가 완료된다.
④ 매도인은 매수인의 요청에 따라 매수인의 위험과 비용으로 매수인이 운송서류를 획득하는 데 협조하여야 한다.

59. 다음의 지식재산권 중에 산업재산권(industrial property)으로 분류되지 않는 것은?
① 저작권(copyright)
② 특허권(patent)
③ 상표권(trademark)
④ 실용신안권(utility model)

60. 정기선 운송의 부대운임에 관한 설명으로 옳은 것은?
① Demurrage는 화주가 컨테이너를 규정된 시간에 반환하지 못할 경우 운송업체에 지불해야 하는 비용이다.
② Detention Charge는 화주가 CY에 장치된 컨테이너를 정해진 기간 내에

목적지로 반출해가지 않을 경우 부과된다.

③ CAF는 선박연료인 벙커유의 가격변동에 따른 손실을 보전하기 위해 부과하는 할증료이다.

④ THC는 화물이 CY에 입고된 순간부터 선측까지 컨테이너 화물의 이동에 따른 비용이다.

61. 무역클레임에서 소송과 중재를 비교한 것이다. 옳지 않은 것을 고르시오.

① 소송의 판결과 달리 중재판정은 단심제로 법원의 확정판결과 동일한 효력을 갖는다.

② 중재합의의 당사자는 중재절차의 개시 전 또는 진행 중에 법원에 보전처분을 신청할 수 있다.

③ 소송이 법원에서 계속 중인 경우, 중재판정부는 중재절차를 개시 또는 진행하거나 중재판정을 내릴 수 없다.

④ 중재합의가 된 분쟁에 대하여 소가 제기된 경우, 피고가 중재합의가 있다는 항변을 하면 법원은 소를 각하하여야 한다.

62. 중계무역에서 중계무역업자가 실수요자와 실공급자를 모르게 하기 위해 사용하는 선하증권은?

① Stale B/L ② Switch B/L

③ Red B/L ④ Surrender B/L

63. 대외무역법상 국제평화 및 안전유지와 국가안보를 위하여 수출허가가 필요한 물품은 다자간 국제수출통제체제에 따라 제한된다. 다음 중 다자간 국제수출통제체제가 아닌 것은?

① Biological Weapons Convention

② Chemical Weapons Convention

③ Australia Group, Kimberly Process Certification Scheme

④ Missile Technology Control Regime, Nuclear Suppliers Group

64. 외국환거래법상의 거주자와 비거주자에 대한 구분 중 비거주자에 해당되는 것은?

① 비거주자였던 대한민국 국민으로서, 입국하여 국내에 3개월 이상 체재하고 있는 경우
② 일반 외국인으로서 국내에서 영업활동에 종사하고 있는 자
③ 외국에서 영업활동에 종사하고 있는 대한민국 국민
④ 일반 외국인으로서 6개월 이상 국내에서 체재하고 있는 자

65. 무역대금결제방식에 대한 다음 설명 중 옳지 않은 것은?
① CAD 방식에서 선적서류가 은행을 통하여 수입자에게 전달되는 경우를 유럽형 D/P라 하는데, 이는 환어음이 발행되지 않는다는 점에서 D/P방식과 구별된다.
② 추심지시서에 추심의 종류를 기재하지 않은 경우에는 D/P로 해석되며, 30 days after sight와 같이 기재된 경우에는 D/P로 해석해야 한다.
③ 추심결제방식의 경우 품질불량을 이유로 대금결제를 거절할 가능성이 있으므로 외상방식을 요구하는 경우에는 D/A보다는 Usance L/C로 유도하는 편이 적절하다.
④ 추심방식하에서 수입업자 거래은행(추심은행)이 수입화물선취보증서(L/G)를 발행했다면, 수입자가 만기에 대금지급을 거절한 경우 추심은행은 대금을 지급해야 한다.

66. 아래 보기의 내용에 적합한 컨테이너 터미널의 시설은?

본선 입항 전에 미리 입안된 선내 적치계획에 따라 선적예정 컨테이너를 순서대로 쌓아두기 위한 곳으로, 컨테이너 터미널 운영에 있어 중심이 되는 장소이다.

① Apron ② Container Yard
③ Marshalling Yard ④ Container Freight Station

67. 국제물품매매계약에 관한 UN협약(CISG)상 계약위반에 관한 설명으로서 옳은 것은?
① 매도인의 본질적 계약위반이 있어야만 매수인은 이행청구를 할 수 있다.
② 매도인의 본질적 계약위반이 있어야만 매수인은 대체물인도를 청구할 수

있다.

③ 매도인의 본질적 계약위반이 있어야만 매수인은 치유청구를 할 수 있다.

④ 매도인의 본질적 계약위반이 있어야만 매수인은 이행정지를 할 수 있다.

68. Incoterms 2010의 개별 규칙에 관한 다음 설명 중 올바른 것은?

① EXW, FCA, CPT, CIF 규칙은 선적지인도규칙에 해당되며, 복수의 운송방식에 사용가능한 규칙이다.

② DAT, DAP, DDP, CIP 규칙은 선적지인도규칙에 해당되며, 복수의 운송방식에 사용가능한 규칙이다.

③ CFR, CIF, CPT, CIP 규칙은 선적지인도규칙에 해당되며, 해상운송방식에 사용가능한 규칙이다.

④ FAS, FOB, CFR, CIF 규칙은 선적지인도규칙에 해당되며, 해상운송방식에 사용가능한 규칙이다.

69. Incoterms 2010에 준거하여 매매당사자 사이의 비용분담을 바르게 설명한 것은?

① FOB에서 매도인은 자신의 비용으로 물품이 인도된 사실을 매수인에게 통지하여야 한다.

② CFR에서 매수인은 강제적인 선적전검사에 드는 비용을 부담하여야 하며, 또한 그러한 검사가 수출국에 의하여 강제되는 경우에도 마찬가지이다.

③ DDP에서 매수인은 매도인에 대하여 수출국이나 수입국에 의하여 강제되는 선적전검사에 드는 비용을 부담할 의무가 없다.

④ EXW에서 매도인은 해당되는 경우에 물품의 수출에 부과되는 모든 관세, 세금 기타 공과금 및 수출통관비용을 부담하여야 한다.

70. 신용장거래에서 은행의 서류심사기준에 관한 설명 중 맞지 않는 것은?

① 은행은 최종서류의 도착익일로부터 최대한 제5은행영업일내의 상당한 시간을 향유할 수 있다.

② 제시된 서류 상호간에 문면상 일치하지 않으면 이는 신용장조건과 일치하지 않는 것으로 본다.

③ 제시된 서류만에 기초하여 서류가 신용장조건, UCP 규정, 국제표준은행

관습 등에 일치하는지 심사한다.

④ 운송서류를 포함할 경우 1통 이상의 원본이 늦어도 선적일후 21일과 유효기일까지 제시되어야 한다.

71. 적하보험계약과 관련된 다음 설명 중 옳은 것은?

① CIF조건의 경우 원칙적으로 보험계약자와 피보험자가 동일인이다.

② 보험계약의 대상인 재화자체를 피보험이익이라 한다.

③ Cover Note는 보험자가 발행한다.

④ FPA조건에서는 SSB사고로 인한 단독해손을 담보한다.

72. 다음 중 외국으로부터 대외지급수단을 차입하거나 자본재, 원자재 등을 장기결제방식으로 도입하는 것을 목적으로 하는 계약은?

① 차관계약 ② 리스계약

③ 팩토링계약 ④ M&A 계약

73. 전자적 형태의 무체물 수출입에 관한 설명으로 가장 올바른 것은?

① 전자적 형태의 수출실적 인정은 외국환은행장이 발급한 수출입확인서에 의해 외국환은행이 입금 확인한 금액이다.

② 전자적 형태의 무체물의 수출실적의 인정시점은 외국환은행이 수출대금을 입금확인한 일자이다.

③ 소프트웨어를 노트북컴퓨터에 내장한 채 휴대반출하는 경우에도 무체물의 수출범위에 포함된다.

④ 전자적 형태의 무체물도 수출입 실적으로 인정하여 무역금융 등의 제도적 지원을 받을 수 있다.

74. 기술의 도입이나 수출에 있어 거래대상에 관한 설명으로서 틀린 것은?

① 기술의 매매 또는 양도 : 기술소유권의 이전(순수기술, 응용기술, 개발기술 등의 순수 매매)

② 라이센스 제공 : 특허권, 실용실안 및 디자인 등에 대한 사용허락

③ 기술정보 : 도면, 규격서, 매뉴얼, 기술데이터 등 각종 기술관련 자료 등

④ 기술정보 : 기술연수에 필요한 각종 데이터, 공정도, 매뉴얼, 도면 및 기

술연수 등

75. 전자무역계약의 성립에 관한 설명으로 가장 올바른 것은?
   ① 전자무역계약은 2인 이상의 당사자간에 전자적 매체를 이용한 전자적 의사표시의 단독행위에 의하여 성립되는 법률행위이다.
   ② 전자무역계약에 있어서 계약당사자간의 분쟁해결 및 법적 구속력을 위한 계약조건을 고려할 필요가 있다.
   ③ 전자무역계약은 전자청약에 대한 승낙의 메시지가 수신자가 지정한 정보시스템으로 발송되는 순간 성립된다.
   ④ 전자무역계약은 정보시스템을 통해 거래가 이루어지기 때문에 상대방의 권리능력 여부는 전혀 문제가 되지 않는다.

무역영어 모범답안(1회)

문항번호	1회 1급 답안번호	문항번호	1회 1급 답안번호	문항번호	1회 1급 답안번호
1번	4	26번	4	51번	4
2번	1	27번	3	52번	4
3번	1	28번	2	53번	2
4번	3	29번	4	54번	2
5번	4	30번	1	55번	1
6번	1	31번	3	56번	4
7번	4	32번	1	57번	3
8번	4	33번	1	58번	4
9번	2	34번	1	59번	3
10번	1	35번	4	60번	4
11번	4	36번	2	61번	1
12번	2	37번	2	62번	4
13번	3	38번	1	63번	2
14번	1	39번	3	64번	4
15번	3	40번	3	65번	4
16번	3	41번	1	66번	4
17번	3	42번	4	67번	1
18번	4	43번	2	68번	3
19번	4	44번	3	69번	4
20번	3	45번	1	70번	2
21번	3	46번	2	71번	4
22번	3	47번	1	72번	2
23번	4	48번	4	73번	2
24번	3	49번	1	74번	4
25번	2	50번	4	75번	1

문항번호	1회 2급	문항번호	1회 2급	문항번호	1회 2급
	답안번호		답안번호		답안번호
1번	3	26번	4	51번	3
2번	4	27번	2	52번	3
3번	4	28번	2	53번	3
4번	모두정답	29번	1	54번	1
5번	3	30번	1	55번	2
6번	2	31번	1	56번	3
7번	4	32번	1	57번	2
8번	4	33번	1	58번	1
9번	2	34번	1	59번	1
10번	4	35번	3	60번	4
11번	1	36번	3	61번	3
12번	3	37번	1	62번	2
13번	3	38번	4	63번	3
14번	3	39번	4	64번	3
15번	1	40번	4	65번	2
16번	4	41번	3	66번	3
17번	4	42번	2	67번	2
18번	3	43번	1	68번	4
19번	1	44번	1	69번	3
20번	1	45번	2	70번	1
21번	3	46번	4	71번	4
22번	4	47번	2	72번	1
23번	3	48번	4	73번	4
24번	4	49번	1	74번	4
25번	2	50번	3	75번	2

* "정답없음" 의 문항은 해당 문항에 대해 모두 맞게 처리함.

[부록 II]

INCOTERMS 2010의 개관

2011년 1월 1일부터 시행된 「INCOTERMS 2010」은 관세가 없는 무역권의 계속적인 확장, 상거래에 있어 전자통신의 사용 증대, 물품 이동에 있어 안전에 대한 관심의 고조 그리고 운송실무의 변화 등과 같은 국제무역 환경변화에 대응하여 내용을 개정하였다.

1. INCOTERMS 2010의 주요 특징

「INCOTERMS 2010」이 기존 「INCOTERMS 2000」에 비해 달라진 중요한 특징을 살펴보면 다음과 같다.

1) 정형거래조건의 축소

「INCOTERMS 2000」의 13개 조건 중 DDU, DEQ, DES, DAF의 4개 조건이 폐지되고 대신에 DAT(Delivered at Terminal)와 DAP(Delivered at Place)의 2개의 규칙이 신설되어 「「INCOTERMS 2010」의 규칙은 모두 11개의 조건으로 기존 조건보다 2개가 축소되었다.

첫째, DAT(Delivery at Terminal, 도착터미널인도)는 「INCOTERMS 2000」에서의 DEQ조건의 대용이며, 목적항 또는 지정목적지에 있는 지정터미널에서 도착된 운송수단으로부터 일단 하역된 후 물품을 수입통관을 하지 않고 매수인의 임의처분상태로 인도하는 조건이다. 이 조건을 사용할 경우 DAT 뒤에 목적항 또는 목적지의 지정터미널을 표시한다.

둘째, DAP(Delivery at Place, 도착장소인도)는 「INCOTERMS 2000」에서의 DAF, DES, DDU조건의 대용이며, 지정목적지에서 수입통관을 필하지 않은 계약물품을 도착된 운송수단으로부터 하역준비가 완료된 후, 매수인의 임의처분상태로 되었을 때에 매도인으로부터 매수인에게 물품이 인도되는 것이다. 이 조건을 사용할 경우 DAP 뒤에 지정목적지를 표시한다.

셋째, DAP조건과 DAT조건의 주된 차이점은 인도조건이다.

즉 DAP조건의 경우 매도인은 지정장소에서 도착된 운송수단으로부터 양하하지 않은 상태로 매수인의 임의처분상태로 물품을 인도하면 되는데 이 때 도착된 운송수단은 선박, 지정목적지는 항구가 될 수 있다. 한편 DAT조건에서는 지정터미널에서 물품이 일단 선박이나 기타 운송수단으로부터 양하된 후 매수인의 임의처분상태로 물품이 인도되는데 이 때 지정터미널은 항구에 있을 수 있다.

2) 정형거래조건의 구분 변경

기존 「INCOTERMS 2000」은 전체 13가지 거래조건을 실무적으로 이해하기 쉽게 각기 공통점을 기준으로 E그룹, F그룹, C그룹, D그룹의 4그룹으로 분류하였지만, 「INCOTERMS 2010」은 현대의 상거래 현실을 반영하여 전체 11개 거래조건을 운송방식에 따라 ① 「모든 운송방식을 위한 규칙」(즉 복합운송: EXW, FCA, CPT, CIP, DAT, DAP 및 DDP)과 ② 「해상 및 내수로 운송을 위한 규칙」(즉 해상운송조건: FAS, FOB, CFR 및 CIF)의 2개 그룹으로 구분하고 있다.

① Rules for Any Mode of Modes of Transport
〈모든 운송방식을 위한 규칙〉

EXW〔EX Works(insert named place of delivery)〕
: 공장인도(지정인도장소 기입)

FCA〔Free Carrier(insert named place of delivery)〕
: 운송인인도(지정인도장소 기입)

CPT〔Carriage Paid To(insert named place of destination)〕
: 운송비지급인도(지정목적지 기입)

CIP〔Carriage and Insurance Paid to(insert named place of destination)〕
: 운송비 · 보험료지급인도(지정목적지 기입)

DAT〔Delivered At Terminal(insert named terminal at port or place of destination)〕
: 도착터미널인도(목적지 항구 또는 장소의 지정터미널 기입)

DAP〔Delivered At Place(insert named place of destination)〕
: 도착장소인도(지정목적지 기입)

DDP〔Delivered Duty Paid(insert named place of destination)〕
: 관세지급인도(지정목적지 기입)

② **Rules for Sea and Inland Waterway Transport**
〈해상 및 내수로 운송을 위한 규칙〉

FAS〔Free Alongside Ship(insert named port of shipment)〕
: 선측인도(지정선적항 기입)

FOB〔Free On Board(insert named port of shipment)〕
: 본선인도(지정선적항 기입)

CFR〔Cost and Freight(insert named port of destination)〕
: 운임포함인도(지정목적항 기입)

CIF〔Cost, Insurance and Freight(insert named port of destination)〕
: 운임 · 보험료포함인도(지정목적항 기입)

3) FOB, CFR 및 CIF조건에서의 위험과 비용부담의 분기점 변경

「INCOTERMS 2000」에서 FOB, CFR 및 CIF조건에서의 위험과 비용부담의 분기점은 「본선의 난간」(ship's rail)을 통과하는 시점으로 규정하고 있었으나, 「INCOTERMS 2010」에서는 물품이 본선 상에 「적재된」(on board) 시점으로 규정하고 있다. 이것은 현대 상거래의 현실을 반영한 것으로 이러한 변경을 통해 위험이 가상의 수직선을 통과할 때 이전된다는 시대에 뒤떨어진 관념을 피할 수 있게 되었다.

2. INCOTERMS 2010의 기타 변경사항

1) 국내거래에 대한 적용 공식화

Incoterms 규칙은 전통적으로 물품이 국경을 통과하는 국제매매계약에 사용되어 왔다. 그러나 세계 각처에서 유럽연합과 같은 자유무역지대(trade bloc)의 등장으로 국제거래에서 국경의 의미가 퇴색되었다. 이렇게 상인들이 순수한 국내매매계약에도 사용하고 있는 현실을 반영하여 「INCOTERMS 2010」에서는 국내매매계약에도 사용될 수 있음을 공식적으로 인정하고 있다. 이러한 취지에서 「INCOTERMS 2010」의 부제를 「ICC Rules for the Use of Domestic and International Trade Terms (국내 및 국제 거래조건의 사용에 관한 ICC 규칙)」라고 하였다. 따라서 「INCOTERMS 2010」은 여러 곳에서 수출/수입통관을 이행할 의무는 '해당되는 경우' (where applicable)한하여 존재함을 명시한다.

2) 사용지침(Guidance Note)의 도입

「INCOTERMS 2010」에서는 Incoterms 사용자들이 특정거래에서 적절한 조건을 선택하여 사용하는데 도움을 주고자 각 조건의 앞부분에 「사용지침」을 두고 있다. 사용지침은 「INCOTERMS 2010」의 실질규칙의 일부를 구성하지 않으며, 단지 사용자들로 하여금 당해 거래에 적합한 Incoterms 규칙을 정확하고 효율적으로 사용할 수 있도록 유도하고자 하는 목적을 갖는다. 사용지침은 각각의 Incoterms 규칙에 대해 언제 사용되어야 하고, 언제 위험이 이전되며, 또 비용은 매매당사자 사이에 어떻게 배분되는지 등 기본적인 사항을 설명하고 있다.

3) 전자통신에 종이서류와 동일한 효력 부여

이전의 Incoterms 규칙에서는 EDI 문서에 의하여 대체가능한 서류를 명시하였다. 그러나 「INCOTERMS 2010」의 각 규칙 A1/B1에서는 당사자들이 합의하거나 관습적인 경우, 전자통신 수단에 대하여 종이에 의한 통신과 동일한 효력을 부여하고 있다. 이러한 개정은 「INCOTERMS 2010」규칙의 시행기간 중에 새로운 전자적 절차의 개발을 활성화한다.

4) 2009년 협회적하약관에 관한 규정 반영

「INCOTERMS 2010」은 협회적하약관(Institute Cargo Clauses : ICC)이 개정된 이후로는 Incoterms 규칙의 최초버전이므로 그 약관의 개정사항을 반영하였다. 운송계약과 보험계약을 다루고 있는 각 A3/B3에서 보험에 관한 정보제공의무를 부과한다. 이러한 규정은 「INCOTERMS 2000」의 각 A10/B10에 내재하던 일반적 규정에서 여기로 이동한 것이다. 보험에 관하여 A3/B3에 사용된 문구는 이러한 점에 관하여 당사자들의 의무를 명확히 하기 위하여 변경되었다.

5) 보안에 관련된 규정 도입

9.11테러 이후 물류상 보안에 관한 우려가 증대하였고, 그에 따라 물품이 그 고유한 성질 외의 이유로 생명이나 재산에 위협이 되지 않는다는 확인이 요구되었다. 따라서 「INCOTERMS 2010」규칙에서는 각 Incoterms 규칙의 A2/B2와 A10/B10 규정에서 매도인과 매수인 사이에 보관사슬정보(chain of custody information)를 입수하는 것과 같이 보안관련 통관을 완료하거나 그 완료에 협

조할 의무를 할당하였다.
예컨대 EXW조건에서 매도인은 매수인의 요청과 위험 및 비용부담으로 자기가 가지고 있는 물품의 안전 확인(security clearance)을 위해 필요한 정보를 제공하여야 한다.

6) 터미널취급수수료(THC)의 취급에 관련된 규정 추가

「INCOTERMS 2010」의 CPT, CIP, CFR, CIF, DAT, DAP 및 DDP 조건에서 터미널취급수수료(THC)를 매매당사자들에게 명확히 할당함으로써 이와 관련된 분쟁을 회피할 수 있도록 하고 있다. 그 운임은 매도인이 부담하지만, 그러한 운송비용은 통상 매도인의 총 매매가격에 산입되어 있기 때문에, 실제로는 매수인이 부담하게 된다. 운송비용은 간혹 항구나 컨테이너터미널 내에서 물품을 취급하고 운반하는 데 드는 비용을 포함하며, 운송인과 터미널 운영자는 일반적으로 이러한 비용을 물품을 수령하는 매수인에게 청구한다. 이러한 상황에서, 매수인은 동일한 서비스에 대한 이중지급, 즉, 총 매매가격의 일부로서 매도인에게 한 번 지급하고 그와 별도로 운송인이나 터미널운영자에게 또다시 지급하게 되는 것을 피하고자 한다.
「INCOTERMS 2010」은 A6/B6의 관련 Incoterms 규칙에서 그러한 비용을 명확히 할당함으로써 이중지급이 발생하지 않도록 도모한다.

7) 연속매매(string sales)와 관련된 규정 도입

제조물(manufactured goods)의 매매와 달리 상품의 매매(sale of commodity)에서는 종종 적하가 운송되는 도중에 "연속적으로" (down a string) 수차례 전매된다. 이러한 경우 중간에 판매한 매도인은 물품이 이미 첫번째 매도인에 의해 선적되어 있기 때문에 물품을 「선적」하지는 않는다. 따라서 연속매매의 경우 중간에 있는 매도인은 매수인에 대한 자기의 의무를 물품을 선적하는 것이 아니라 선적된 물품을 「조달」(procure)함으로써 이행한다. 이를 명확히 하기 위해 「INCOTERMS 2010」에서는 관련 규칙에서 매도인은 물품을 선적할 의무의 대안으로서「선적된 물품을 조달」(procuring goods shipped) 할 의무를 신설하였다.

3. INCOTERMS 2010의 적용

Incoterms 규칙은 물품매매계약 분야에서 기업간 거래실무를 반영하는 세 문자로 이루어진 일체의 정형거래조건을 설명한다. Incoterms 규칙은 주로 매도인과 매수인 사이에서 물품인도에 관한 업무와 비용 및 위험을 기술한다.

1) 「INCOTERMS 2010」규칙이 매매계약에 편입되도록 할 것

「INCOTERMS 2010」은 2011년 1월 1일부터 시행되었다. 따라서 2011년 1월 이후 매매계약에서 「INCOTERMS 2000」을 계속 사용하고자 하는 당사자들은 매매계약에 「INCOTERMS 2000」을 명시하여야 한다. 최신판 Incoterms를 적용하고자 하는 경우에도 당분간 분쟁을 피할 수 있도록 매매계약에 단순히 'Incoterms'가 아닌「INCOTERMS 2010」를 적용하는 경우에는 그러한 취지를 계약에서 명확히 하여야 한다.

2) 적절한 Incoterms 규칙을 선택할 것

선택된 Incoterms 규칙은 당해 물품과 그 운송방법에 적합하여야 하고, 무엇보다도 운송계약이나 보험계약의 체결에 관한 의무와 같은 추가적 의무를 매도인과 매수인 중에서 누가 부담하도록 의도하는지에 적합하여야 한다. 각 Incoterms 규칙의 사용지침(Guidance Note)에서는 특히 이러한 선택을 하는데 유익한 정보가 담겨있다. 그러나 어떠한 Incoterms 규칙이 선택되든지 간에, 당사자들은 당해 계약에서 이용되는 항구나 장소에 특유한 관습에 의하여 계약의 해석이 영향을 받을 수 있다는 것을 명심하여야 한다.

3) 당해 장소나 항구를 가급적 정확하게 명시할 것

선택된 Incoterms 규칙은 당사자들이 그에 관한 장소나 항구를 지정하는 때에만 작동할 수 있고, 당사자들이 그러한 장소나 항구를 가급적 정확하게 명시하는 경우에 가장 잘 작동한다.

EXW, FCA, DAT, DAP, DDP, FAS, FOB 조건의 Incoterms 규칙에서, 지정장소(the named place)는 인도가 일어나는 장소이자 위험이 매도인에게서 매수인에게로 이전하는 장소이다. 그러나 CPT, CIP, CFR, CIF 조건에서 지정장소는 인도장소와 다르다. 후자의 4가지 Incoterms 규칙에서, 지정장소는 목적지이고 거기까지의 운임이 지급되어야 한다. 장소나 목적지의 표시는 의문이나 논란을 피할 수 있도록 그러한 장소나 목적지 내의 정확한 지점(point)을 명시하는 것이 좋다.

4) Incoterms 규칙이 매매계약을 완벽하게 해주는 것은 아님을 유념할 것

Incoterms 규칙은 매매계약의 어느 당사자가 운송계약이나 보험계약을 체결할 의무를 부담하는지, 매도인은 매수인에게 언제 물품을 인도하는지, 각 당사자는 어떠한 비용을 부담하는지를 규정한다. 그러나 Incoterms 규칙은 매매대금이나 그 지급방법에 대하여는 언급이 없다. 또한 Incoterms 규칙은 물품 소유권의 이전이나 계약위반의 효과를 다루지 않는다. 이러한 사항들은 당해 매매계약상의 명시조건이나 그 준거법에 의하여 다루어진다. 더욱이 당사자들은 매매계약(선택된 Incoterms 규칙 포함)의 어느 측면에서도 국내법의 강행규정이 우선한다는 것을 유의하여야 한다.

[부록 Ⅲ] Western Business Idioms

1. In a Jam

Dialogue

Doug : I hear you're in a jam.

Larry : I want to get out of an agreement with that fly-by-night organization. I don't think they're on the level.

Doug : You should have double-checked before you put your John Hancock on the contract. Now your company will end up financially in the red.

Larry : I guess I'll have to chalk it up to experience.

Vocabulary

in a jam	adj) in trouble 궁지에 빠지다
get out of	v) withdraw 철회하다
fly-by-night	adj) unreliable, untrustworthy 믿을 수 없는, 무책임한(금전적으로)
on the level	adj) honest 정직하게/공평하게
double-check	v) reinvestigate thoroughly, look again for errors 재확인하다
John Hancock	n) signature 서명
end up	v) finish 청산/정리하다, 끝나다
in the red	adv. or adj) losing money 적자를 내고 있는
chalk up	v) record, score 마음에 새기다/(득점 등을) 기록으로 적어두다

Exercise Ⅰ. *Complete the sentences with the correct idiom.*

a) John Hancock b) get out of c) in a jam d) double-check f) on the level g) in the red h) fly-by-night I) end up

1. I'm always getting in trouble. Why am I always__________?

2. I don't trust that company. I think they're a__________organization.

3. They're not telling you the whole story. I don't think they're________.
4. They want my__________on that contract.
5. I heard he raced in the marathon. How did he__________?
6. I don't remember locking the door. Let me__________.
7. They're getting married next month but she doesn't really love him. I think she'll__________it.
8. That company keeps losing money. It's__________.
9. She studied hard this year and __________ some good grades.

Exercise Ⅱ. ***Rewrite the phrases in italics, using the proper idiomatic expression.***

1. Put your ***signature*** right here.
2. It doesn't sound ***honest*** to me.
3. Don't try to ***cancel*** your doctor's appointment.
4. They keep ***losing money***.
5. That company is ***new and has a bad reputation***.
6. Are you sure that's the right amount? Let's ***look again***.
7. That new team ***won*** another victory.
8. I'm in ***trouble***.
9. You worked very hard in that course. How did you ***finish***?

2. Having a Ball

Dialogue

Tina : I feel like having a ball. Let's splurge.

Barbara : Forget it. I'm broke.

Tina : Don't worry. I'll pick up the tab. I'm loaded today. I'll treat you.

Barbara : No. we'll go Dutch. I don't like to freeload.

Vocabulary

have a ball	v) enjoy oneself, have a good time 즐겁게/유쾌히 지내다
splurge	v) spend a lot of money for something 과시하다/(돈을) 물쓰듯하다
broke	adj) having no money 무일푼/돈이 없는
pick up the tab	v) pay the bill 값을 지불하다
loaded	adj) having lots of money 돈을 많이 가지고 있는
treat	v) pay for someone else 대접하다/한턱내다
go Dutch	v) each pay for himself or herself 각자부담하다
freeload	v) get things that others pay for 공짜식사, (음식물)공짜로 먹는 것

Exercise Ⅰ. *Complete the sentences with the correct idiom.*

a) pick up the tab b) broke c) loaded d) splurge e) treat f) go Dutch g) freeload h) have a ball

1. I don't want pizza tonight. Let's go to a fancy restaurant. Let's ___________.
2. I have so much money today. I'm___________.
3. You're going to a party?___________.
4. I don't have any money. I'm ___________.
5. You pay for your meal. I'll pay for mine. We'll___________.
6. This dinner was good. You don't have to pay. I'll___________.
7. She always eats dinner with us, and never invites us to eat at her house. She always___________ .
8. Don't pay for that. I'll___________.

Excrcise Ⅱ. *Rewrite the phrases in italics, using the proper idiomatic expression.*

1. They always ***get others to pay for them.***
2. I want to ***pay for you.***
3. We will ***each pay our own bill.***
4. Sometimes I ***spend a lot of money*** on clothes.
5. After payday, ***I always have a lot of money.***
6. Who ***paid*** the check?

7. When I go to a party, I usually ***have a good time.***
8. After I pay all my bills, ***I have no money.***

3. Ripped Off

Dialogue

Debbie : Why are you down in the dumps?

Mike : I bought some hot merchandise and got ripped off. The man conned me and I fell for it.

Debbie : You're kidding! Why can't you size people up?

Mike : I guess I'm still wet behind the ears. I fall for any snow job.

Vocabulary

down in the dumps	adj) unhappy 울적하여/우울하여
hot	adj) stolen (also means 'in great demand' : He's the hottest actor in town.) 부정으로 입수한/훔쳐낸/목하인기중인
rip off	v) cheat, rob 사취하다
con	v) lie, swindle, trick 사기의/협잡의
fall for	v) believe a false story (기만적인 진술)믿어버리다
You're kidding!	Really? Is it true? 농담하다/조롱하다
size up	v) form an opinion, assess 의견을 정하다/한눈으로 (인물) 평가하다
wet behind the ears	adj) inexperienced 미숙한/무경험의
snow job	n) insincere or exaggerated talk intended to trick or impress 감언이설

Exercise Ⅰ. *Complete the sentences with the correct idiom.*

a) size him up b) fell for it c) conned d) hot e) snow job) f) You're kidding! g) ripped off h) down in the dumps I) wet behind the ears

1. Joe didn't any work all day but he told his boss he had been working very hard. He gave him a__________.
2. I lost all my money. That's why I am__________.

3. The used-car salesman___________the man. He told him the car was in excellent shape.
4. When you meet someone for the first time, you usually __________.
5. He told me he was a millionaire and I__________.
6. I paid too much for those boots. I saw them cheaper in another store. I was__________.
7. Don't buy that watch. It's stolen. It's__________.
8. You found $1,000 in the street?__________.
9. He can't manage the office; he's still__________.

Exercise Ⅱ. ***Rewrite the phrases in italics, using the proper idiomatic expression.***

1. She lost her job. Now she is ***unhappy.***
2. That watch is ***stolen.***
3. I thought I bought a diamond but it was glass. I was ***cheated.***
4. The salesman told me it was a good car, but the transmission was bad. He ***tricked*** me.
5. You're getting married? Is it ***really true***?
6. How did you ***assess*** his qualifications?
7. You can tell him anything. He'll ***believe your story***.
8. I wouldn't have gotten the job with the truth, so I gave him ***an exaggerated*** story.
9. She doesn't ***have enough experience***.

4. Hitting the Bottle

Dialogue

Lisa : They were only married for a year before they broke up.

Elaine : What was her beef?

Lisa : She said he was hitting the bottle too much.

Elaine : Do you think they'll patch things up?

Lisa : Only if he turns over a new leaf.

Elaine : He won' t. He's going to keep on drinking. He has no will power.
Lisa : He can do it if he goes cold turkey.

Vocabulary

break up	v) separate 교제(관계)를 끊다/헤어지다
beef(s)	n) complaint 불평/불만
hit the bottle	v) drink alcohol 술을 많이 마시다/취하다
patch up	v) fix (싸움)수습하다
turn over a new leaf	v) change one's conduct for the better 마음을 고치다/새생활을 시작하다
keep on	v) continue 계속하다
will power	n) strength of mind 의지력/정신력
go cold turkey	v) stop abruptly 돌연히 중지하다/갑자기(마약/담배) 끊기

Exercise Ⅰ. *Complete the sentences with the correct idiom.*

a) your beef b) cold turkey c) patch things up d) hit the bottle e) turns over a new leaf f) will power g) break up h) keep on

1. He gave up smoking. He has more __________than I do.
2. I don't want to argue. Let's__________ .
3. Why are you angry? What's__________?
4. They aren't happy together. They're going to __________.
5. He lost his job because he__________.
6. He just got out of jail. I hope he__________.
7. He stopped smoking right away. he went__________.
8. If you're not hungry, don't__________eating.

Exercise Ⅱ. *Rewrite the phrases in italics, using the proper idiomatic expression.*

1. What's your ***complaint?***
2. Let's ***fix everything.***
3. Don't smoke another cigarette. ***Stop now.***
4. He's ***drinking liquor*** again.
5. If I want to quit smoking, I can. I have the ***strength.***

6. They ***aren't seeing each other any more.***
7. He's ***never going to lie or steal again.***
8. It's not 5 P.M.-***continue*** working.

5. Bringing home the Bacon

Dialogue

Judy : Today I'm under the weather.
Ann : Play hooky. I won't spill the beans.
Judy : I can't I'm swamped with work. My job is no picnic.
Ann : Well, hang in there. In the long run, you'll be sitting pretty.
Judy : I hope so. I have to bring home the bacon.

Vocabulary

under the weather	adj) not feeling well 기분이 언짢은/몸상태가 좋지 않은
play hooky	v) stay away from school or work without permission (학교/직장)빼먹다
spill the beans	v) tell a secret, inform 비밀을 누설하다
swamped	adj) overwhelmed 압도/압승하다
no picnic	adj) not pleasant 불쾌한
hang in there	v) be patient, wait 곤란을 버티다/견디다
in the long run	adv) in the end, as a result 결과적으로
sitting pretty	adj) in a favorable situation 유리(우세)한 입장에 있다/성공하다
bring home the bacon	v) earn the family's income 생활비를 벌다/성공을 거두다

Excrcise Ⅰ. *Complete the sentences with the correct idiom.*

a) brings home the bacon b) no picnic c) under the weather d) swamped e) hang in there f) spilled the beans g) played hooky h) in the long run I) sitting pretty

1. It's the busy season and I'm __________with work.
2. Raising children today is__________.
3. His wife works and he stays home and takes care of the children. She __________.
4. Get a college education because__________ you'll make more money.
5. I can't go to work today. I'm getting a cold and feeling __________.
6. She didn't know about the surprise party until somebody__________.
7. The children didn't go to school. They__________.
8. She married a very nice, rich, handsome man. Now she's __________.
9. I know you want to go and have fun with your friends, but and finish your homework.

Exercise Ⅱ. *Rewrite the phrases in italics, using the proper idiomatic expression.*

1. ***I don't feel very well.***
2. ***I have too much work.***
3. Her husband died. Now she has to ***support the family.***
4. They worked very hard and now ***they have a good life.***
5. His wife was planning a surprise brithday party and by mistake his best friend ***told him.***
6. He didn't feel like going to school today, so he ***stayed out*** and went to a movie instead.
7. I know you'll get the job you want. Just be ***patient.***
8. He works outside. It's ***not pleasant*** in the winter time when it's cold and icy.
9. You should get a leather wallet instead of a plastic one because ***in the end,*** leather is superior.

[부록 Ⅳ] Enrich Your Word Power

> "Wasting time is worse than wasting money".
> "You can never recapture time once gone, but
> you can always make more money."

1. absorb : take in (흡수하다)
   adsorb : cause to adhere (흡착하다)
2. accede : yield (동의하다, 양보하다)
   exceed : surpass (초과하다)
3. accept : receive (받아들이다)
   except : take or leave out (~을 제외하고)
4. acetic : acid (신 맛이 나는)
   ascetic : austere (금욕적인)
5. adapt : adjust (조정하다)
   adept : skillful (능숙한)
6. adverse : unfavorable (부정적인, 불리한)
   averse : unwilling, disinclined (~을 반대하는)
7. affect : influence (영향을 미치다)
   effect : result (영향)
8. affective : emotional (정서적인)
   effective : producing a desired result (효과적인)
9. aid : assist, assistance, assistant (원조, 지원)
   aide : assistant, esp, military or naval (보좌관)
10. all ready : prepared (준비가 되어 있는)
    already : previously (이미, 벌써)
11. alternate : every other(time, object, etc) (번갈아 생기는)
    alternative : choice(or one of two) (대안)
12. apprise : inform (알리다)
    apprize : appraise (~을 평가하다)
13. ascent : rise (상승)
    assent : consent (찬성)

14. awhile : for a short time (잠깐)
    a while : a some time (얼마간)
15. bazaar : a fair (상점가)
    bizarre : fantastic (기이한)
16. biweekly : every two weeks (격주로)
    semiweekly : twice a week (주 2회의)
17. born : brought into existence (태어나다)
    borne : carried (가져온)
18. bouillon : soup (부용)
    bullion : metal (금괴)
19. callus(noun) (굳은살)
    callous(adjective) (굳은살이 박힌)
20. canvas : cloth (캔버스 천)
    canvass : solicit (유세하다)
21. capital : city (수도)
    capitol : building (국회 의사당)
22. carat : weight (캐럿)
    caret : insertion mark (탈자 기호)
23. caster : roller (바퀴)
    castor : oil (피마자유)
24. casual : accidental, incidental (평상시의)
    causal : producing a result (결과를 초래하는)
25. climactic : pertaining to a climax (절정의)
    climatic : pertaining to climate (기후의)
26. complacent : satisfied (자기만족적인)
    complaisant : obliging (남의 뜻에 잘 따르는)
27. complement : that which completes (보완물)
    compliment : flattery (칭찬)
28. comprehensible : intelligible (이해할 수 있는)
    comprehensive : large in scope (포괄적인)
29. comprise : include (포함하다)
    constitute : make up (구성하다)
30. condole : sympathize (동정하다)
    condone : excuse (용납하다)

31. confidant : one who is, confided in (비밀을 털어놓는 친구)
confident : sure (확신하는)
32. connotation : suggestive, meaning (함축적 의미)
denotation : explicit, meaning (명시적 의미)
33. contemptible : deserving contempt (경멸을 받을 만한)
contemptuous : showing contempt (경멸하는)
34. continual : lasting, but, with interruptions (지속적인, 중단과 함께)
continuous : lasting, without interruptions (지속적인, 중단 없이)
35. councilor : member of a council (평의원)
counselor : adviser (상담전문가)
36. decent : respectable (예의 바른)
descent : decline (하강) dissent : oppose (반대하다)
37. depravation : corruption (타락)
deprivation : depriving or being deprived (박탈)
38. device(noun) (장치)
devise(verb) (고안하다)
39. discreet : prudent (신중한)
discrete : distinct (별개의)
40. disinterested : not influenced by personal considerations (사심이 없는)
uninterested : indifferent (무관심한)
41. dyeing : coloring (염색)
dying : losing life (죽어가는)
42. elicit : draw out (끌어내다)
illicit : unlawful (불법의)
43. emigrate : move from one' s country (이민을 가다)
immigrate : move to another country (이민을 오다)
44. envelop(verb) (감싸다)
envelope(noun) (봉투)
45. dual : twofold (이중의)
duel : contest between two opponents (결투)
46. equable : uniform, calm (차분한)
equitable : fair (공평한)
47. expose(noun) (노출, 폭로)
expose(verb) (폭로하다)

48. extant : in existence (현존하는)
extent : range (범위)
49. farther : at a greater distance (더 멀리)
further : to a greater degree, in addition (더 멀리, 추가적인)
50. fewer : denoting numbers(fewer letters) (숫자를 나타낼 때)
less : denoting quantity(less responsibility) (양을 나타낼 때)
51. forbear : endure (참다)
forebear : ancestor (조상)
52. forgo : relinquish (포기하다)
forego : precede (앞서다)
53. guarantee(verb) (보장하다)
guaranty (보증)
54. guerrilla : (member of) irregular fighting band (게릴라)
gorilla : ape (고릴라)
55. healthful : producing health (건강에 좋은)
healthy : having health (건강한)
56. homogeneous : consisting of similar parts (동질의)
homogenous : alike in origin (역사적 상동의)
57. indict : accuse (기소하다)
indite : compose (시나 글 등을 짓다)
58. inequity : unfairness (불공평)
iniquity : sin (부당성)
59. ingenious : skillful (기발한)
ingenuous : simple (순진한)
60. interment : burial (매장)
internment : detention (유치)
61. lath : wooden slat (욋가지)
lathe: machine (선반)
62. liable : exposed to risk of something undesirable (법적 책임이 있는)
likely : probable (~할 것 같은)
63. linage : number of written or printed lines (일렬 정렬)
lineage : descent (자손)
64. liquor : an alcoholic beverage (술)
liqueur : a particular type of alcoholic beverage (리큐어)

65. loath : reluctant (꺼리는)
    loathe : detest (혐오하다)
66. luxuriant : abundant (풍부한)
    luxurious : appealing to sense, usually costly(사치스러운)
67. maize : corn (옥수수)
    maze : labyrinth (미로)
68. mantel : shelf (선반)
    mantle : cloak (망토)
69. millenary : pertaining to a thousand (1000과 관련된)
    millinery : hats (모자)
70. mucus(noun) (점액)
    mucous(adjective) (점액을 분비하는)
71. official : authorized (공식적인)
    officious : meddlesome (거들먹거리는)
72. ordinance : regulation (법령)
    ordnance : military supplies (대포)
73. peremptory : decisive (독단적인)
    preemptory : preference (선매의)
74. perquisite : privilege (특권)
    prerequisite : requirement (전제 조건)
75. personal: private (개인적인)
    personnel : group of employed people (인사, 인원)
76. perspective : view (관점)
    prospective : expected (유망한)
77. phosphorous(adjective) (인을 함유한)
    phosphorus(noun) (인)
78. practicable : feasible (실현 가능한)
    practical : suitable for use (실용적인)
79. precedence : priority (우선)
    precedents : examples for future action (판례)
80. principal : chief (주된)
    principle : tenet (원리, 이론)
81. prophecy(noun) (예언)
    prophesy(verb) (예언하다)

82. scent : odor (향기)
    cent : coin (센트) sent : shipped (발송된)
83. selvage : edging (가장자리)
    salvage : save (구조)
84. sensual : indulging the senses (감각적인)
    sensuous : appealing to the senses (오감을 만족시키는)
85. sewage : waste (오물)
    sewerage : drain system (하수 처리 시설)
86. sometime : formerly, at some unspecified time (언젠가)
    sometimes : occasionally (때때로)
87. spacious : roomy (널찍한)
    specious : plausible (그럴 듯한)
88. specie : coin (정금)
    species : variety (종)
89. stationary : fixed (정지된)
    stationery : paper (문구류)
90. statue : sculpture (조각상)
    stature : height (키)statute : law (법규)
91. therefor : for it (그것을 위해)
    therefore : for that reason (그러므로)
92. timber : wood (목재)
    imbre : tone (음색)
93. tortuous : twisting (길고 복잡한)
    torturous : painful (고통스러운)
94. troop : an armed force, group of people (군대)
    troupe : a company of actors (극단)
95. valance : drapery (장식용 천)
    valence : chemical combining power (원자가)
96. waiver : release (포기)
    waver : hesitate between choices (망설이다)

[부록 V] 무역용어 약어표 (Commonly-used Abbreviations of Trade Terms)

【A】

AA. item	Automatic Approval item	자동승인품목
A.A.R	Against All Risks(marine)	전위험부담(해상)
A/C, a/c	Account/Account Current	계정/상호계산
@	ad(Latin)at, to	~와 교환으로, 단가를 ~으로, ~에 따라
A.C.U	Asian Currency Unit	아시아 통화단위
A.D	Anno Domini	서력 기원
A. E	Account Executive	거래처 담당자, 광고주 담당자
AFKN	American Forces Korean Network	주한미군방송
AID	Agency for International Development	미국국제개발국
AIDA	Attention, Interest, Desire, Action	주의, 흥미, 욕망, 행동
a. l. s	autograph letter, signed	서명이 있는 자필편지
A.M	forenoon(Ante Meridien)	오전
ANICs	Asian Newly Industrialized Countries	아시아중진국(한국, 대만, 싱가포르, 홍콩 등)
APO	apoderado(Spanish)-Empowered, attorney	위임받은 대리인
	cf) A.P.O Army Post Office	군우체국
A.R	All Risks	위험담보
A/S	Account Sales	매출계산서(매상계산서)
ASA	American Standards Association	미국규격협회
ASAP	as soon as possible	지급
ASEAN	Association of South-East Asian Nations	동남아시아 국가연합
ASEM	Asia Europe Summit Meeting	아시아유럽정상회의
ASP	American Selling Price	미국 판매가격
A/V	Ad Valorem	종가
A/W	Actual Weight, All Water	실제중량/전로수로

AWB	Airway Bill	항공화물운송장

【 B 】

BA	Banker's Acceptance	은행인수어음
B.C.	Before Christ	기원전
B/E	Bill of Exchange	환어음
BEP	Break-Even Point	손익분기점
BFDC	Bureau of Foreign and Domestic Commerce	(미상무성 내의) 내외통상국
BIS	Bank for International Settlements	국제결제은행
BIBOR	Bahrain Interbank offered Rate	바레인 은행간 대출금리
B/L	Bill of Lading	선화증권
B.O	Buyer's Option, By the order of	구매자의 선택/~의 지시식으로
BOK	Bank of Korea	한국은행
B.O.P.	Balance of International Payment	국제수지표
B.P	Bills Purchased	추심전 매입
B' PAY(B/P)	Bills Payable	지급어음
B' REC(B/R)	Bills Receivable	받을어음
B/S	Balance Sheet	대차대조표
B.S.S	British Standard Specification	영국 표준규격
BTU	British Thermal Unit	영국 열단위
B.W	Bonded Warehouse	보세창고
BWT	Bonded Warehouse Transaction	보세창고거래

【 C 】

C/A	Capital Account	자본계정
CAD	Cash Against Documents	선적서류상환현금불
C/B	Cash Book	현금출납장

CBD	Cash Before Delivery	선적전 현금불
	Central Business District	중심상업지구
CBM	Cubic Meter	입방 미터
C. C	Carbon Copy Notation	사본 배부처
C. D	Certificate of Deposit	양도성 예금증서
Cet Par	Ceteris Paribus(Latin)-other things being equal	여러 조건이 변하지 않고, 다른 조건을 고정시키고
CF ; c/f	Carried Forward	차기이월
CFI	Cost, Freight and Insurance	운임, 보험료포함가격
CFR	Cost and Freight	운임포함가격조건
CFS	Container Freight Station	컨테이너 화물의 적입 및 분배용 운송인 지정 화물조작소
CFT	Cubic Feet	입방 피트
C.H	Customs House	세관
CHIPS	Clearing House Interbank Payment System	컴퓨터에 의해 자동화된 은행간 자금결제시스템
CIF	Cost, Insurance and Freight	운임, 보험료포함가격
CIF & C	Cost, Insurance, Freight and Commission	운임, 보험료, 수수료 포함가격
CIF & I	Cost, Insurance, Freight, Insurance, Commission and Interest	운임, 보험료, 수수료 및 이자포함가격
CIF & E	Cost, Insurance, Freight, Interest and Exchange	운임, 보험료, 수수료, 이자 및 환비용 포함가격
CIP	Carriage and Insurance Paid to	운송비 및 보험료 지급인도조건
	Corporate Identity Program	기업 위상 프로그램
CIS	Commonwealth of Independent States	독립국가연합
CISG	Contracts for the International Sales of Goods	국제물품매매계약
C/N	Credit Note	대변표
C/O	Certificate of Origin	원산지증명서
	Country of Origin	원산국
COEX	Convention & Exhibition Center	코엑스(한국종합전시장)

c/o	care of	~方
COD	Cash On Delivery(영)	현금상환인도조건
	Collect On Delivery(미)	대금 인환
Con. Inv	Consular Invoice	영사송장
COOC	Contact with Oil and Other Cargo	유류 및 타화물과의 접촉
COS	Cash On Shipment	선적불
CP	Commercial Paper	상업어음
C/P	Charter Party	용선계약
C.P.A	Certified Public Accountant	공인회계사
C.P.I	Consumer Price Index	소비자가격지수
CPT	Carriage Paid To	운임지급인도조건
C/S	Cases	상자(복수)
CT	Container Terminal	컨테이너취급 적양시설 장소
CTA, C/A	Current Account	당좌계정
CVS	Convenience Store	편의점
CWO	Cash With Order	현금불 주문
CY	Container Yard	컨테이너의 인수, 인도 및 저장용 운송인 지정 야적장

【 D 】

DA;d,a,d/a	Days after Acceptance	인수후 ~일
	Decument attached	첨부서류
D/A	Document against Acceptance	인수인도조건
DAF	Delivered At Frontier	국경인도조건
DC	Domestic Credit	국내 여신
D/D	Demand Draft	요구불어음, 송금수표
	Delivered Docks	인도 부두
D.D.D	Direct Distance Dialing	장거리 자동전화
DDP	Delivered Duty Paid	관세 지급인도조건
DDU	Delivered Duty Unpaid	관세 미지급인도조건
DES	Delivered Ex Ship	착선인도조건
DEQ	Delivered Ex Quay	부두인도조건
DIN	Deutsche Industrie Normen	독일 공업품 표준규격

	(German Industry Standard)	
DM	Direct Mail	직접우편(광고)
DN	Debit Note	차변표
DO	Delivery Order	인도지시서(창고)
do : dto	ditto-the same	(동상)
D.O.T	Department of Overseas Trade	해외무역국(영)
D/P	Document against Payment	지급인도조건
D.P	Duty Paid	세금 지급필
D.P.L	Deposit Placement Limit	예금거래한도
D/R	Dock Receipt	부두 수취증
D/s	days after sight ; day's sight (cf. d/d=days after date)	일람후~일
DTC	Deposit Taking Company	예금수취회사
D/W	Dock Warrant	(부두)창고증권
DZ	Dozen	다스(타, 12개)

【E】

E.C	East Central Postal district(London)	영국 런던의 동부중앙 우편 지역
ECA	Economic Cooperation Administration	경제협력국(미)
ECAFE	Economic Commission for Asia and Far East	아시아극동경제위원회
ECOSOCO	Economic and Social Council of United Nations	국제연합경제사회이사회
ECU	European Currency Unit	유럽통화단위
E/D	Export Declaration	수출신고
EFTA	European Free Trade Association	유럽자유무역협회
e.g	exempli gratia(Latin)-For Instance	예를 들면
E/L	Export License	수출승인
E & O.E	Errors and Omissions are excepted	오류와 누락분은 제외
E.o.h.p	Excepted otherwise herein provided	본문 중 별도규정은 제외
e.o.m	end of the month	월말

EST	Eastern Standard Time	동부 표준시(미)
ETA	Estimated Time of Arrival	도착예정시간
ETC	et cetera(Latin)-and so forth	등등
ETD	Estimated Time of Departure	출발예정시간
et seq	et sequentes(Latin)-and the following	및 이하 참조
EX	out of	~로부터, ~에서
EX. Cont	from contract	계약서로부터
EXW	EX Works	공장인도조건

【 F 】

FA	Factory Automation	공장자동화
FAA	Free of All Average	전해손부담보(해상보험)
FDA	Food and Drug Administration	식품의약청
FAQ	Fair Average Quality	중등품, 평균중등품질
FAS	Free Alongside Ship	선측인도조건
FCA	Free Carrier	운송인인도조건
FCL	Full Containerload Lot	컨테이너 만재화물
FCFS	First Come, First Served	선착순
f.f.	following	다음의, 하기의
FFA	Free From Alongside	선복인도
FGA	Free of General Average	공동해손부담보(보험)
FI	Free In	적화비 선주무부담
FIO	Free In and Out	적화비, 양화비 선주 무부담
FO	Firm offer, Free Out	확정오퍼, 양화비 선주 무부담
FOB, fob,	f.o.b, Free on Board	본선인도조건
FOC	Free of Charge	비용 무료
FOQ	Free on Quay	부두도
FOS	Free on Steamer	기선인도
FOT	Free on Truck	화물인도
FPA	Free from Particular Average	단독해손부담보
FRB	Federal Reserve Bank	연방준비은행
FTC	Federal Trade Commission	연방거래위원회

FTW	Free Trade Wharf	자유무역부두
FV	folio verso(Latin)-on the back of the page	뒷면에, 후면에
FY	Fiscal Year	회계연도

【G】

G/A	General Average	공동해손(보험)
GATT	General Agreement on Tariff & Trade	관세 및 무역에 관한 일반협정
GBP	Great Britain Pounds	영국통화
GIS	Galvanized Iron Sheet	아연을 도금한 판
G.M.Q	Good Merchantable Quality	양호품, 판매적격품질
G.M.S	General Merchandise Stores	일반 상품점
G.M.T	Greenwich Mean Time	그리치니 표준시
GNP	Gross National Product	국민총생산
GSP c/o	Generalized System of Preference Certificate of Origin	일반특혜 관세용 원산지 증명서
G.T	Gross Ton	영국 톤, 대톤(2,240lbs)
G.W	Gross-Weight	총중량

【H】

H.A	Home Automation	가정자동화
h.a	hoc anno(Latin)-in this year	금년에
HKD	Hong Kong dollar	홍콩통화
H.O	Head Office	본사
H.P	Horse Power	마력
H.S	Harmonized Commodity Description and Coding System	신국제통일상품분류

【 I 】

IAEA	International Atomic Energy Agency	국제원자력기구
Ibid ; Ib	ibidem(Latin)-from the same place (chapter)	동소에서, 같은 원천에서
IBRD	International Bank for Reconstruction and Development	국제부흥개발은행
ICC	Institute Cargo Clause	협회적화약관
	International Chamber of Commerce	국제상업회의소
ICU	International Code Used	만국 전신 암어사용
I.d	idem (Latin)-the same	같이, 동
i.e	id est(Latin)-that is	즉
ITF	International Trade Fair	국제무역박람회
I/L	Import License	수입승인
IMF	International Monetary Fund	국제통화기금
INC	Incorporated	법인, 주식회사
INCOTERMS	International Rules for the Interpretation of Trade Terms	무역조건의 해석에 관한 국제규칙
ITE	Inland Transit Extension	내륙운송연장
IOU	I Owe You	차용증
IPA	Including Particular Average	단독해손을 포함하는
IPO	International Post Office	국제우체국 사서함
IQ	Intelligence Quotient	지능지수
IRR	Internal Rate of Return	내부수익률
I/S	Income Statement	손익계산서
ISO	International Standard Organization	국제표준화기구
ITO	International Trade Organization	국제무역기구
I.W.W	Industrial Workers of the World	세계산업노동자

【 J 】

JETRO	Japan External Trade Organization	일본 무역진흥회

JIS	Japan Industrial Standard	일본 공업규격
Jt. a/c	Joint account	공동계산
JWOB	Jettison Washing Over Board	투하, 갑판유실담보조건
KATUSA	Korean Augumentation Troops to United States Army	(주한) 미육군에 배속된 한국군인
KBS	Korea Broadcasting System	한국방송공사
KCAB	Korea Commercial Arbitration Board	대한상사중재원
KCGF	Korea Credit Guarantee Fund	한국신용보증기금
KDI	Korea Development Institute	한국개발연구원
KEB	Korea Exchange Bank	한국외환은행
KITA	Korea International Trade Association	한국무역협회
KIST	Korea Institue of Science and Technology	한국과학기술연구원
	cf) KAIST Korea Advanced Institute Science and Technology	한국과학기술원
KIT	Korea International Telecommunications	국제전신전화국
Km	kilometer(s)	킬로미터
KOTRA	Korea Trade-Investment Promotion Agency	대한무역투자진흥공사
KOSDAQ	Korea Securities Dealers Automated Quotation	한국장외주식거래시장
KS	Korean(Industrial) Standards	한국공업규격
KTA	Korea Telecommunication Authority	한국전기통신공사
KW	kilowatt	킬로와트
KWH	kilowatt-hour	시간당 킬로와트

【 L 】

L/A	Letter of Authority	어음매입수권서
LASH	lighter-aboard-ship	화물을 적재한 부선을 선박에 탑재하여 수송하는 방식

Lb	Libra(Latin)-Pound in weight	중량
L/C	Letter of Credit	신용장
LCL	Less than Container Load	화물이 컨테이너를 채울 수 없는 소량화물
L.D.C.	Less Developed Country	저개발국
LDDC	Least Developed Among Developing Countries	후진개발도상국
L/G	Letter of Guarantee	화물선취보증서
LI	Letter of Indemnity	(파손화물)보상장
LIBOR	London Inter Bank offered Rate	런던은행간 대출금리
LIP	Life Insurance Policy	생명보험증권
Loco	on the spot	현장인도조건
LST	Local Standard Time	현지표준시간
LT	Letter Telegram	서신 전보
L.T	Long Ton(2,240Lb)	톤
LTD.	Limited	유한회사

【 M 】

MD;m/d	month after date	일부후~월
MFA	Multi-Fiber Arrangement	다자간 섬유협정
MFN	Most Favored Nation Trading	무역최혜국
MIA	Marine Insurance Act	해상보험법(영)
MIP	Marine Insurance Policy	해상보험증권
MITI	Ministry of International Trade and Industry	통산성(일본)
M/L Clause	More or Less Clause	과부족용인조항
M.M.A	Merchandise Marks Act	상표조례
MND	Ministry of National Defense	국방부
MOFE	Ministry of Finance and Economy	재정경제부
m.o.m	middle of month	월의 중간
MOTIE	Ministry of Trade, Industry and Energy	산업자원부

m.p.h	miles per hour	시속
M/R	Mate's Receipt	본선수취증
Mrs.	Mistress	부인(경칭)
M.S	Motor Ship	발동기선
	Months after sight	일람후~월
MSA	Merchant Shipping Act	상선조약
MT	Mail Transfer	우편송금
M/T	Metric Ton	미터 톤
M.V	Motor Vessel	전기발동기선
MVP	Most Valuable Player	최우수 선수

【N】

N/A	new account	신규계정
	no account	계좌거래 없음
	no advice	통지 없음
	no acceptance	인수거절
NAFTA	North America Free Trade Agreement	북미자유무역협정
NATO	North Atlantic Treaty Organization	북대서양조약기구
NASDAQ	National Association of Securities Dealers Automated Quotation	미국장외주식거래시장
NB	Nota Bene(Latin)-Note Well	주의
NC	No Circuit	회선 없음
NG	No Good	불량
NHK	Nippon Hoso Kyokai	일본방송협회
NM	No Mark	무화인
N/P	Non-Payment	지급 거절
NPT	Non-Proliferation Treaty	핵비확산조약
NSF	Non-Sufficient Fund	예금잔고부족
NTB	Non-Tariff Barrier	비관세장벽
NTWT	Net Weight	순중량
NYT	New York Times	뉴욕타임즈

【 O 】

OA	Office Automation	사무자동화
O/A	On Account of	~의 계산으로
O.B	Old Boy	졸업생
OCP	Overland Common Point	선적에 있어 목적지 표시 방법
OCR	Optical Character Reader(or Rcognition)	광학문자판독기
O/D	On Demand	요구불
OECD	Organization for Economic Cooperation and Development	경제협력개발기구
OEM	Original Equipment Manufacturing	주문자상표 부착상품생산
OJT	On-the-job Training	현장실무교육
O/No	Order Number	주문번호
OPEC	Oranization of Petroleum Exporting Countries	석유수출국기구
ORD	Ordinary Telegram	통상정보
OSROK	Office of Supply, Republic of Korea	대한민국 조달청

【 P 】

p.a	per annum(Latin), yearly, by the year	1년마다
PANDL	Profit and Loss	손익계산서
P/AV	Particular Average	단독해손
Per Pro	Per Procurationem-by power of authority	대리
p.f	Proforma	형식상의, 견적의
PFC	Private First Class	일등병
P.M	Post Meridian-afternoon	오후
P.M.O	Post Money Order	우편송금환
P.N	Promissory Note	약속어음
P.O	Payment Order	지급지시서

POB	Post Office Box	우편사서함
P.O.B.R	Payable on Receipt	화물상환증
PPD	Postpaid, Prepaid	우편료 선불, 선불필
PPP theory	Purchasing Power Parity theory	구매력평가이론
PPS	Post Postscriptum	재추신
P.R	Parcel Receipt	소포수취증
Proxi	Proximo-next month	다음달
P.S	Postscriptum	추신
P/S	Public Sale	공매
P.S.T	Pacific Standard Time	태평양표준시간
P.T.O	Please Turn Over	이면을 보시오
Pty. Co.	Proprietary(Company)	호주, 남아 등의 주식회사
P.X	Please Exchange	교환바람
	Post Exchange	매점, 물물교환소

【 R 】

R/A	refer to acceptor	인수인에게 조회하다
R/D	refer to drawer	발행인 회부
R&D	Research and Development	연구개발
R.F.D	Rural Free Delivery	지방무료우편 배달(미)
R.F.W.D.	Rain & Fresh Water Damage	우수 및 단수 피해
RO/RO	Roll on/Roll off	선수, 선측 또는 선내의 Ramp(경사)로부터 컨테이너 또는 트레일러로 수평으로 적재하거나 양륙하는 하역방식
R.O.G	Receipt of Goods	현품인수
RP	Repurchase Agreement	환매조건부증권
RPM	Revolution Per Minute	매분 회전수
RPT	Reply Prepaid Telegram	회신료 선납전보

R.S.V.P	Respondez, S'il Vous Plait (프)-Please Reply	회신요망
R.T	Rye Term	호밀의 거래
Rt. Hon.	Right Honorable	각하

【 S 】

S/A	Statement of Account	계정명세서
SBU	Strategic Business Unit	전략사업단위
S/D	Sight Draft, Sea Damage	일람출급어음, 해수에 의한 분손(보험)
SDR	Special Drawing Right	특별인출권
SG	Ship and Goods	선박 및 적화
SHEX	Sundays and National Holidays are excepted	일요일과 공휴일은 일수에서 제외
SIBOR	Singapore Interbank Offered Rate	싱가포르 은행간 대출금리
SIMEX	Singapore International Monetary Exchange	싱가포르 국제 통화거래소
SKU	Stockkeeping Unit	재고유지단위
SOHO	Small Office Home Office	재택소규모창업
SOFA	Status of Forces Agreement	한·미주둔군지위협정
S.N	Shipping Note	적출통지서
S.O	Shipping Order, Seller's Option	선적지시서/판매자의 선택
S.O.S	Save Our Ship	해난신호
SPA	Subject to Particular Average	단독해손담보
SPQR	Small Profit and Quick Returns	박리다매
S/R	Shipping Request	선적요청
SRCC	Strikes, Riots and Civil Commotions	태업, 폭동 및 소요로 인한 화물손해를 담보해 주는 조건
S.S	Steam Ship	기선
SSE	South-South East	남남동
SSW	South-South West	남남서
S/T	Short-Ton	미국식톤(2000파운드)

STG	Sterling Pound	영국통화
Sub.Cap	Subscribed Capital	응모자본금
SWIFT	Society for Worldwide Interbank Financial Telecommunication	국제 은행간 컴퓨터 통신 시스템

【T】

T.B	Trial Balance, Treasury Bill	시산표, 재정증권
T.C	Traveller's Check	여행자수표
T/D	Time Deposit	정기예금
T.L.O	Total Loss Only	전손(만)부담
TMO	Telegraph Money Order	전신환
T.P.N.D	Theft, Pilferage & Non-delivery	도난, 좀도둑, 불착의 위험
T.Q	Tale Quale(프)-of condition on arrival	운송중의 손해 매수인 부담
T/R	Trust Receipt	화물대도(선인도)
T/S	Transhipment	환적
TSR	Trans-Siberian Railroad	시베리아횡단철도수송
T.S.V.P	Tournez S'il Vous Plait(프)-Please Turn Over	이면을 보십시오
TOEFL	Test of English as a Foreign Language	토플
TOEIC	Test of English for International Communication	토익
T.T	Telegraphic Transfer	전신송금
T.U	Trade Union	노동조합

【U】

U/A	Underwriting Account	보험계정
UCP	Uniform Customs and Practice for Documentary Credit	화환신용장에 관한 통일규칙 및 관행
U.D	Ut Dictum (Latin)-as directed	지시대로
U.i	Ut infra (Latin)-as below	아래와 같이

U.K	United Kingdom	영국
Ult	Ultimo	지난달
UNCTAD	United Nations Conference on Trade and Development	유엔무역개발회의
UNESCO	United Nations Educational Scientific and Cultural Organization	유엔 교육, 과학, 문화기구
UNICEF	United Nations International Children's Emergency Fund	국제아동구호기구
UR	Uruguay Round	우루과이라운드
U.S	Ut Supra (Latin)-as above	상기와 같이
U.S.P	Unique Selling Proposition	특수판매소구점
U.S.Q	Usual Standard Quality	보통품질조건
U.S.W	Und So Weiter(German)-and so forth	등등

【 V 】

VAT	Value Added Tax	부가가치세
VER	Voluntary Export Restraints	수출자율규제
Via	by way of(Latin)	~경유로
VIP	Very Important Person	요인(要人)
Viz	Videlicet (Latin)-namely	즉
VP	Vice President	부사장, 차장
VS	versus(Latin)-against	~대, ~와 대비하여
V.V	Vice Versa	반대로

【 W 】

W.A	With Average	단독해손담보
W/B	Way Bill. Warehouse Book	화물운송장/창고입고장
W.C	Without Charge	무료
Whs. rec	Warehouse Receipt	창고증권(미)

W/M	Weight of Measurement	용적중량
W/P	Without Prejudice	편견없이, 권리침해없이
WPA	With Particular Average	단독해손담보
WPM	word per minute	1분간의 타자기 타자수
W/R	War Risk	전쟁위험
WW	Warehouse Warrant	창고증권
W.W.D	Weather Working Days	호천후 하역일
W.T.O	World Trade Organization	세계무역기구

【 X 】

X	ex(Latin)-out of	인도, ~으로
X.M.P	Extra Message Paid	초과통신료 지불필
XX	all of double strength, good quality	이중강도/양질
XXX	all of triple strength, very good quality	삼중강도/매우 양질
XXXX	best quality	극상

【 Y 】

Y.A.R	York Antwerp Rules	요크앤트워프규정(공동해손에 관한)
Y.B	Year Book, Year Boy	연보, 재학생

【 Z 】

ZBB	Zero-Base Budgeting	제로베이스 예산편성
ZEG	Zero Economic Growth	경제의 제로성장
ZIP	Zone Improvement Program	우편번호

참고문헌

1. Business Communications, Kathryn Rentz, MaGraw-Hill, 2014.
2. Business Communications Essentials, Courtland L., Bovee Prentice Hall, 2013.
3. Business Grammar, Style & Usage, Alicia Abell, Thomson West, 2013.
4. Business English, Mary Ellen Guffy, Cengage Learning, 2010.
5. Communicating in Business English, Bob Dignen, Compass publishing, 2013.
6. Business Letter For All Occasions, Alan Bond, Barron's, 1998.
7. English for Business Studies, Lan Mackenzi, Cambridge University Press, 1999.
8. You're in Business!, John Thomas French, Addison-Wesley Publishing Company, 1998.
9. New International Business English, Leo Jones, Cambridge University Press, 1999.
10. The New Oxford Dictionary of English, Oxford Univ. Press, 1998.
11. English for Business Communication, Simon Sweeney, Cambridge Univ. Press, 1998.
12. Effective Business Communications, Herta A. Murphy & Herbert W. Hildebrant, McGraw-Hill Book Company, 1980.
13. How to Write Business Letters, Urabe Shigeo, Nam Woon Dang, 1989.
14. How to Write Better Resumes, Gary Joseph Grappo and Adele Lewis, Baron's, 1998.
15. Commercial English & Trade Practice, Bruce. S. Stewart, Learning Publishing, Co., Ltd, 1991.
16. Commercial Correspondence, A, Ashley, Oxford Univ. Press, 1986.
17. Letter Perfect, Abraham Allenbogan, Macmillan Publishing Co., Inc., 1990.

18. Longman Dictionary of Contemporary English, Longman Group Ltd., 1995.
19. Business English, 3rd Edition, Andrea B. Geffner, Barron's, 1998.
20. Common Problems in Korean English, David Kosofsky, Foreign Language Service, 1987.
21. Practical English for Foreign Exchange Business, Joe A. Collins, KBI, 1998.
22. Effective Fax Communications, Francis J. Kurdayla, The Korea Herald, 1996.
23. NTC's English Idioms Dictionary, Richard A. Spears, NTC Publishing Group, 1998.
24. Black's Law Dictionary, Seventh Edition, Bryan A. Garner, West Group, 1990.
25. 대한상공회의소 무역영어 검정시험 기출문제
26. 외환실무영어, 고명규, 한국금융연수원, 1990.
27. 국제무역영어, 고명규, 도서출판 청람, 2012.
28. 신영어학 개론, 박의재, 한신문화사, 1999.
29. 미국영어의 역사, 김윤경, 한국문학사, 2000.
30. 영어연설의 이론과 실제, 한동만, 백산출판사, 2005.
31. 비즈니스인문학, 조승연, 김영사, 2015.

찾아보기

저자약력

고명규

고대부속고등학교 졸업
중앙대학교 문리과대학 영어영문학과(문학사)
중앙대학교 국제경영대학원(경영학석사)
중앙대학교 대학원 경영학과(경영학박사)
중앙대학교 The Chung-ang Herald 편집부장
First Interstate Bank of California 외환세미나과정 수료
영국 Aston University BI Leadership Program 연수
중앙대학교 경영대학 강사
한국금융연수원 외환 및 실무영어 강사
한·일 경상학회, 한국창업보육협회, 대한상사중재인협회,
영중유아학교, 한국문화산업학회 이사
한국무역통상학회 부회장
한국물류학회 부회장
서울창업보육센터협의회 회장
관세청 관세사 자격시험 선정위원
대한상공회의소 무역영어 검정시험 출제위원
국제물류사 출제위원
배화여자대학교 교무처장, 학생처장 겸 산학협력처장
대학평의원회 의장 역임
대한상사중재원 국제중재인(외환분야) 역임
현) 배화여자대학교 국제무역과 교수
필리핀 라이시엄 대학교 명예교수
한국구매경영학회(KSPM) 회장

[저서 및 논문]

외환실무영어, 한국금융연수원, 1990.
국제무역영어, 삼영사, 2000.
글로벌시대의 외환실무, 도서출판 두남, 2002.
은행의 서비스 마케팅에 관한 실증적 연구
우리나라 시중은행의 마케팅전략에 관한 연구
은행의 서비스품질과 시장세분화 방법론에 관한 연구
고객만족과 은행의 서비스품질 구성요인에 관한 연구
외환금융실무, 도서출판 두남, 2012.
국제무역영어, 도서출판 청람, 2012.

글로벌 무역영어

2015년 2월 25일 1판 1쇄 발행
2016년 1월 28일 1판 2쇄 발행

저　　자 | 고명규
발 행 인 | 이수영
발 행 처 | 도서출판 청람
서울시 마포구 독막로 288(대흥동, 세양상가 109호)
전　　화 | 02)3272-2601~2
팩　　스 | 02)3272-2603
홈페이지 | www.crbooks.co.kr
이 메 일 | crbooks@hanmail.net
등　　록 | 2000년 8월 26일 제6-0509호

ISBN 978-89-5972-426-0 93320 [정가 25,000원]